JESSICA JONES
ALIAS

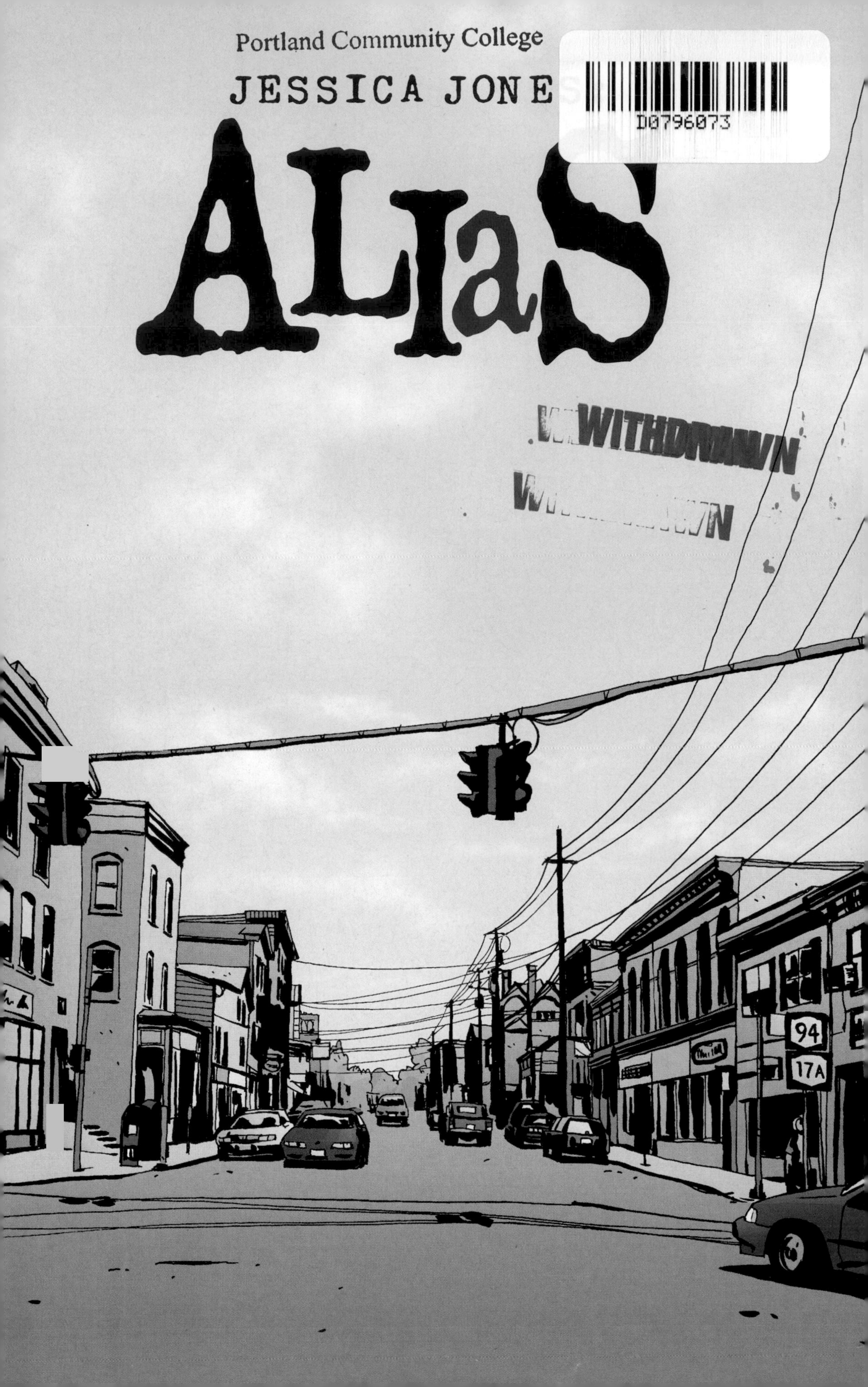
94
17A

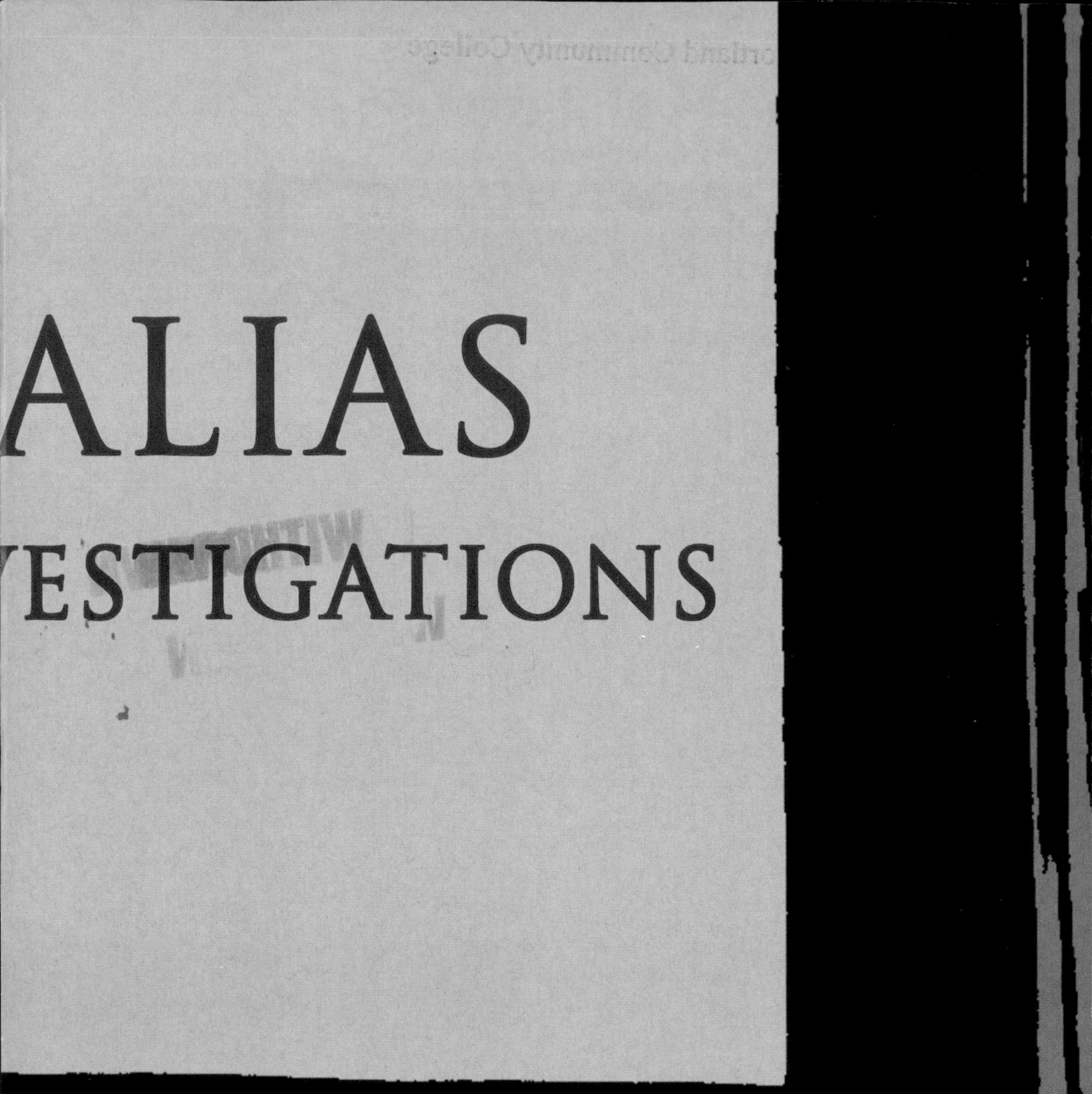

ALIAS

ＶESTIGATIONS

Collection Editor: **Jennifer Grünwald**
Associate Editor: **Sarah Brunstad**
Associate Managing Editor: **Alex Starbuck**
Editor, Special Projects: **Mark D. Beazley**
VP, Production & Special Projects: **Jeff Youngquist**
SVP Print, Sales & Marketing: **David Gabriel**
Book Designer: **Jay Bowen**

Editor in Chief: **Axel Alonso**
Chief Creative Officer: **Joe Quesada**
Publisher: **Dan Buckley**
Executive Producer: **Alan Fine**

JESSICA JONES: ALIAS VOL. 2. Contains material originally published in magazine form as ALIAS #11-15. Second printing 2016. ISBN# 978-0-7851-9856-7. Published by MARVEL WORLDWIDE, INC., a subsidiary of MARVEL ENTERTAINMENT, LLC. OFFICE OF PUBLICATION: 135 West 50th Street, New York, NY 10020. Copyright © 2015 MARVEL No similarity between any of the names, characters, persons, and/or institutions in this magazine with those of any living or dead person or institution is intended, and any such similarity which may exist is purely coincidental. **Printed in the U.S.A.** ALAN FINE, President, Marvel Entertainment; DAN BUCKLEY, President, TV, Publishing and Brand Management; JOE QUESADA, Chief Creative Officer; TOM BREVOORT, SVP of Publishing; DAVID BOGART, SVP of Operations & Procurement, Publishing; C.B. CEBULSKI, VP of International Development & Brand Management; DAVID GABRIEL, SVP Print, Sales & Marketing; JIM O'KEEFE, VP of Operations & Logistics; DAN CARR, Executive Director of Publishing Technology; SUSAN CRESPI, Editorial Operations Manager; ALEX MORALES, Publishing Operations Manager; STAN LEE, Chairman Emeritus. For information regarding advertising in Marvel Comics or on Marvel.com, please contact Jonathan Rheingold, VP of Custom Solutions & Ad Sales, at jrheingold@marvel.com. For Marvel subscription inquiries, please call 800-217-9158. **Manufactured between 1/13/16 and 2/8/16 by HESS PRINT SOLUTIONS, A DIVISION OF BANG PRINTING, BRIMFIELD, OH, USA.**

1 0 9 8 7 6 5 4 3 2

JESSICA JONES:
ALIaS

Brian Michael Bendis
WRITER

Michael Gaydos
ARTIST

Mark Bagley & Rodney Ramos
JEWEL SEQUENCES

Matt Hollingsworth
COLORIST

David Mack
REBECCA'S JOURNAL ART

**Richard Starkings and
Comicraft's Wes Abbott & Oscar Gongora**
LETTERERS

David Mack
COVER ART

Stuart Moore
EDITOR

Kelly Lamy
ASSOCIATE MANAGING EDITOR

Nanci Dakesian
MANAGING EDITOR

ALIaS CREATED BY BRIAN MICHAEL BENDIS & MICHAEL GAYDOS

2I2-555-[redacted] Ms. [redacted]

ISSUE #11

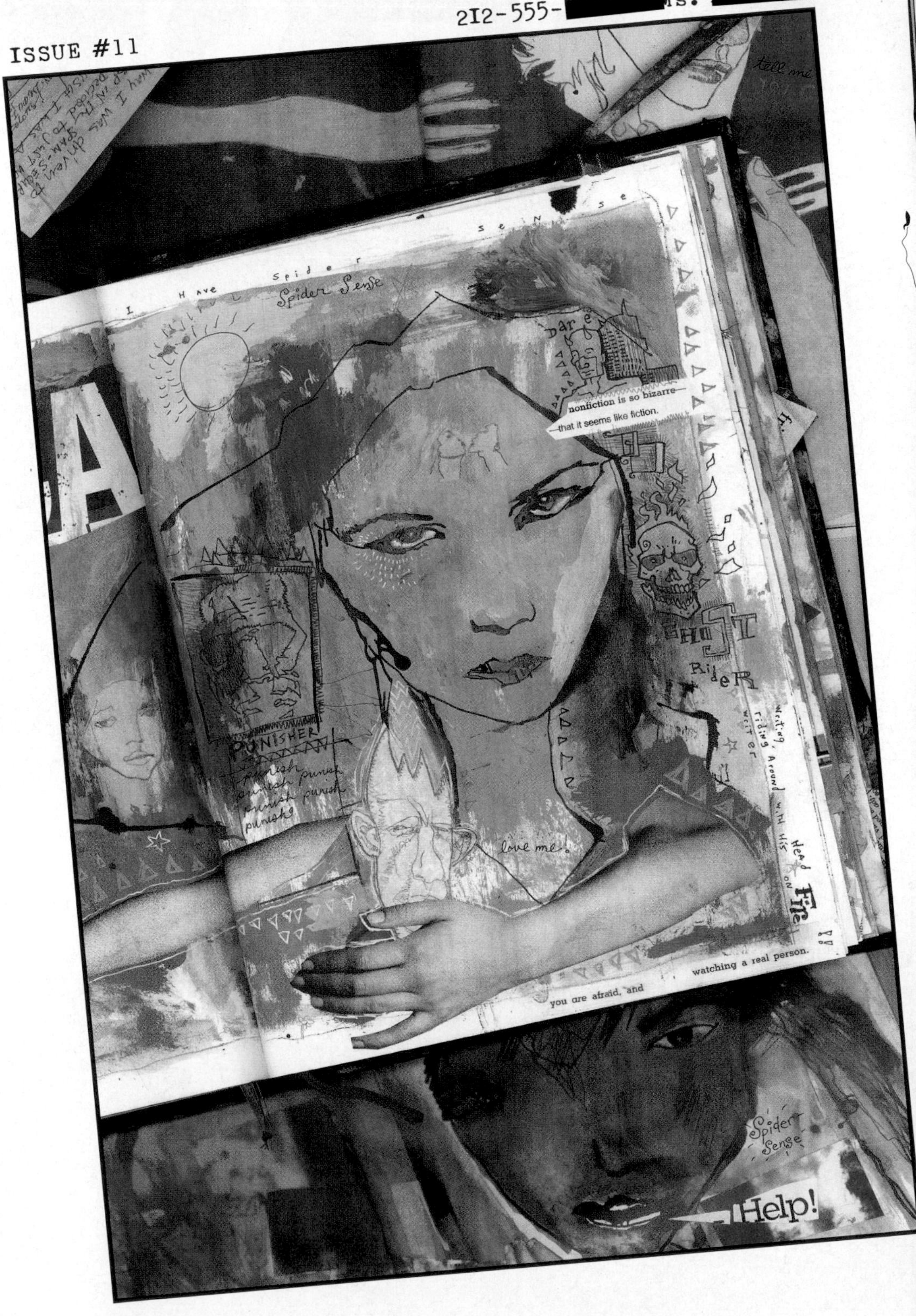

tell me
I HAVE SPIDER SENSE
Spider Sense
Dare
nonfiction is so bizarre—
—that it seems like fiction.
GHOST RIDER
writer
writing riding Around with his Head on Fire
PUNISHER
punish punish punish punish punish punish
love me!
watching a real person.
you are afraid, and
Spider Sense
Help!

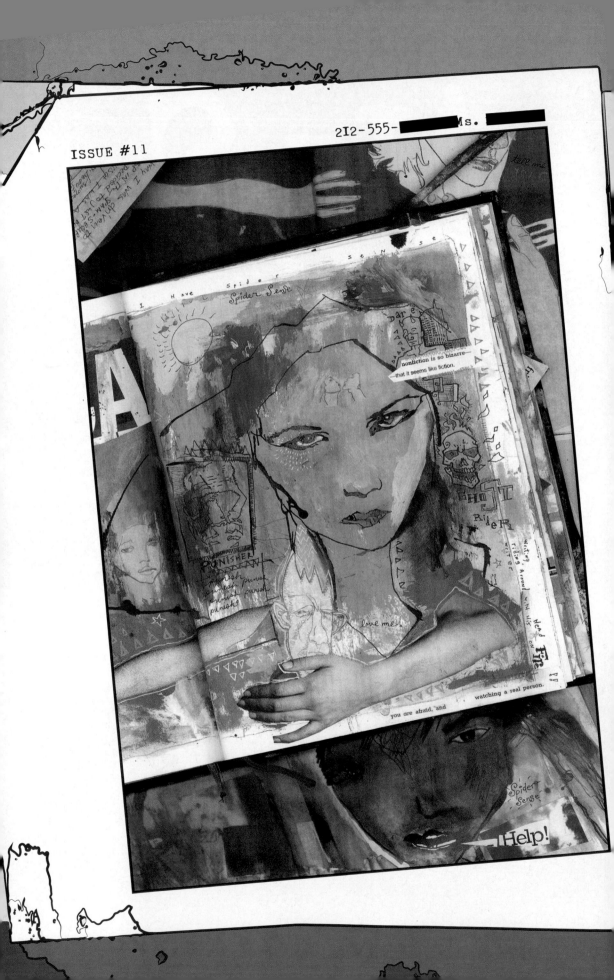

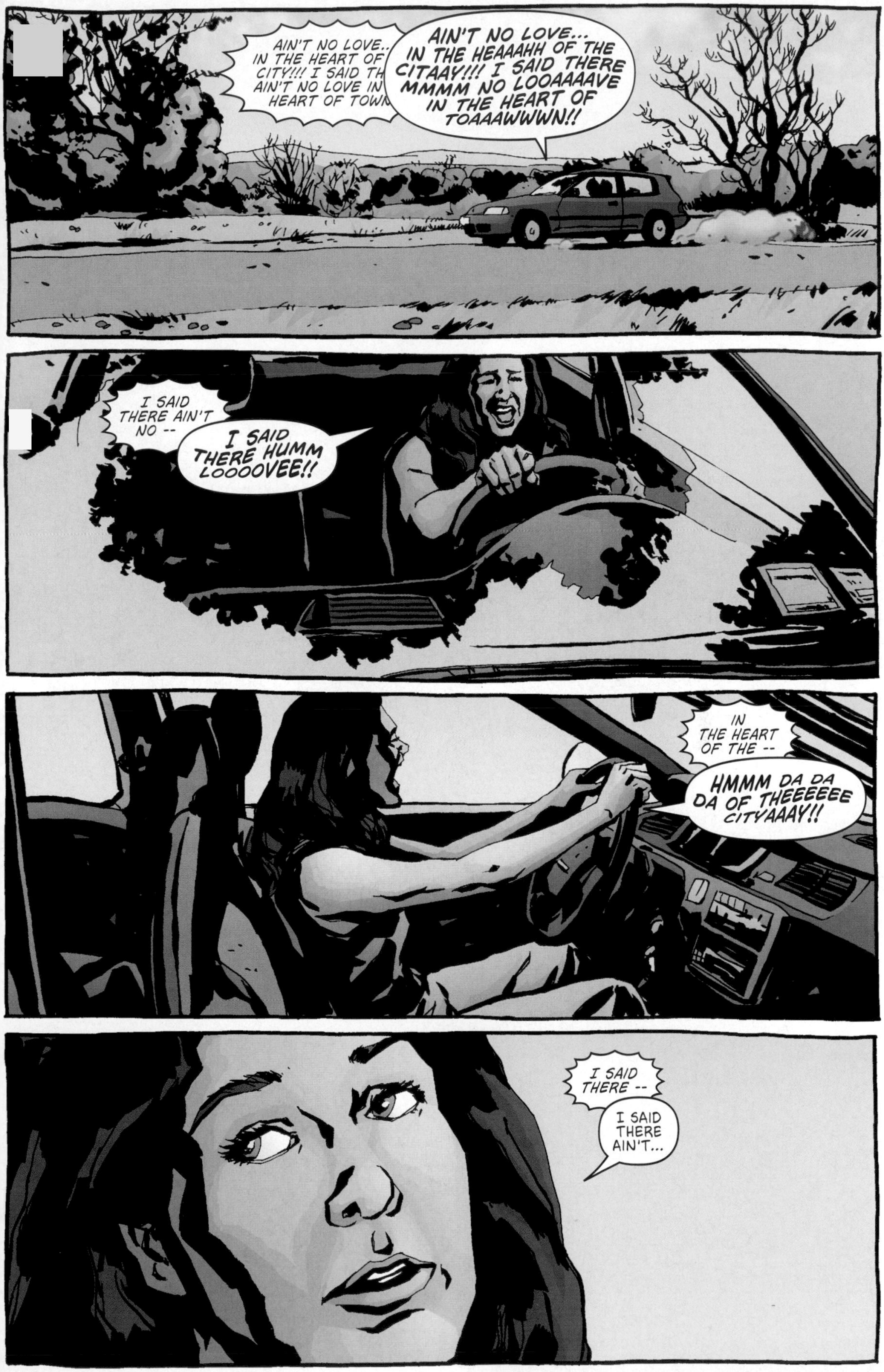
AIN'T NO LOVE... IN THE HEART OF CITY!!! I SAID TH AIN'T NO LOVE IN HEART OF TOWN
AIN'T NO LOVE... IN THE HEAAAHH OF THE CITAAY!!! I SAID THERE MMMM NO LOOAAAAAVE IN THE HEART OF TOAAAWWWN!!
I SAID THERE AIN'T NO --
I SAID THERE HUMM LOOOOVEE!!
IN THE HEART OF THE --
HMMM DA DA DA OF THEEEEEE CITYAAAY!!
I SAID THERE --
I SAID THERE AIN'T...

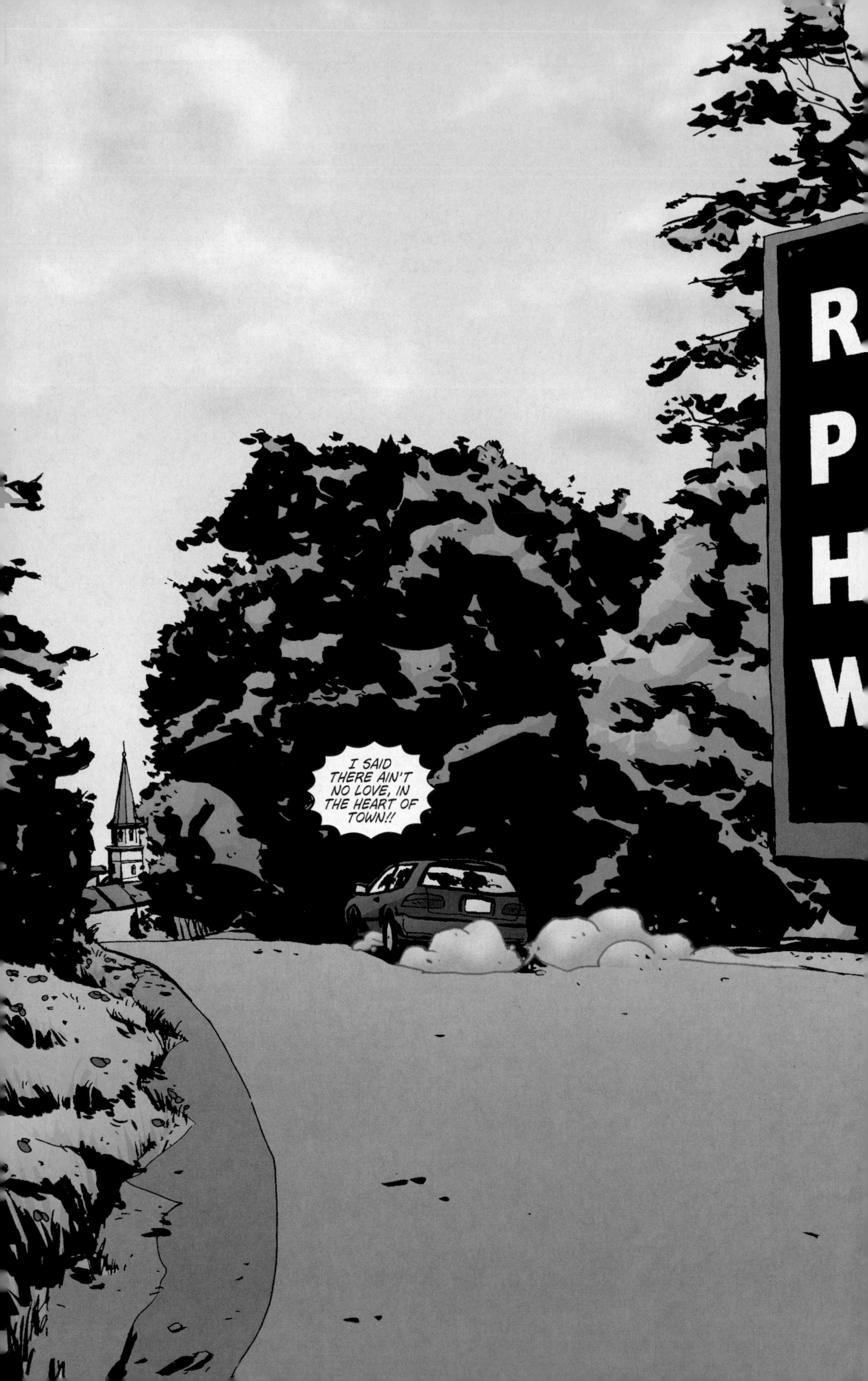
I SAID THERE AIN'T NO LOVE, IN THE HEART OF TOWN!!
R
P
H
W

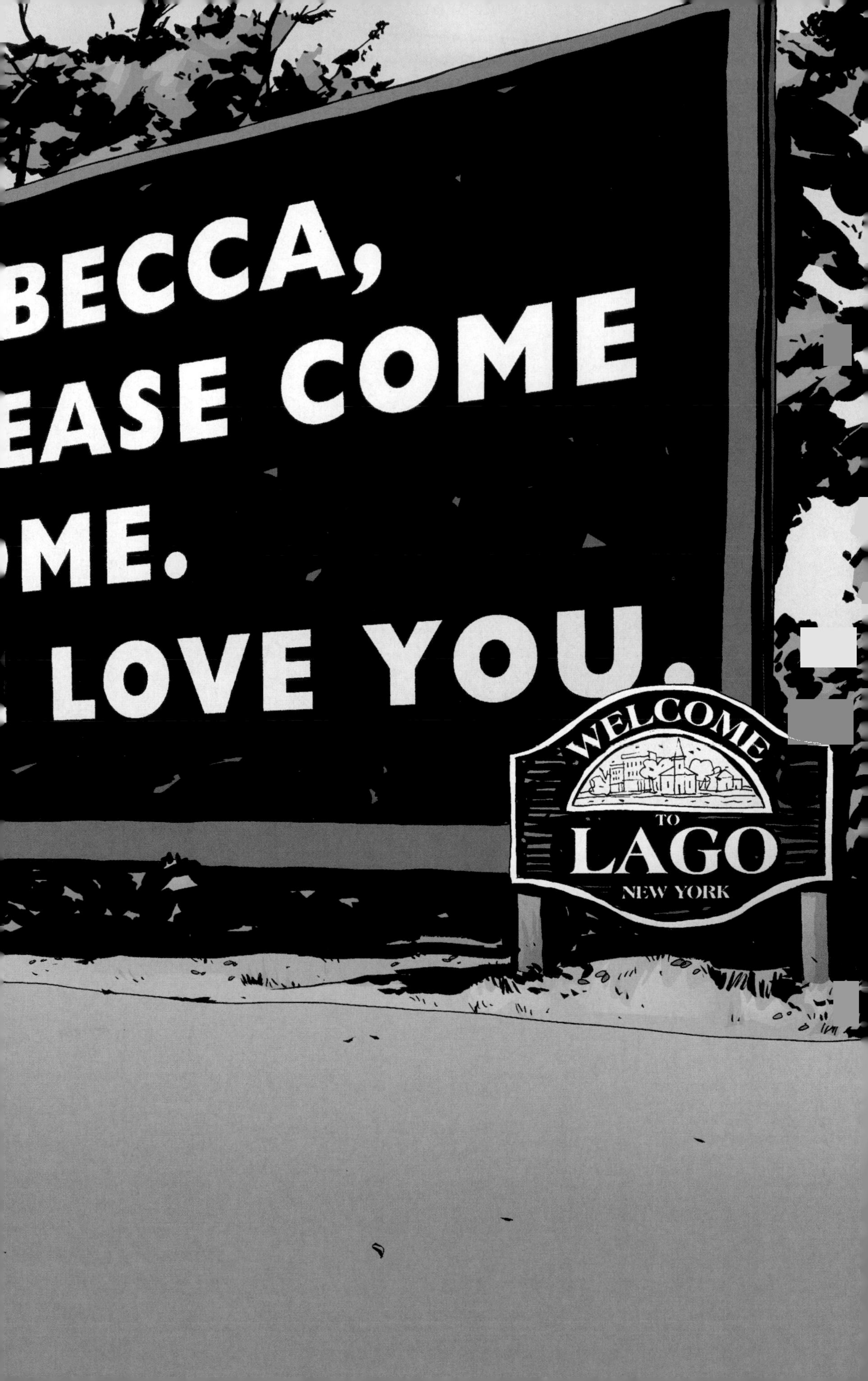
BECCA,
EASE COME
ME.
LOVE YOU.
WELCOME
TO
LAGO
NEW YORK

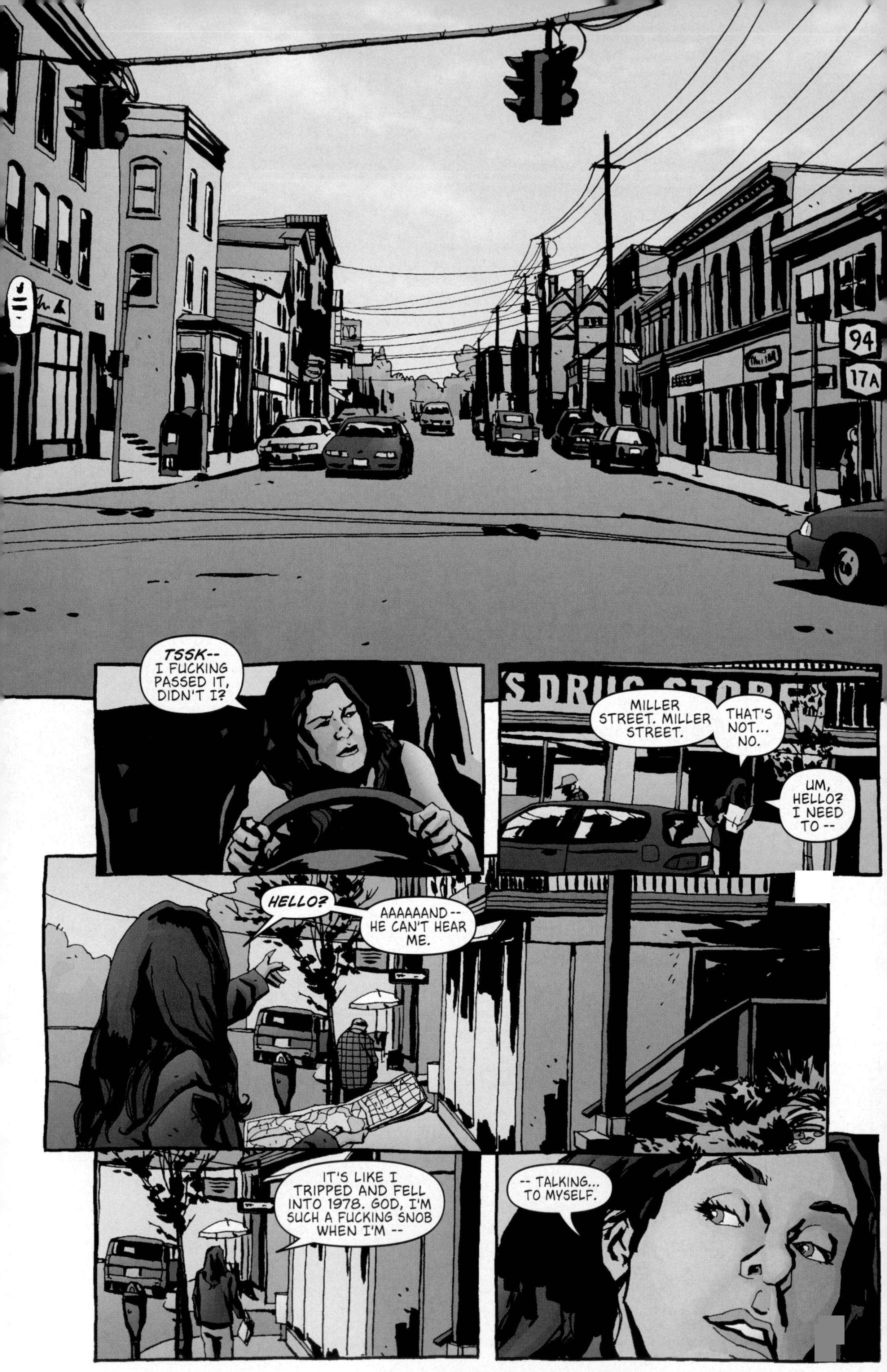
94
17A
S DRUG STORE
TSSK-- I FUCKING PASSED IT, DIDN'T I?
MILLER STREET. MILLER STREET.
THAT'S NOT... NO.
UM, HELLO? I NEED TO --
HELLO?
AAAAAAND -- HE CAN'T HEAR ME.
IT'S LIKE I TRIPPED AND FELL INTO 1978. GOD, I'M SUCH A FUCKING SNOB WHEN I'M --
-- TALKING... TO MYSELF.

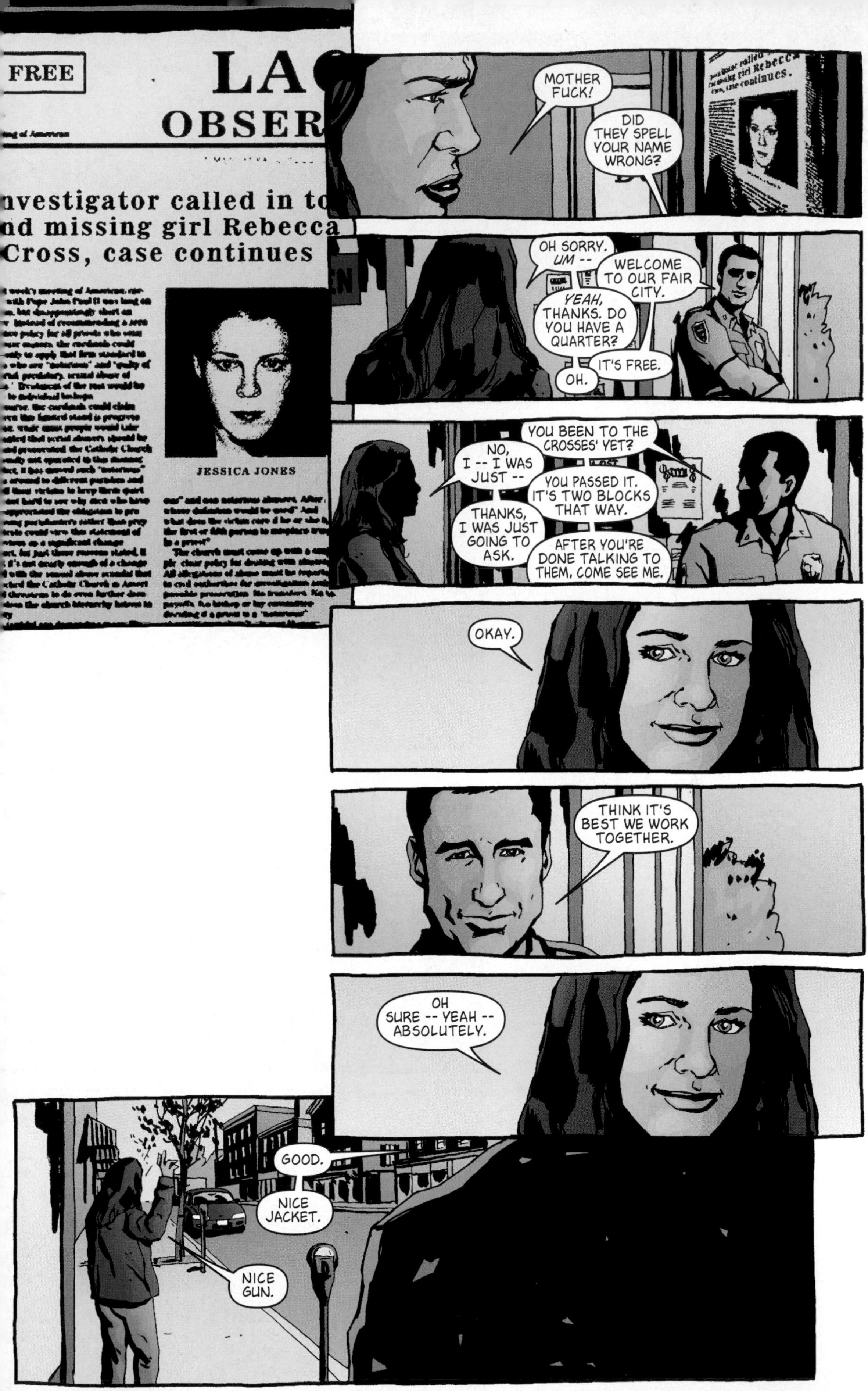

FREE
LA
OBSER
nvestigator called in to
nd missing girl Rebecca
Cross, case continues
JESSICA JONES
MOTHER FUCK!
DID THEY SPELL YOUR NAME WRONG?
OH SORRY. UM --
WELCOME TO OUR FAIR CITY.
YEAH, THANKS. DO YOU HAVE A QUARTER?
IT'S FREE.
OH.
YOU BEEN TO THE CROSSES' YET?
NO, I -- I WAS JUST --
YOU PASSED IT. IT'S TWO BLOCKS THAT WAY.
THANKS, I WAS JUST GOING TO ASK.
AFTER YOU'RE DONE TALKING TO THEM, COME SEE ME.
OKAY.
THINK IT'S BEST WE WORK TOGETHER.
OH SURE -- YEAH -- ABSOLUTELY.
GOOD.
NICE JACKET.
NICE GUN.

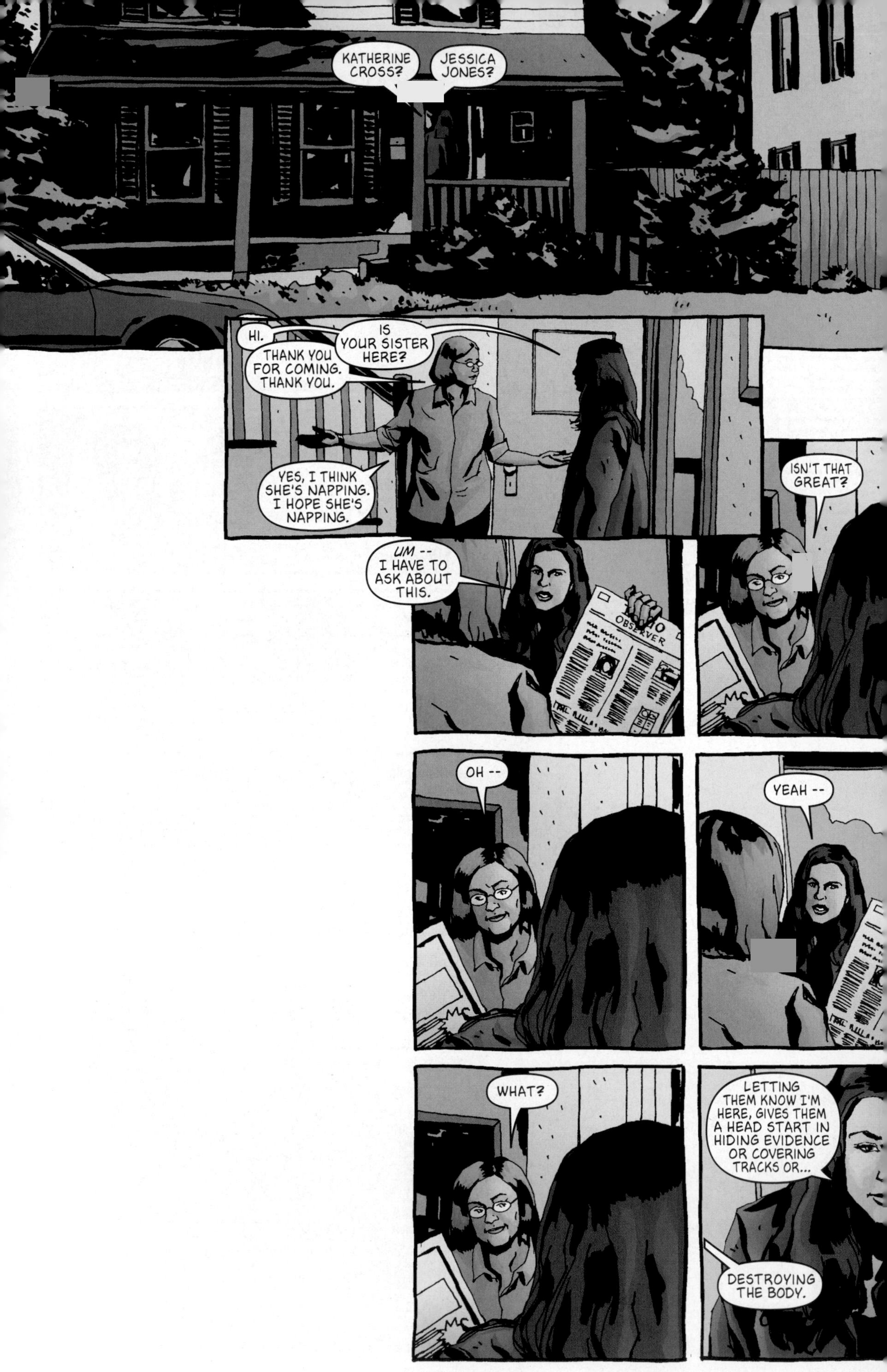
KATHERINE CROSS?
JESSICA JONES?
HI.
THANK YOU FOR COMING. THANK YOU.
IS YOUR SISTER HERE?
YES, I THINK SHE'S NAPPING. I HOPE SHE'S NAPPING.
UM -- I HAVE TO ASK ABOUT THIS.
OBSERVER
ISN'T THAT GREAT?
OH --
YEAH --
WHAT?
LETTING THEM KNOW I'M HERE, GIVES THEM A HEAD START IN HIDING EVIDENCE OR COVERING TRACKS OR...
DESTROYING THE BODY.

YEAH, BUT SEE -- REALLY, I'M YOUR PRIVATE INVESTIGATOR. *"PRIVATE"* BEING THE OPERATIVE ADJECTIVE. I --

OH --

SEE, IT WOULD HAVE BEEN MUCH EASIER FOR ME TO DO MY JOB IF EVERYONE IN TOWN HADN'T BEEN ALERTED TO MY PRESENCE.

WELL...

FRONT PAGE.

SEE, IT WOULD HAVE BEEN MUCH EASIER FOR ME TO DO MY JOB IF EVERYONE IN TOWN HADN'T BEEN ALERTED TO MY PRESENCE.

HOW EXACTLY?

YOUR MISSING NIECE...

IMAGINE -- AND I THINK YOU HAVE OR I WOULDN'T BE HERE -- IMAGINE SOMEONE DID SOMETHING TO HER.

WELL, BY LETTING THEM KNOW I'M HERE...

SEE...

DO YOU THINK YOU'LL FIND MY DAUGHTER?

I'LL TRY.

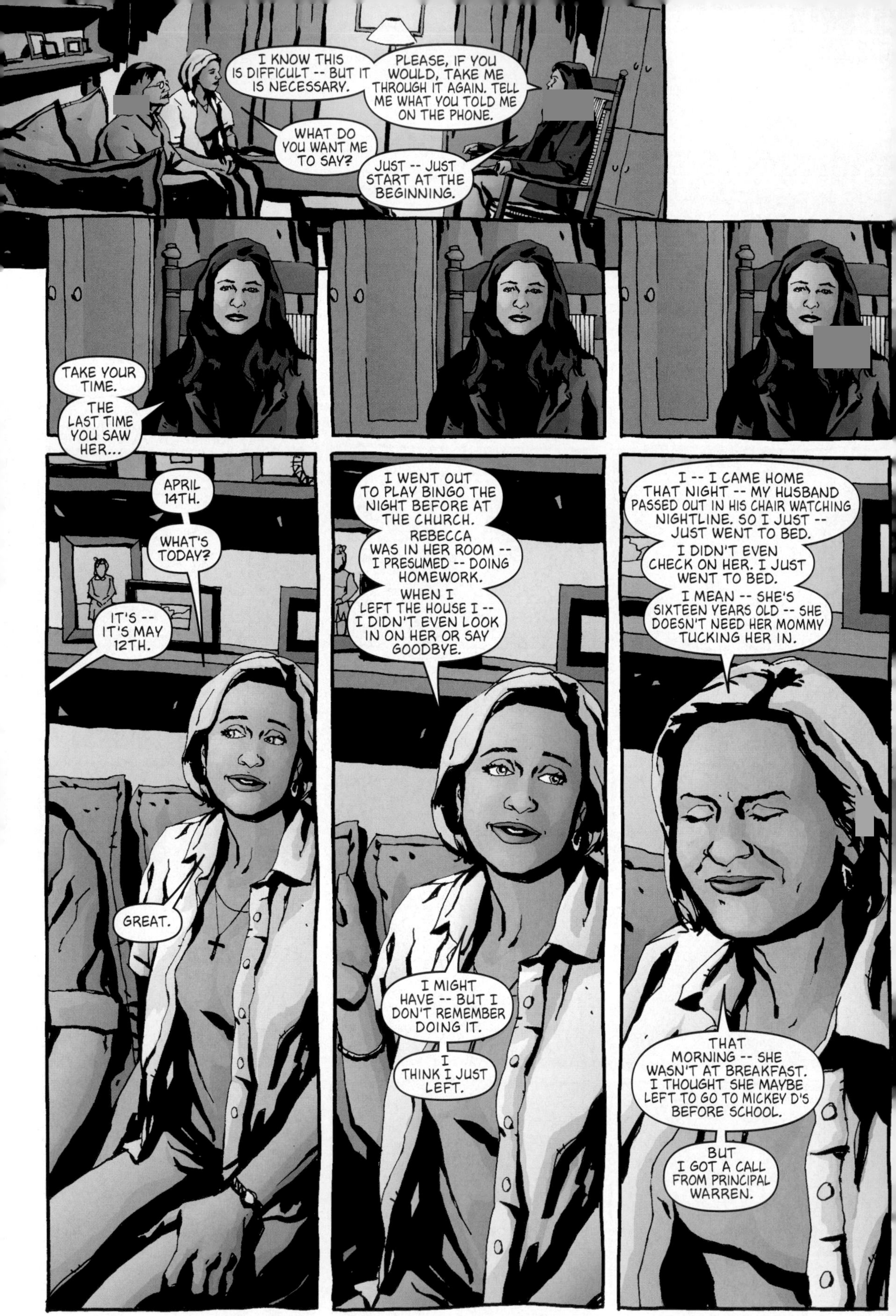
I KNOW THIS IS DIFFICULT -- BUT IT IS NECESSARY.
PLEASE, IF YOU WOULD, TAKE ME THROUGH IT AGAIN. TELL ME WHAT YOU TOLD ME ON THE PHONE.
WHAT DO YOU WANT ME TO SAY?
JUST -- JUST START AT THE BEGINNING.
TAKE YOUR TIME.
THE LAST TIME YOU SAW HER...
APRIL 14TH.
WHAT'S TODAY?
IT'S -- IT'S MAY 12TH.
GREAT.
I WENT OUT TO PLAY BINGO THE NIGHT BEFORE AT THE CHURCH.
REBECCA WAS IN HER ROOM -- I PRESUMED -- DOING HOMEWORK.
WHEN I LEFT THE HOUSE I -- I DIDN'T EVEN LOOK IN ON HER OR SAY GOODBYE.
I MIGHT HAVE -- BUT I DON'T REMEMBER DOING IT.
I THINK I JUST LEFT.
I -- I CAME HOME THAT NIGHT -- MY HUSBAND PASSED OUT IN HIS CHAIR WATCHING NIGHTLINE. SO I JUST -- JUST WENT TO BED.
I DIDN'T EVEN CHECK ON HER. I JUST WENT TO BED.
I MEAN -- SHE'S SIXTEEN YEARS OLD -- SHE DOESN'T NEED HER MOMMY TUCKING HER IN.
THAT MORNING -- SHE WASN'T AT BREAKFAST. I THOUGHT SHE MAYBE LEFT TO GO TO MICKEY D'S BEFORE SCHOOL.
BUT I GOT A CALL FROM PRINCIPAL WARREN.

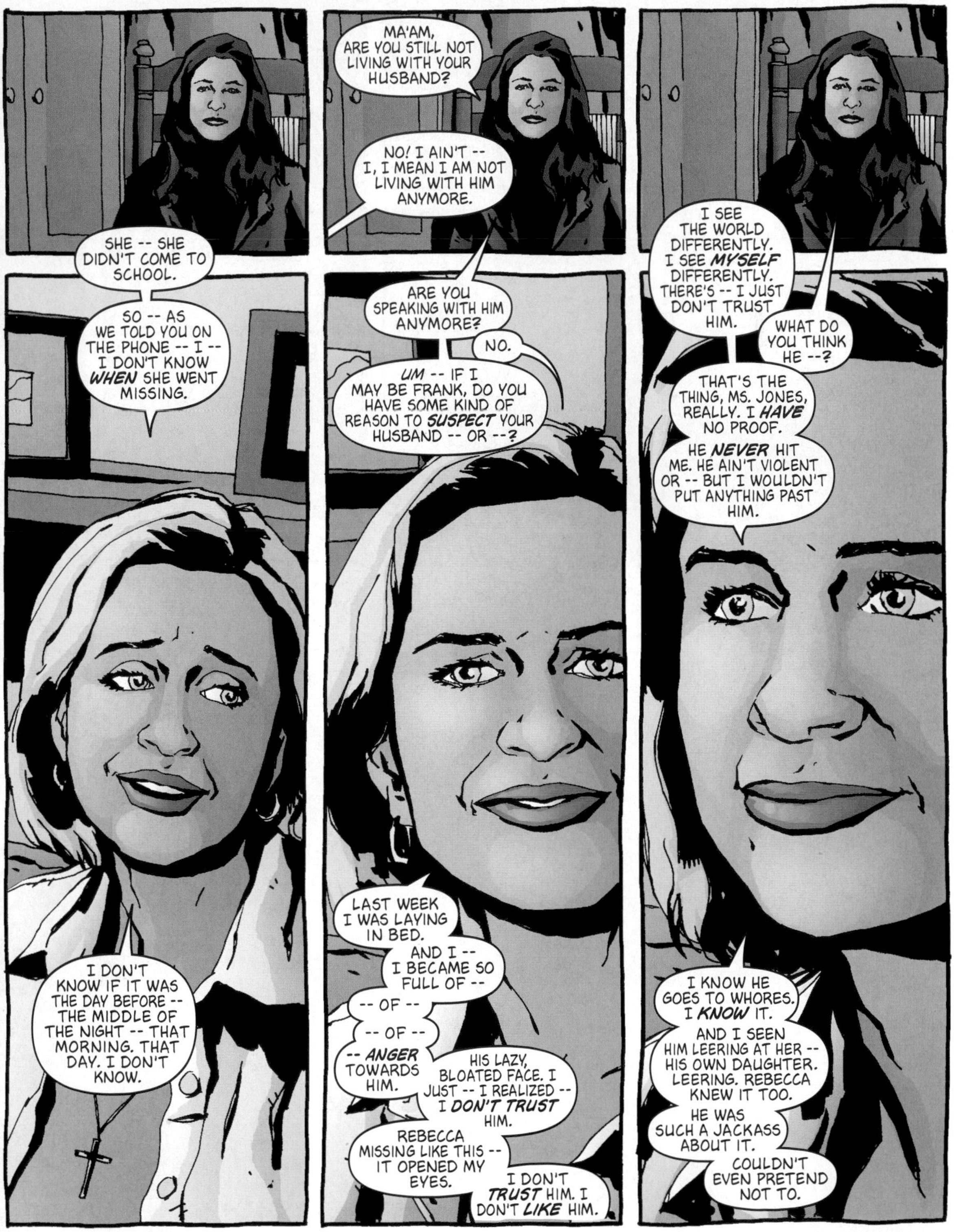
SHE -- SHE DIDN'T COME TO SCHOOL.
SO -- AS WE TOLD YOU ON THE PHONE -- I -- I DON'T KNOW *WHEN* SHE WENT MISSING.
I DON'T KNOW IF IT WAS THE DAY BEFORE -- THE MIDDLE OF THE NIGHT -- THAT MORNING. THAT DAY. I DON'T KNOW.
MA'AM, ARE YOU STILL NOT LIVING WITH YOUR HUSBAND?
NO! I AIN'T -- I, I MEAN I AM NOT LIVING WITH HIM ANYMORE.
ARE YOU SPEAKING WITH HIM ANYMORE?
NO.
UM -- IF I MAY BE FRANK, DO YOU HAVE SOME KIND OF REASON TO *SUSPECT* YOUR HUSBAND -- OR --?
LAST WEEK I WAS LAYING IN BED.
AND I -- I BECAME SO FULL OF --
-- OF --
-- OF --
-- *ANGER* TOWARDS HIM.
HIS LAZY, BLOATED FACE. I JUST -- I REALIZED -- I *DON'T TRUST* HIM.
REBECCA MISSING LIKE THIS -- IT OPENED MY EYES.
I DON'T *TRUST* HIM. I DON'T *LIKE* HIM.
I SEE THE WORLD DIFFERENTLY. I SEE *MYSELF* DIFFERENTLY. THERE'S -- I JUST DON'T TRUST HIM.
WHAT DO YOU THINK HE --?
THAT'S THE THING, MS. JONES, REALLY. I *HAVE* NO PROOF.
HE *NEVER* HIT ME. HE AIN'T VIOLENT OR -- BUT I WOULDN'T PUT ANYTHING PAST HIM.
I KNOW HE GOES TO WHORES. I *KNOW* IT.
AND I SEEN HIM LEERING AT HER -- HIS OWN DAUGHTER. LEERING. REBECCA KNEW IT TOO.
HE WAS SUCH A JACKASS ABOUT IT.
COULDN'T EVEN PRETEND NOT TO.

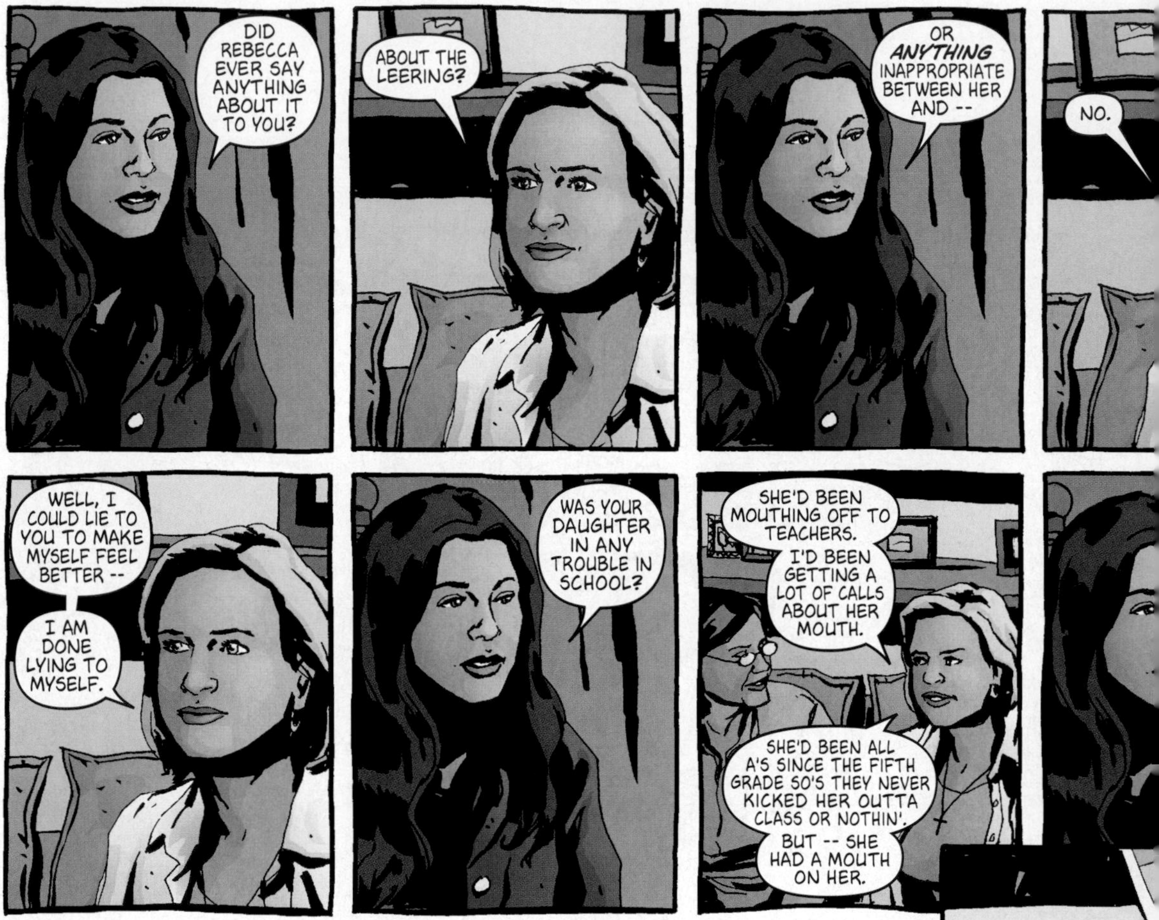
DID REBECCA EVER SAY ANYTHING ABOUT IT TO YOU?
ABOUT THE LEERING?
OR ANYTHING INAPPROPRIATE BETWEEN HER AND --
NO.
WELL, I COULD LIE TO YOU TO MAKE MYSELF FEEL BETTER --
I AM DONE LYING TO MYSELF.
WAS YOUR DAUGHTER IN ANY TROUBLE IN SCHOOL?
SHE'D BEEN MOUTHING OFF TO TEACHERS.
I'D BEEN GETTING A LOT OF CALLS ABOUT HER MOUTH.
SHE'D BEEN ALL A'S SINCE THE FIFTH GRADE SO'S THEY NEVER KICKED HER OUTTA CLASS OR NOTHIN'.
BUT -- SHE HAD A MOUTH ON HER.

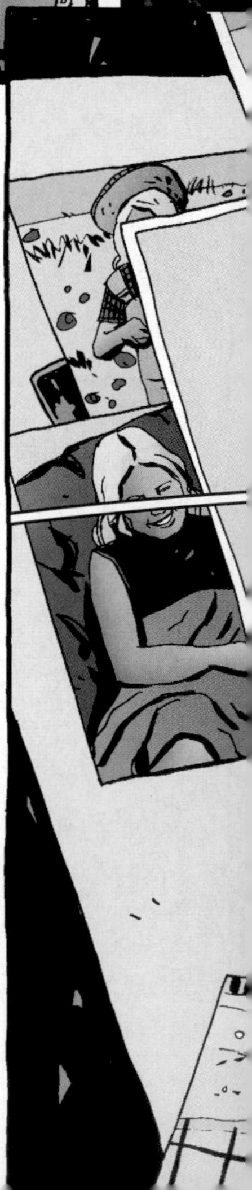

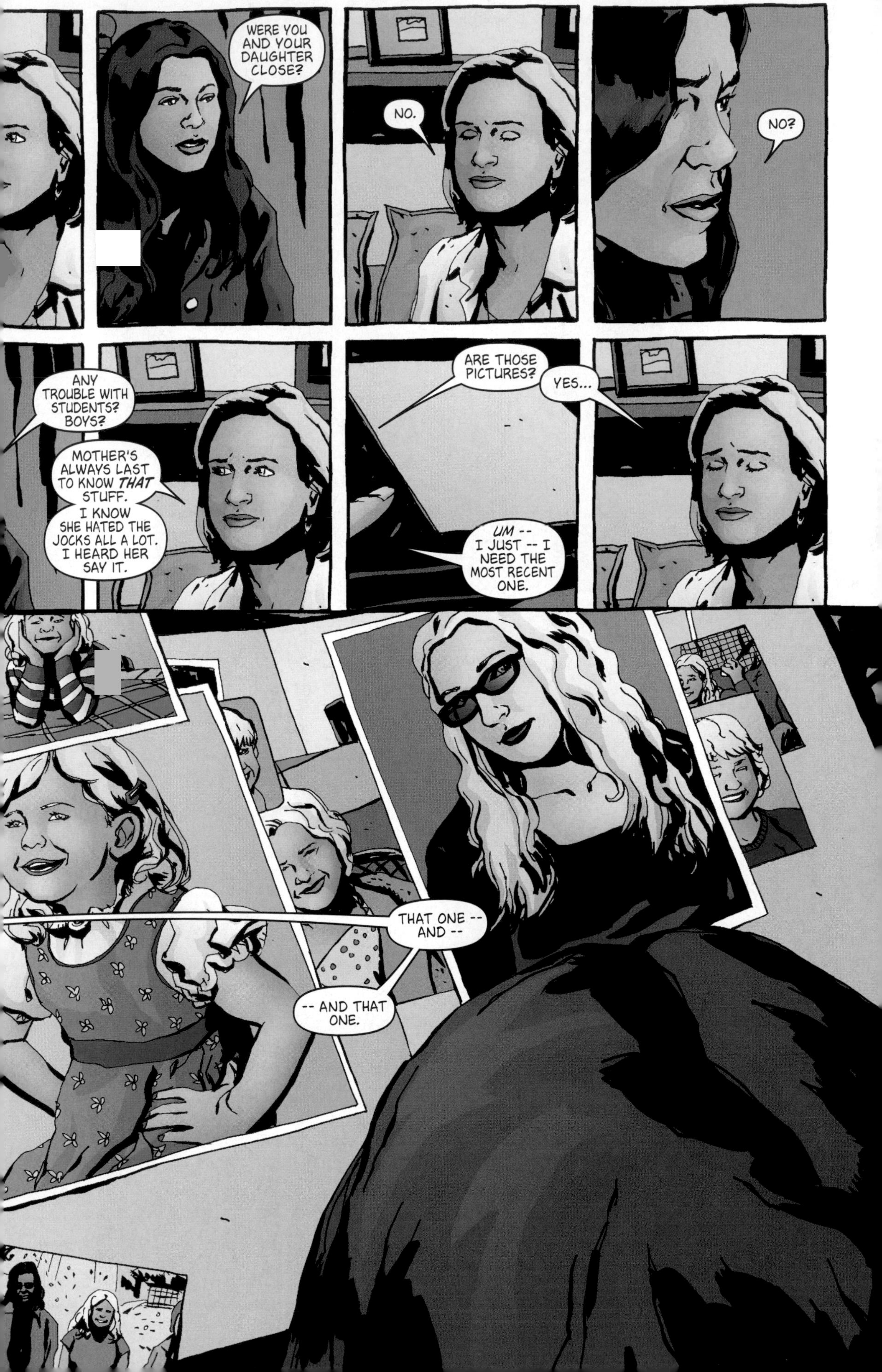
WERE YOU AND YOUR DAUGHTER CLOSE?
NO.
NO?
ANY TROUBLE WITH STUDENTS? BOYS?
MOTHER'S ALWAYS LAST TO KNOW *THAT* STUFF.
I KNOW SHE HATED THE JOCKS ALL A LOT. I HEARD HER SAY IT.
ARE THOSE PICTURES?
YES...
UM -- I JUST -- I NEED THE MOST RECENT ONE.
THAT ONE -- AND --
-- AND THAT ONE.

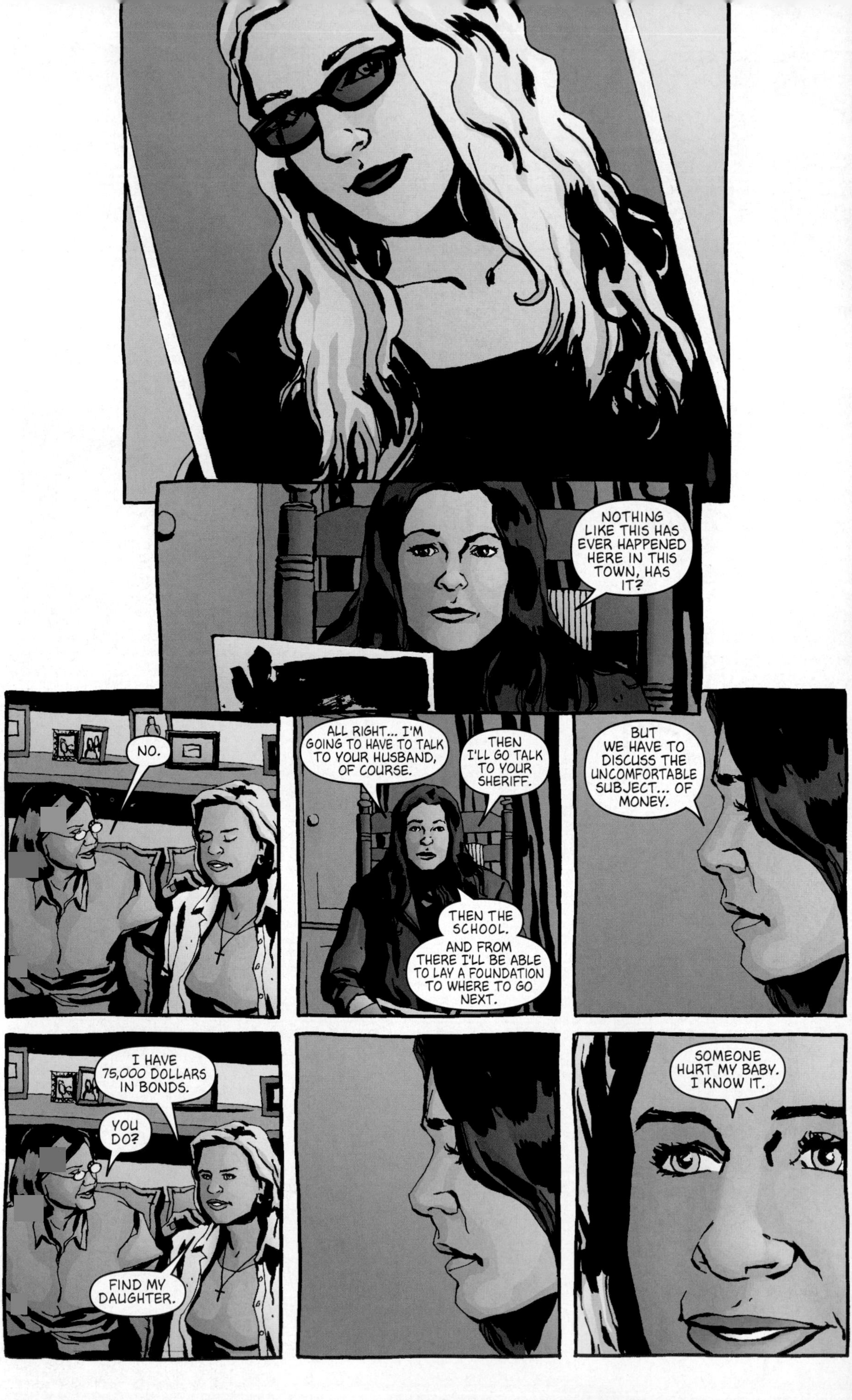
NOTHING LIKE THIS HAS EVER HAPPENED HERE IN THIS TOWN, HAS IT?
NO.
ALL RIGHT... I'M GOING TO HAVE TO TALK TO YOUR HUSBAND, OF COURSE.
THEN I'LL GO TALK TO YOUR SHERIFF.
THEN THE SCHOOL.
AND FROM THERE I'LL BE ABLE TO LAY A FOUNDATION TO WHERE TO GO NEXT.
BUT WE HAVE TO DISCUSS THE UNCOMFORTABLE SUBJECT... OF MONEY.
I HAVE 75,000 DOLLARS IN BONDS.
YOU DO?
FIND MY DAUGHTER.
SOMEONE HURT MY BABY. I KNOW IT.

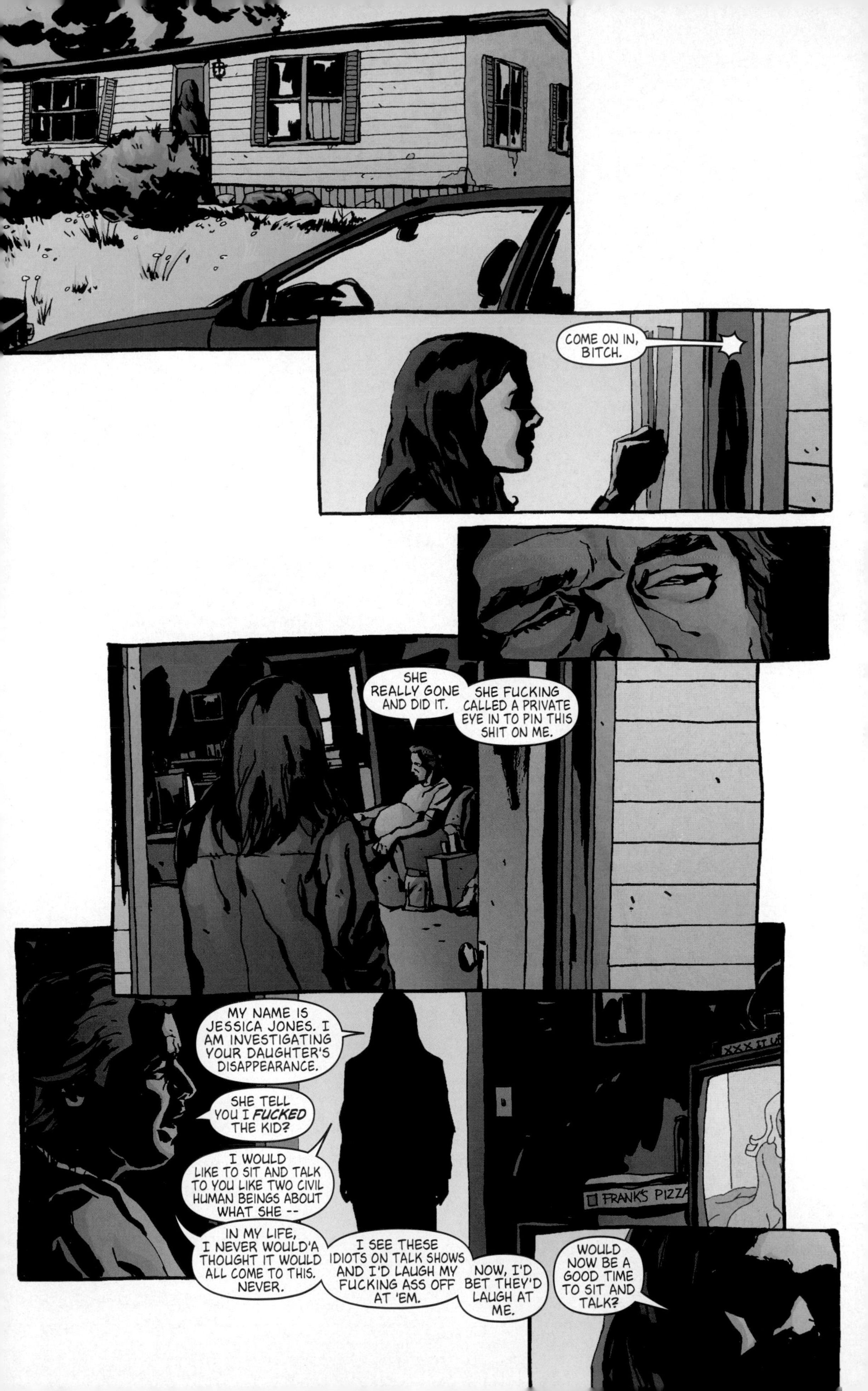
COME ON IN, BITCH.
SHE REALLY GONE AND DID IT.
SHE FUCKING CALLED A PRIVATE EYE IN TO PIN THIS SHIT ON ME.
MY NAME IS JESSICA JONES. I AM INVESTIGATING YOUR DAUGHTER'S DISAPPEARANCE.
SHE TELL YOU I *FUCKED* THE KID?
I WOULD LIKE TO SIT AND TALK TO YOU LIKE TWO CIVIL HUMAN BEINGS ABOUT WHAT SHE --
IN MY LIFE, I NEVER WOULD'A THOUGHT IT WOULD ALL COME TO THIS. NEVER.
I SEE THESE IDIOTS ON TALK SHOWS AND I'D LAUGH MY FUCKING ASS OFF AT 'EM.
NOW, I'D BET THEY'D LAUGH AT ME.
WOULD NOW BE A GOOD TIME TO SIT AND TALK?
FRANK'S PIZZA

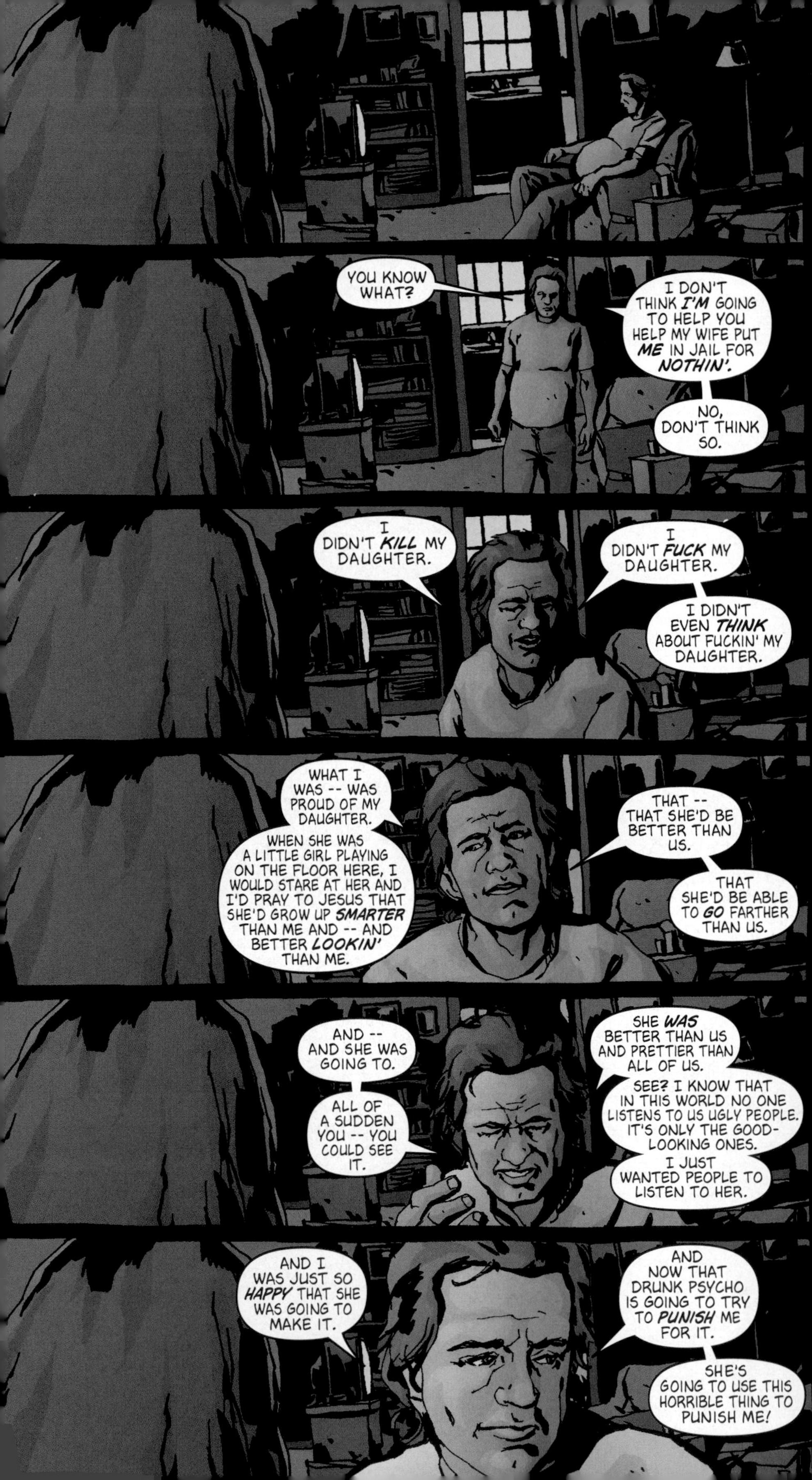
YOU KNOW WHAT?
I DON'T THINK *I'M* GOING TO HELP YOU HELP MY WIFE PUT *ME* IN JAIL FOR *NOTHIN'*.
NO, DON'T THINK SO.
I DIDN'T *KILL* MY DAUGHTER.
I DIDN'T *FUCK* MY DAUGHTER.
I DIDN'T EVEN *THINK* ABOUT FUCKIN' MY DAUGHTER.
WHAT I WAS -- WAS PROUD OF MY DAUGHTER.
WHEN SHE WAS A LITTLE GIRL PLAYING ON THE FLOOR HERE, I WOULD STARE AT HER AND I'D PRAY TO JESUS THAT SHE'D GROW UP *SMARTER* THAN ME AND -- AND BETTER *LOOKIN'* THAN ME.
THAT -- THAT SHE'D BE BETTER THAN US.
THAT SHE'D BE ABLE TO *GO* FARTHER THAN US.
AND -- AND SHE WAS GOING TO.
ALL OF A SUDDEN YOU -- YOU COULD SEE IT.
SHE *WAS* BETTER THAN US AND PRETTIER THAN ALL OF US.
SEE? I KNOW THAT IN THIS WORLD NO ONE LISTENS TO US UGLY PEOPLE. IT'S ONLY THE GOOD-LOOKING ONES.
I JUST WANTED PEOPLE TO LISTEN TO HER.
AND I WAS JUST SO *HAPPY* THAT SHE WAS GOING TO MAKE IT.
AND NOW THAT DRUNK PSYCHO IS GOING TO TRY TO *PUNISH* ME FOR IT.
SHE'S GOING TO USE THIS HORRIBLE THING TO PUNISH ME!

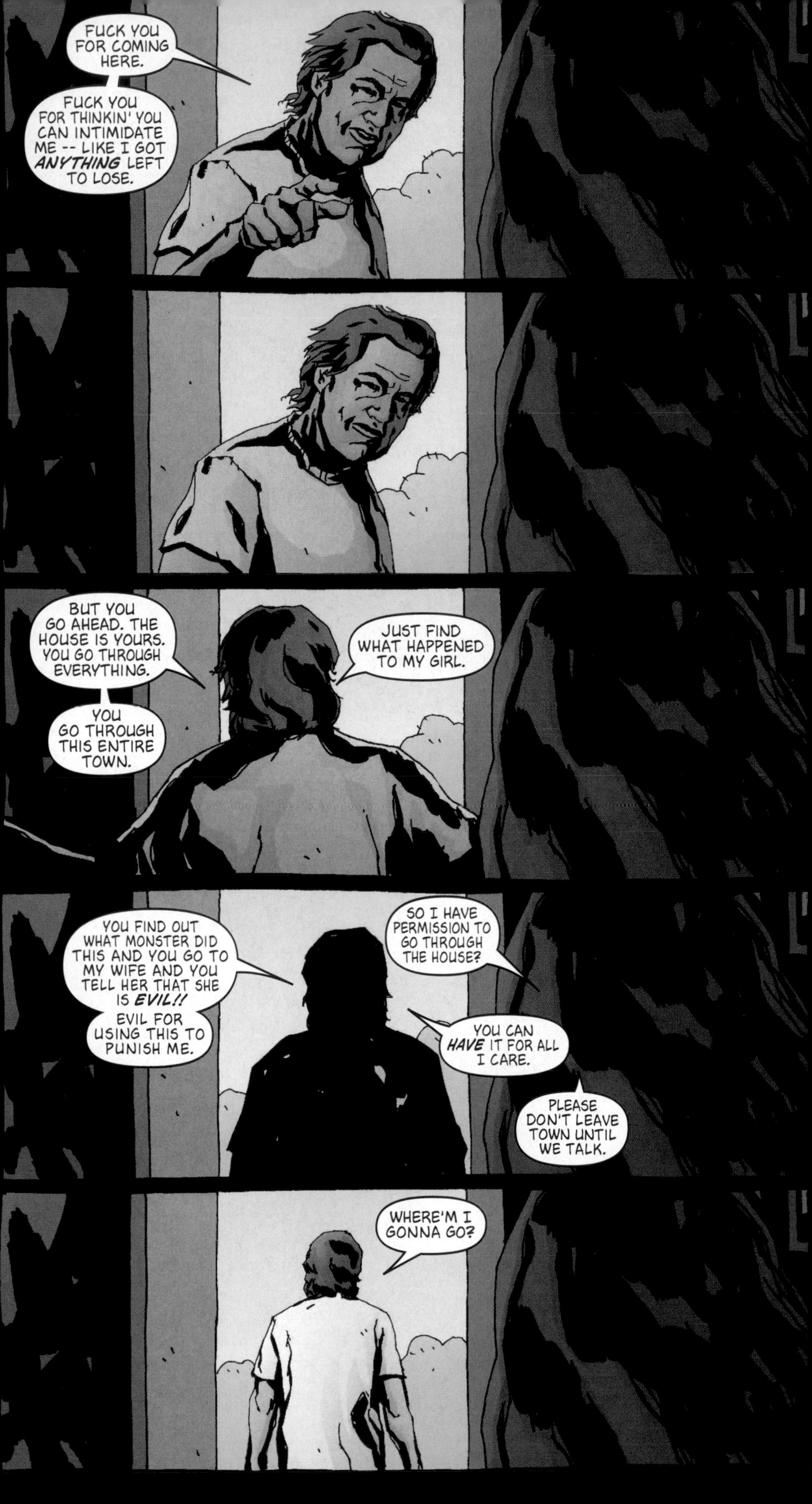
FUCK YOU FOR COMING HERE.
FUCK YOU FOR THINKIN' YOU CAN INTIMIDATE ME -- LIKE I GOT ***ANYTHING*** LEFT TO LOSE.
BUT YOU GO AHEAD. THE HOUSE IS YOURS. YOU GO THROUGH EVERYTHING.
YOU GO THROUGH THIS ENTIRE TOWN.
JUST FIND WHAT HAPPENED TO MY GIRL.
YOU FIND OUT WHAT MONSTER DID THIS AND YOU GO TO MY WIFE AND YOU TELL HER THAT SHE IS ***EVIL!!***
EVIL FOR USING THIS TO PUNISH ME.
SO I HAVE PERMISSION TO GO THROUGH THE HOUSE?
YOU CAN ***HAVE*** IT FOR ALL I CARE.
PLEASE DON'T LEAVE TOWN UNTIL WE TALK.
WHERE'M I GONNA GO?

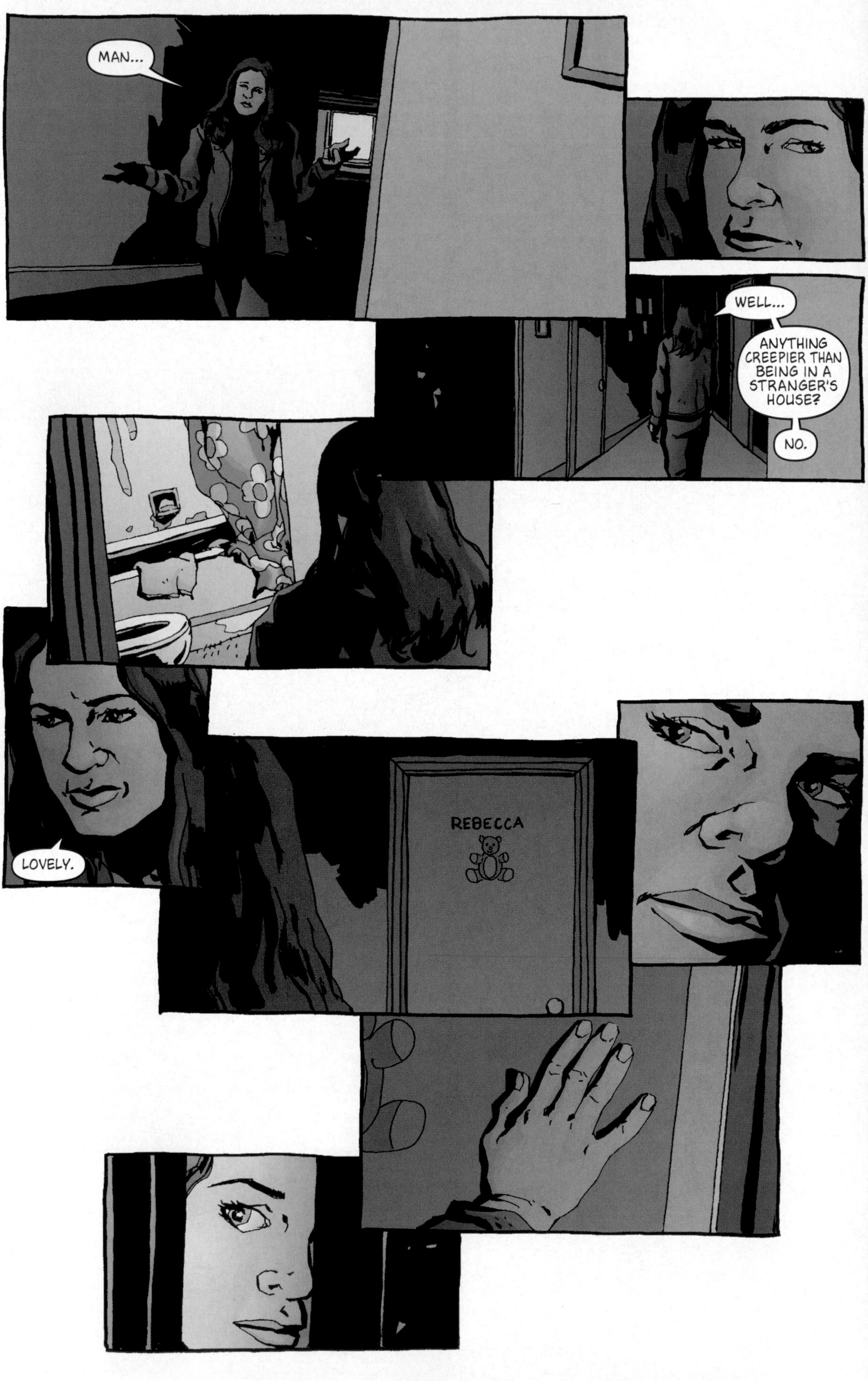
MAN...
WELL...
ANYTHING CREEPIER THAN BEING IN A STRANGER'S HOUSE?
NO.
LOVELY.
REBECCA

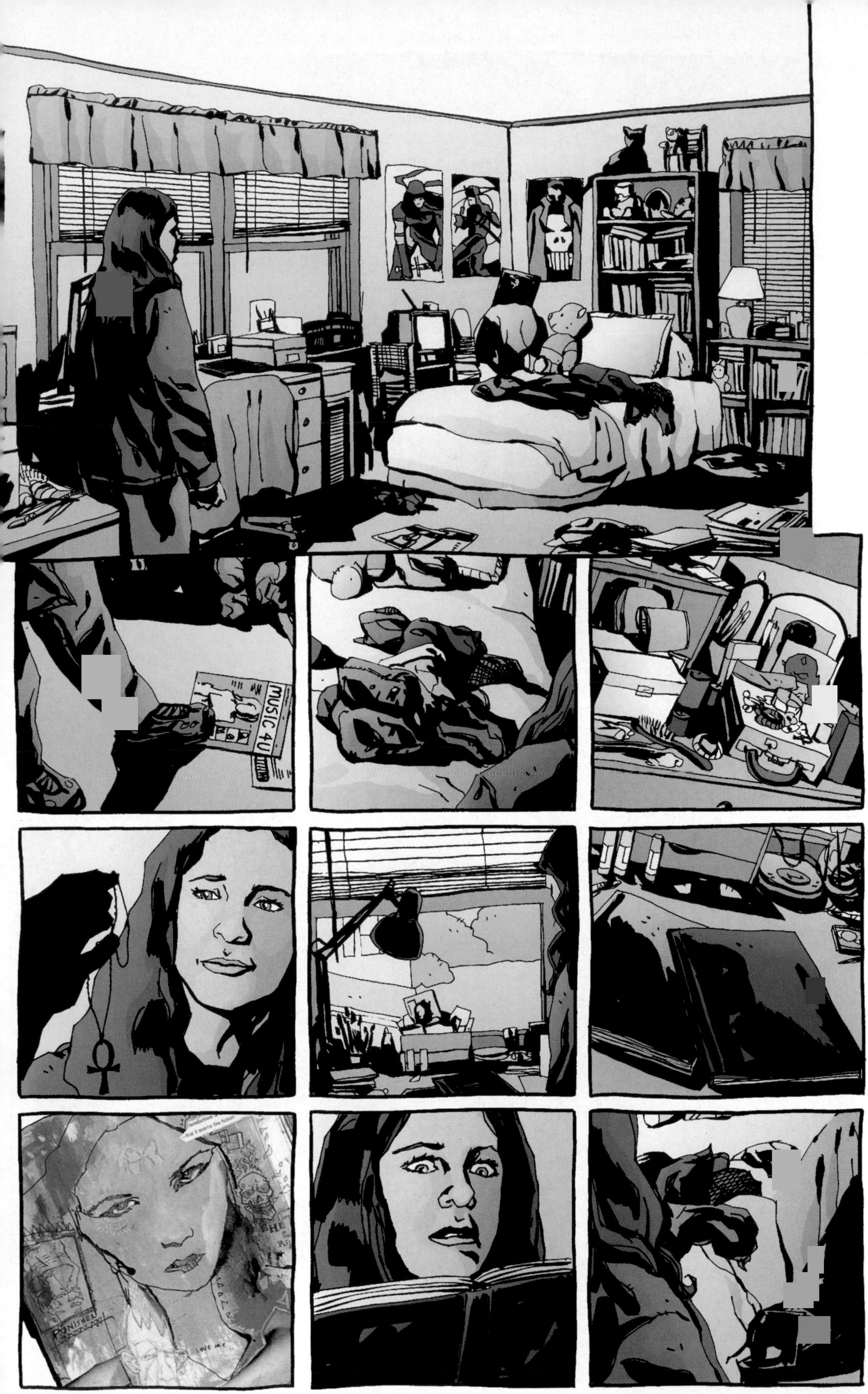
MUSIC 4U
—that it seems like fiction
PUNISHER
LOVE ME

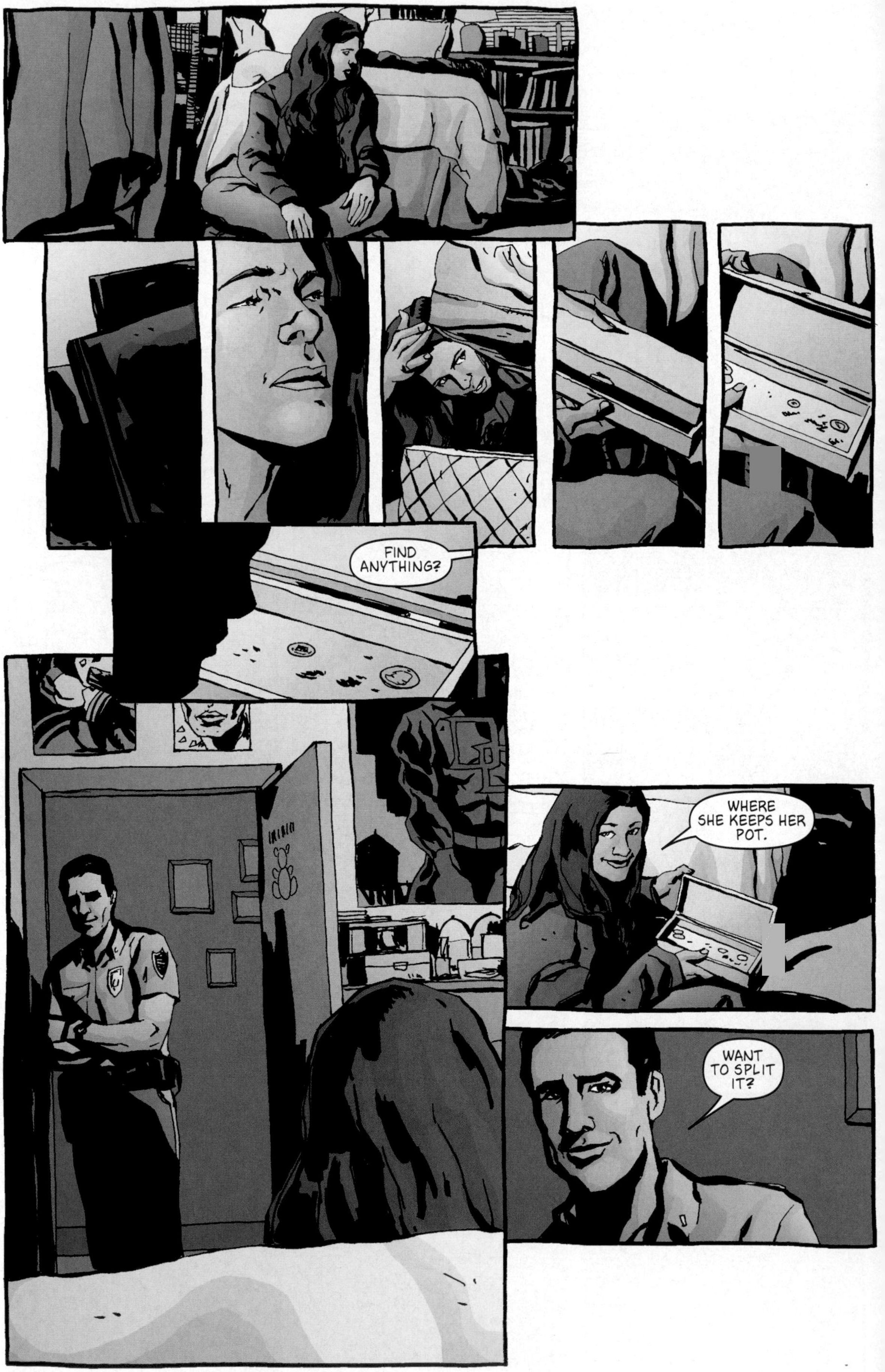
FIND ANYTHING?
WHERE SHE KEEPS HER POT.
WANT TO SPLIT IT?

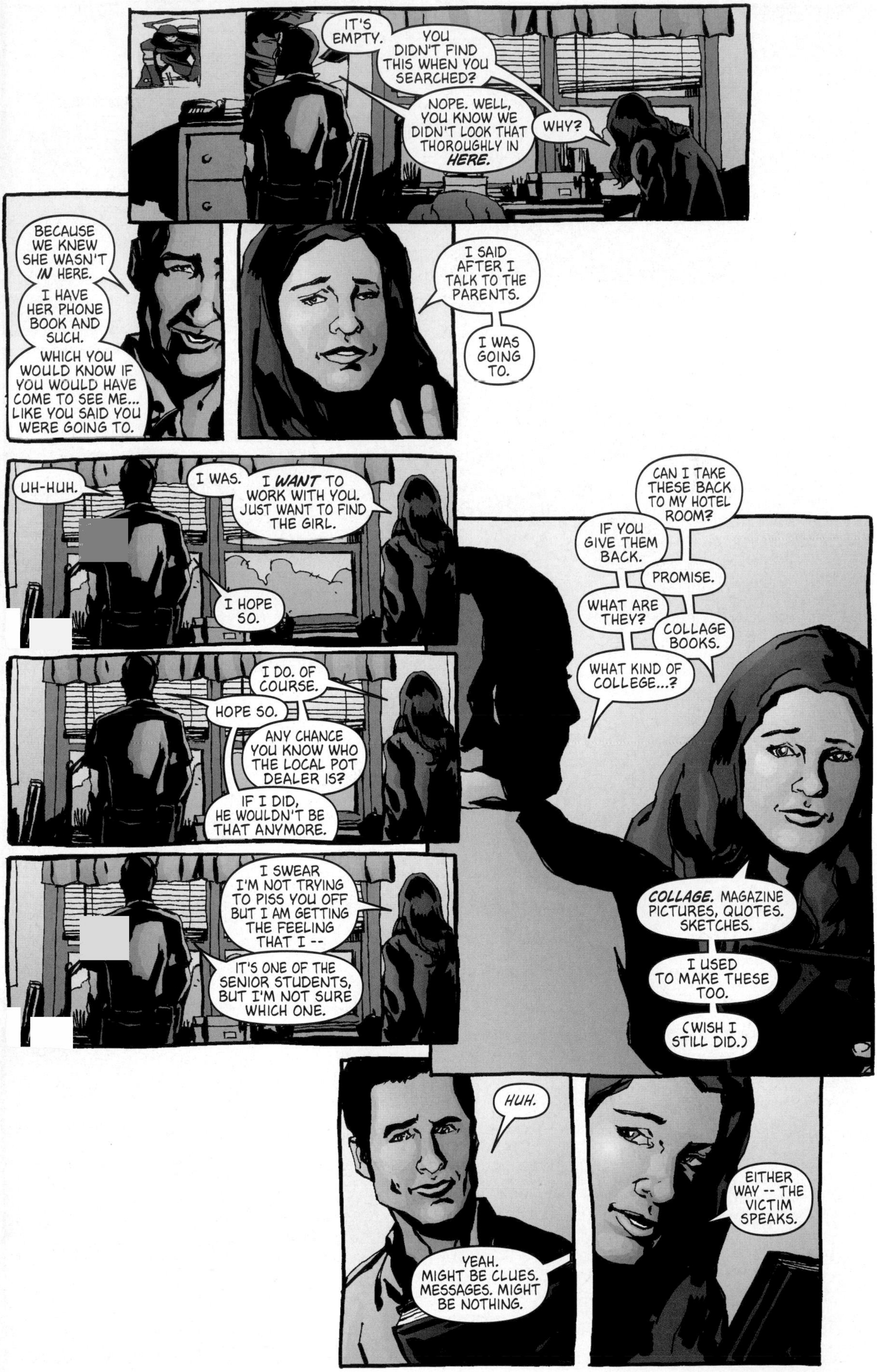
IT'S EMPTY.
YOU DIDN'T FIND THIS WHEN YOU SEARCHED?
NOPE. WELL, YOU KNOW WE DIDN'T LOOK THAT THOROUGHLY IN *HERE.*
WHY?
BECAUSE WE KNEW SHE WASN'T *IN* HERE.
I HAVE HER PHONE BOOK AND SUCH.
WHICH YOU WOULD KNOW IF YOU WOULD HAVE COME TO SEE ME... LIKE YOU SAID YOU WERE GOING TO.
I SAID AFTER I TALK TO THE PARENTS.
I WAS GOING TO.
UH-HUH.
I WAS.
I *WANT* TO WORK WITH YOU. JUST WANT TO FIND THE GIRL.
I HOPE SO.
I DO. OF COURSE.
HOPE SO.
ANY CHANCE YOU KNOW WHO THE LOCAL POT DEALER IS?
IF I DID, HE WOULDN'T BE THAT ANYMORE.
I SWEAR I'M NOT TRYING TO PISS YOU OFF BUT I AM GETTING THE FEELING THAT I --
IT'S ONE OF THE SENIOR STUDENTS, BUT I'M NOT SURE WHICH ONE.
CAN I TAKE THESE BACK TO MY HOTEL ROOM?
IF YOU GIVE THEM BACK.
PROMISE.
WHAT ARE THEY?
COLLAGE BOOKS.
WHAT KIND OF COLLEGE...?
COLLAGE. MAGAZINE PICTURES, QUOTES. SKETCHES.
I USED TO MAKE THESE TOO.
(WISH I STILL DID.)
HUH.
YEAH. MIGHT BE CLUES. MESSAGES. MIGHT BE NOTHING.
EITHER WAY -- THE VICTIM SPEAKS.

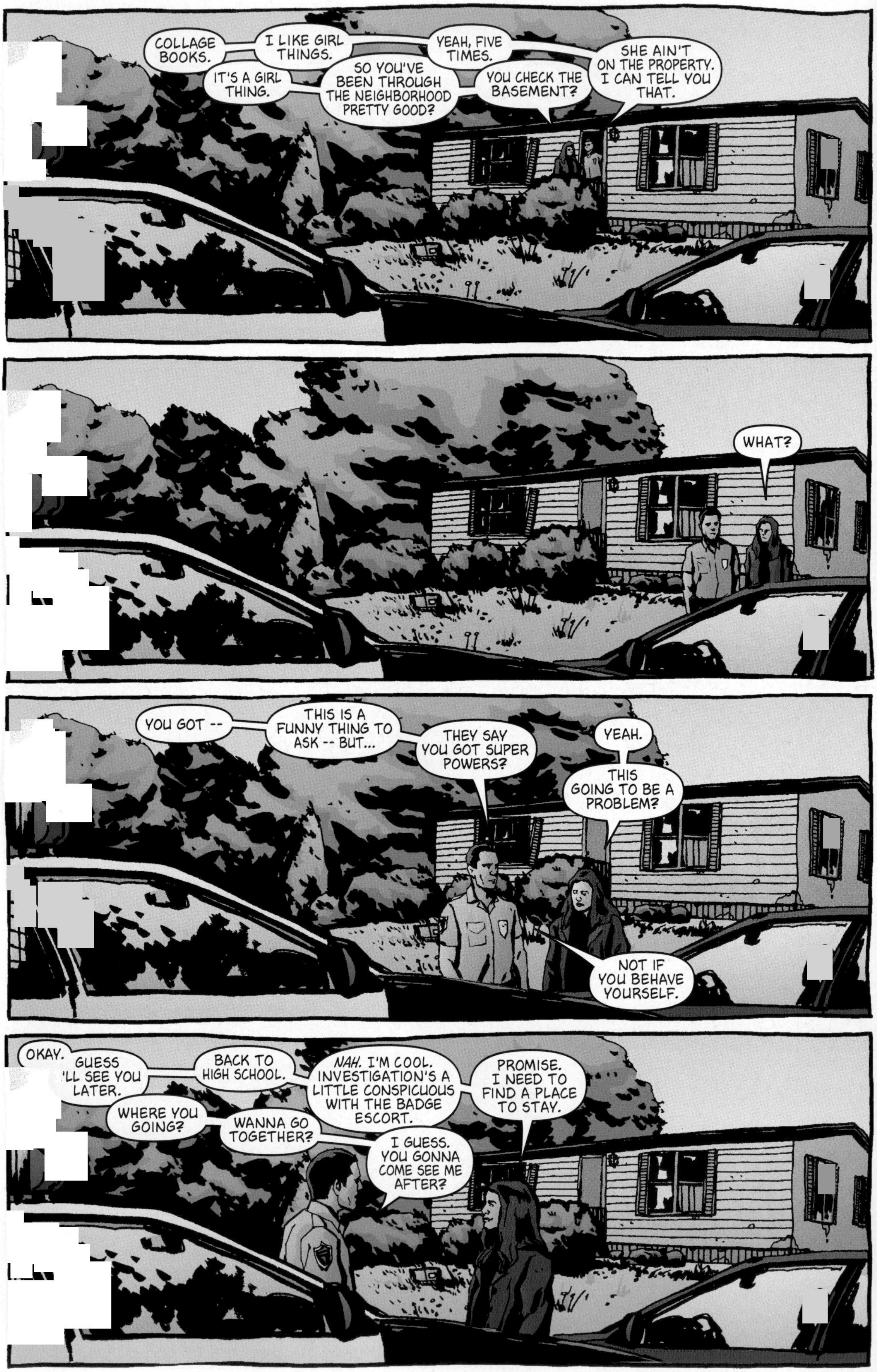
COLLAGE BOOKS.
IT'S A GIRL THING.
I LIKE GIRL THINGS.
SO YOU'VE BEEN THROUGH THE NEIGHBORHOOD PRETTY GOOD?
YEAH, FIVE TIMES.
YOU CHECK THE BASEMENT?
SHE AIN'T ON THE PROPERTY. I CAN TELL YOU THAT.
WHAT?
YOU GOT --
THIS IS A FUNNY THING TO ASK -- BUT...
THEY SAY YOU GOT SUPER POWERS?
YEAH.
THIS GOING TO BE A PROBLEM?
NOT IF YOU BEHAVE YOURSELF.
OKAY.
GUESS 'LL SEE YOU LATER.
WHERE YOU GOING?
BACK TO HIGH SCHOOL.
WANNA GO TOGETHER?
NAH. I'M COOL. INVESTIGATION'S A LITTLE CONSPICUOUS WITH THE BADGE ESCORT.
I GUESS. YOU GONNA COME SEE ME AFTER?
PROMISE. I NEED TO FIND A PLACE TO STAY.

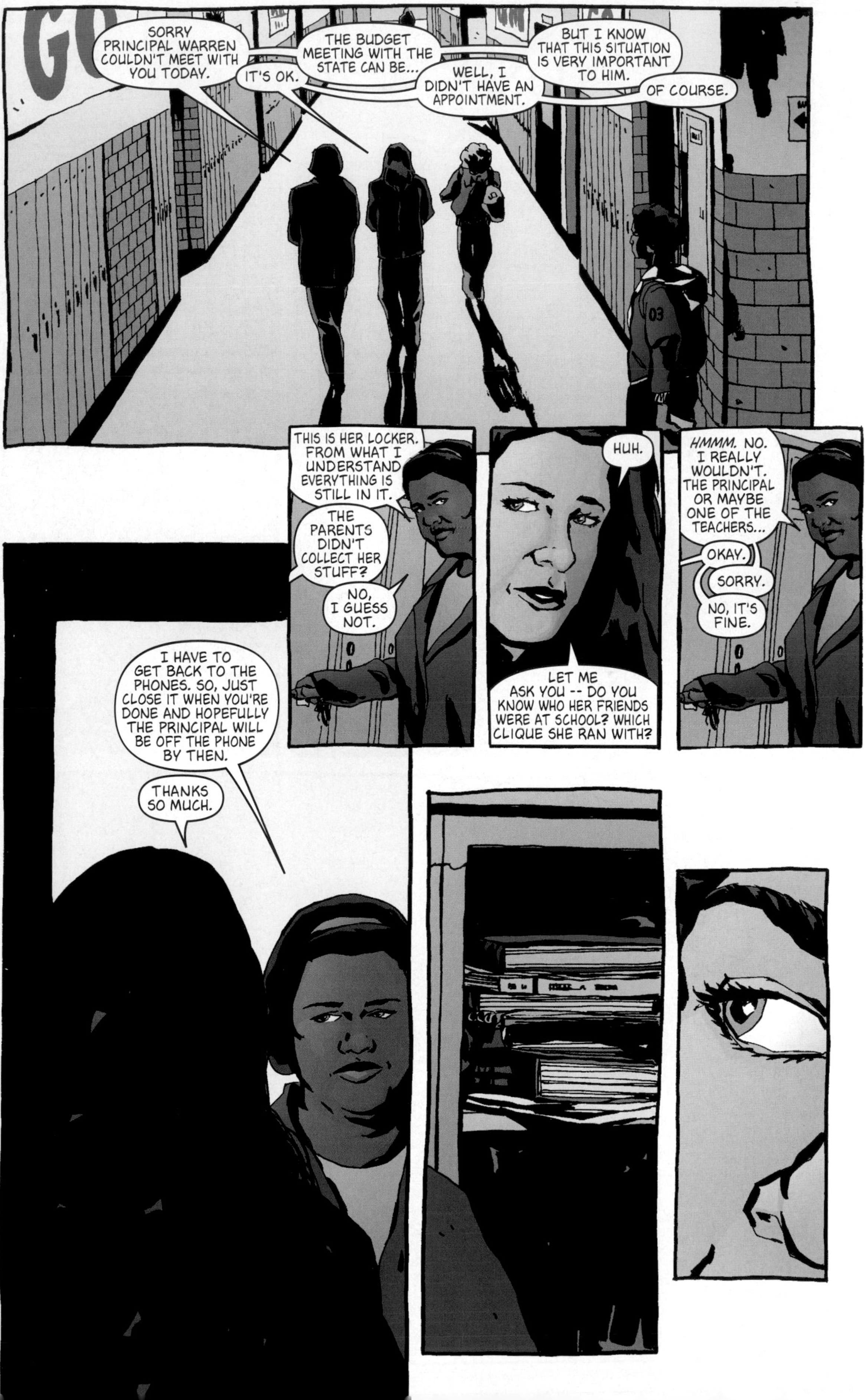
SORRY PRINCIPAL WARREN COULDN'T MEET WITH YOU TODAY.
IT'S OK.
THE BUDGET MEETING WITH THE STATE CAN BE...
WELL, I DIDN'T HAVE AN APPOINTMENT.
BUT I KNOW THAT THIS SITUATION IS VERY IMPORTANT TO HIM.
OF COURSE.
THIS IS HER LOCKER. FROM WHAT I UNDERSTAND EVERYTHING IS STILL IN IT.
THE PARENTS DIDN'T COLLECT HER STUFF?
NO, I GUESS NOT.
HUH.
LET ME ASK YOU -- DO YOU KNOW WHO HER FRIENDS WERE AT SCHOOL? WHICH CLIQUE SHE RAN WITH?
HMMM. NO. I REALLY WOULDN'T. THE PRINCIPAL OR MAYBE ONE OF THE TEACHERS...
OKAY.
SORRY.
NO, IT'S FINE.
I HAVE TO GET BACK TO THE PHONES. SO, JUST CLOSE IT WHEN YOU'RE DONE AND HOPEFULLY THE PRINCIPAL WILL BE OFF THE PHONE BY THEN.
THANKS SO MUCH.

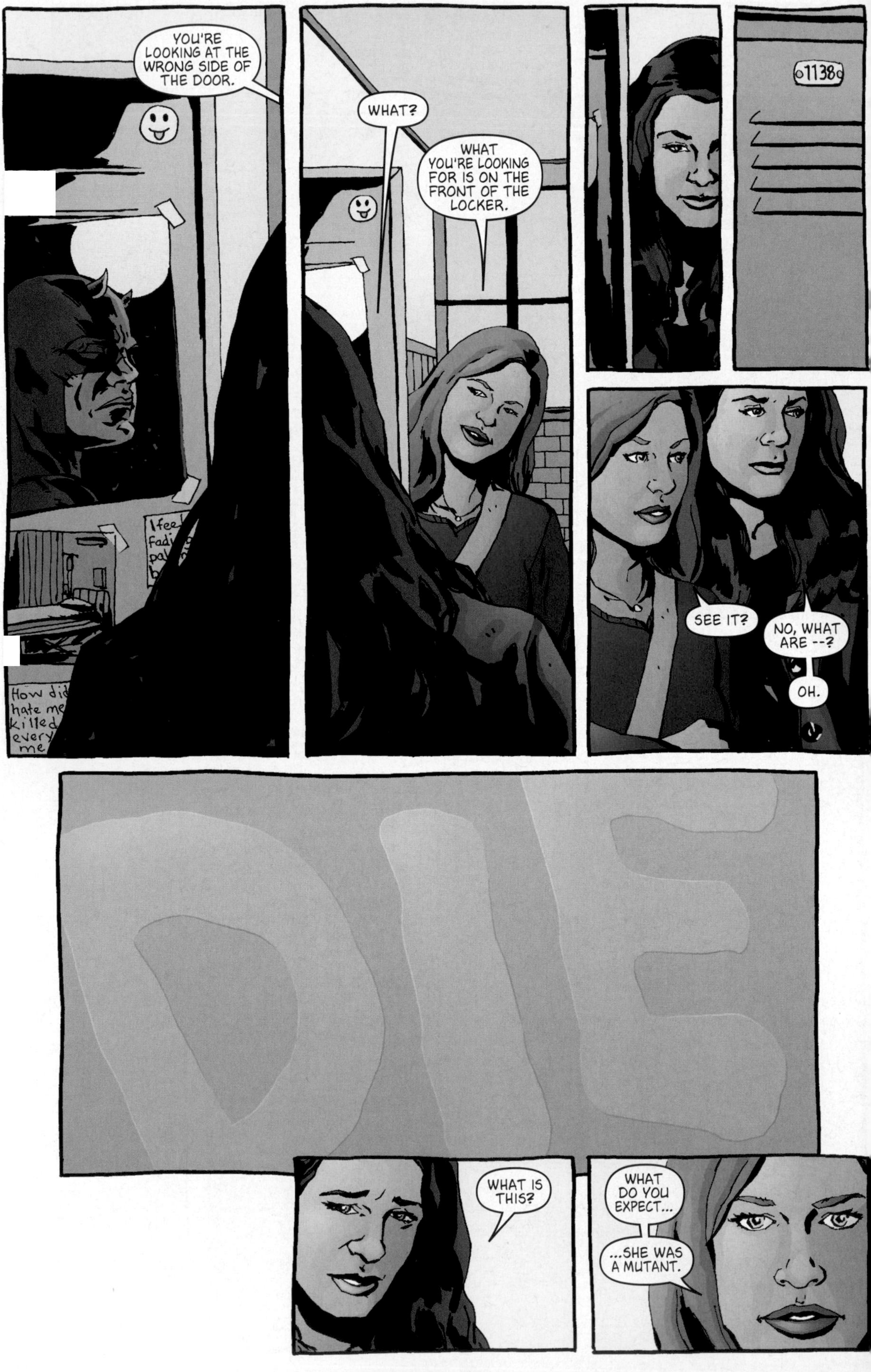
YOU'RE LOOKING AT THE WRONG SIDE OF THE DOOR.
WHAT?
WHAT YOU'RE LOOKING FOR IS ON THE FRONT OF THE LOCKER.
1138
SEE IT?
NO, WHAT ARE --?
OH.
DIE
WHAT IS THIS?
WHAT DO YOU EXPECT...
...SHE WAS A MUTANT.

WELCOME TO [redacted], NY

ISSUE #12

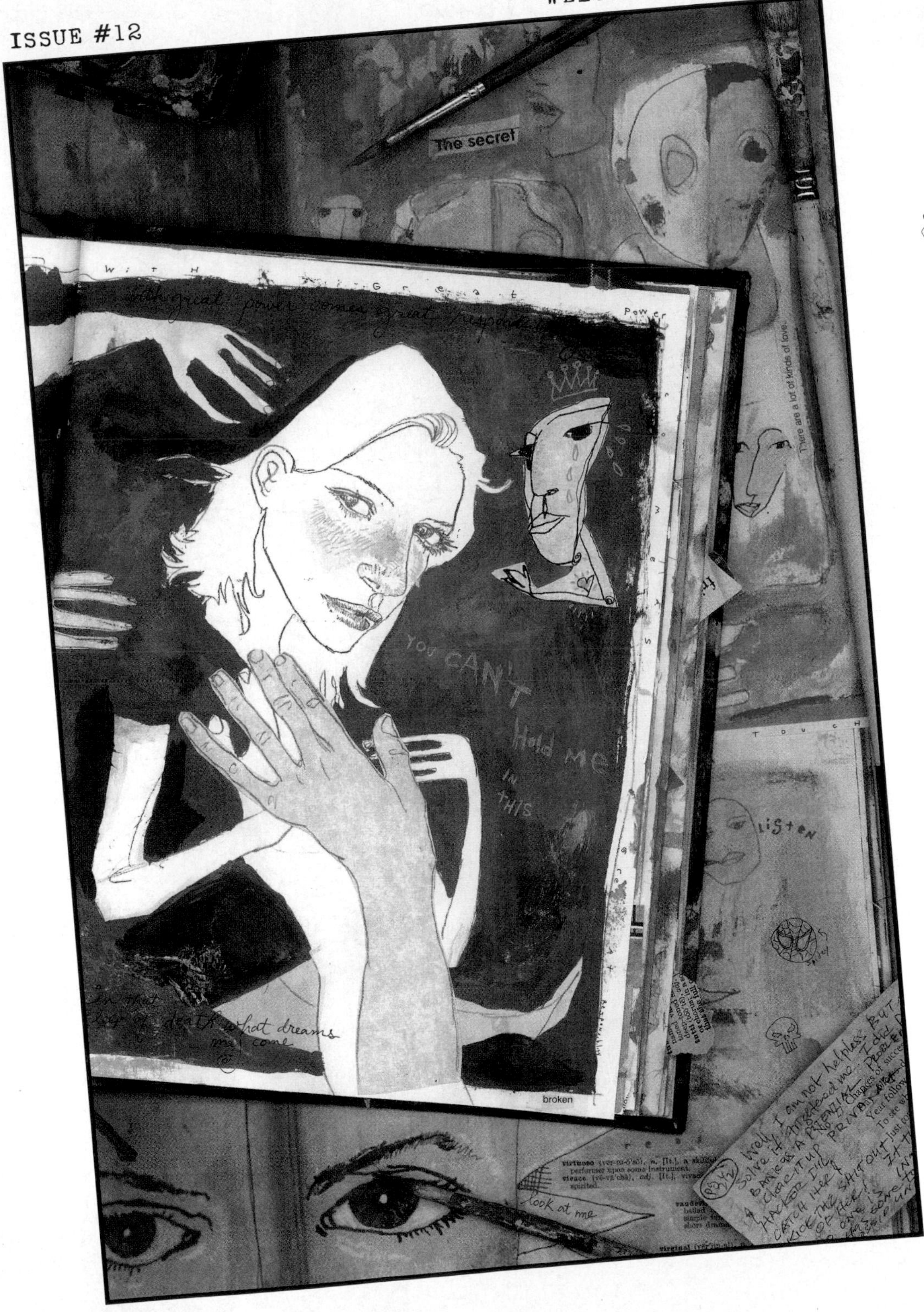

The secret
Power
You CAN'T Hold me IN THIS
There are a lot of kinds of love.
LiSten
broken
look at me

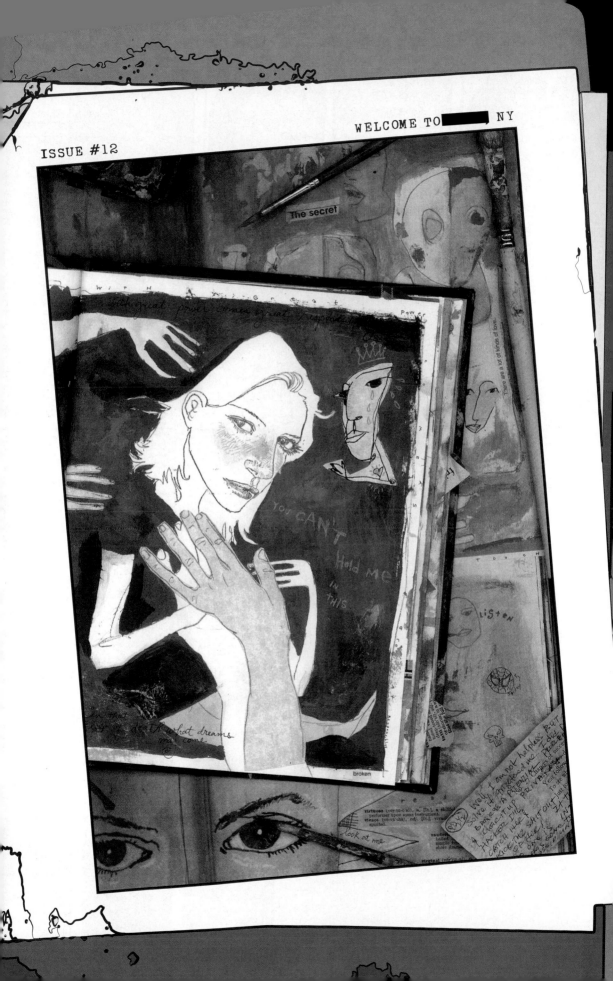

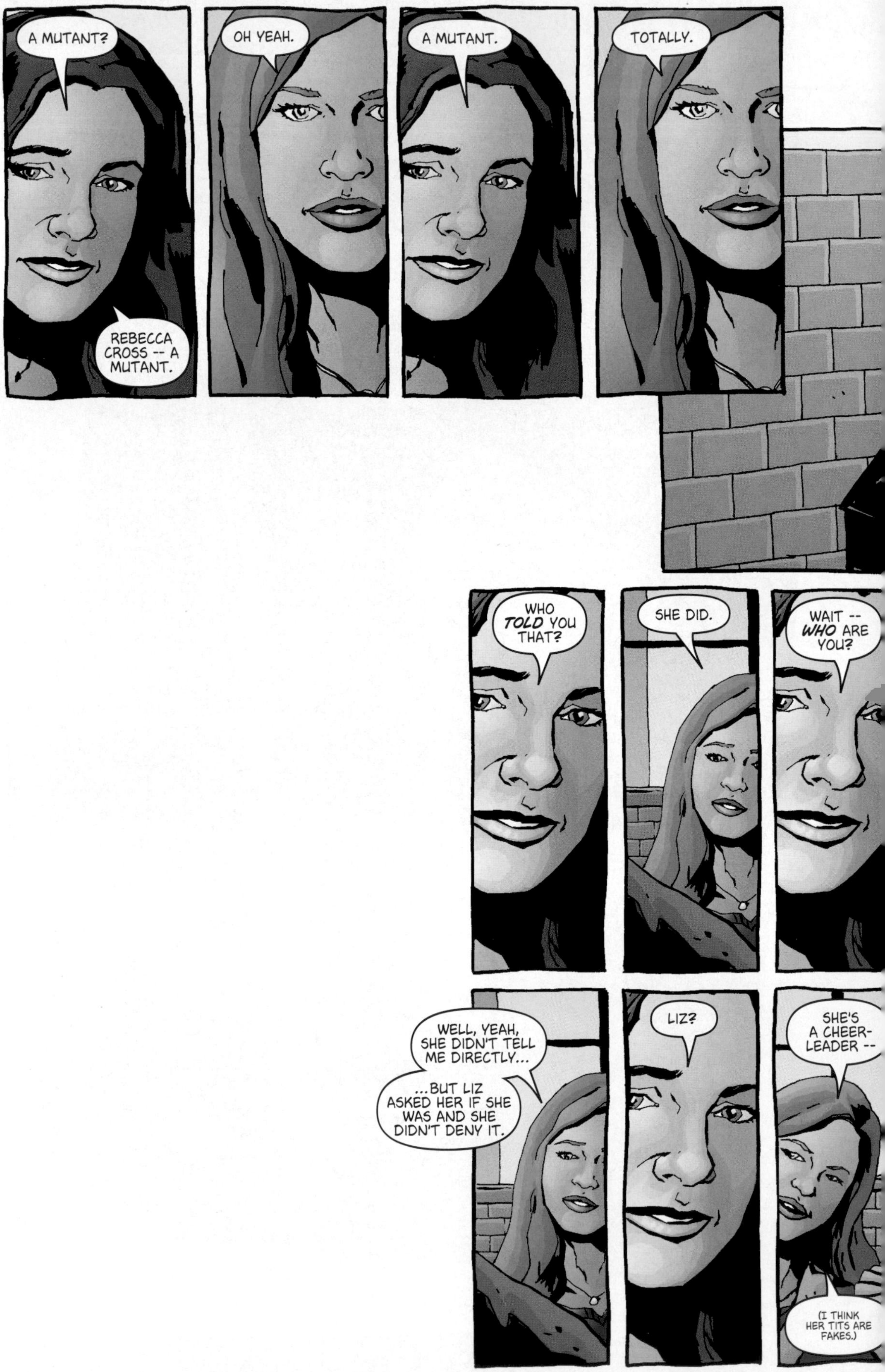
A MUTANT?
REBECCA CROSS -- A MUTANT.
OH YEAH.
A MUTANT.
TOTALLY.
WHO *TOLD* YOU THAT?
SHE DID.
WAIT -- *WHO* ARE YOU?
WELL, YEAH, SHE DIDN'T TELL ME DIRECTLY...
...BUT LIZ ASKED HER IF SHE WAS AND SHE DIDN'T DENY IT.
LIZ?
SHE'S A CHEER-LEADER --
(I THINK HER TITS ARE FAKES.)

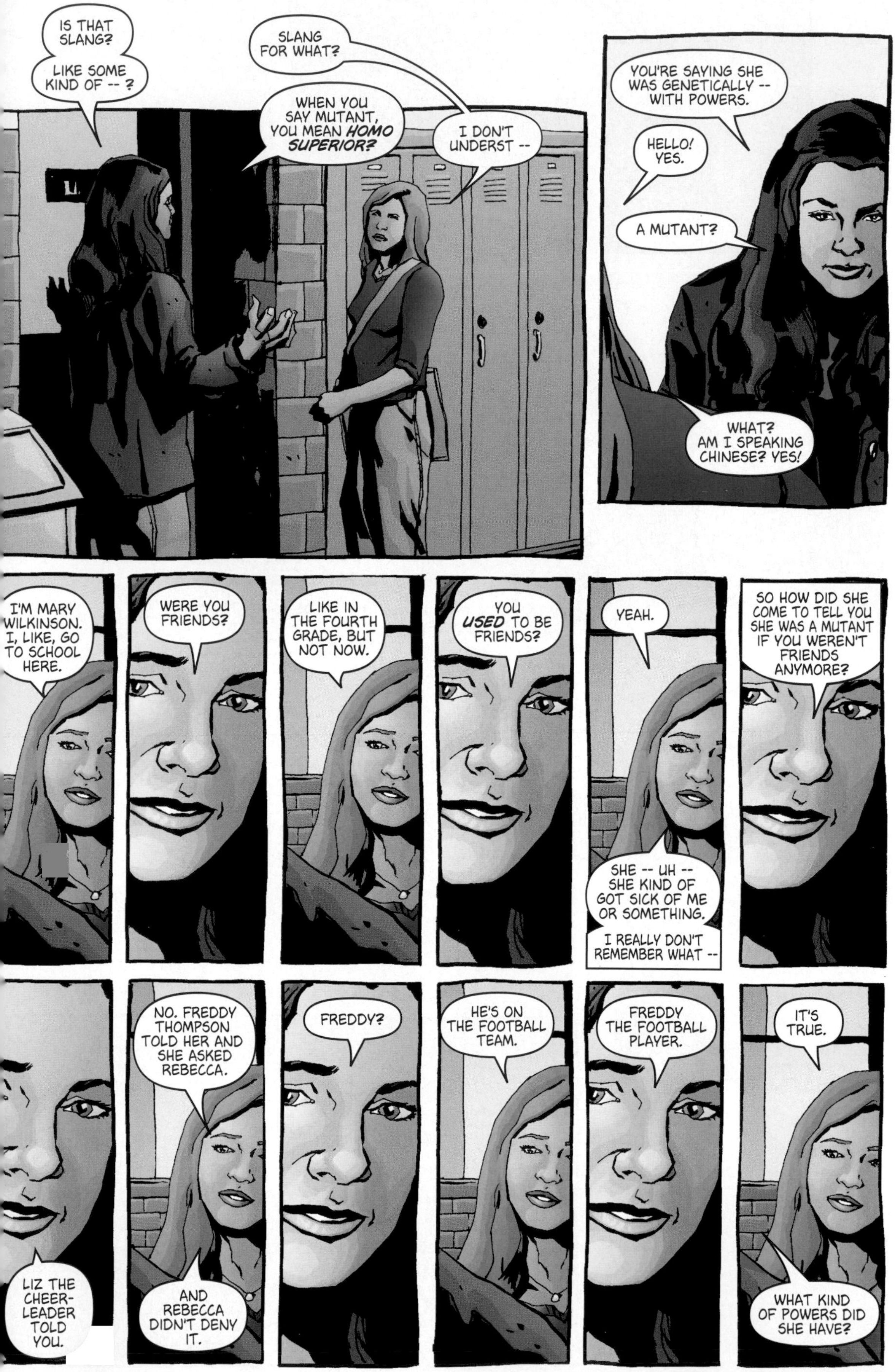
IS THAT SLANG?
LIKE SOME KIND OF -- ?
SLANG FOR WHAT?
WHEN YOU SAY MUTANT, YOU MEAN *HOMO SUPERIOR?*
I DON'T UNDERST --
YOU'RE SAYING SHE WAS GENETICALLY -- WITH POWERS.
HELLO! YES.
A MUTANT?
WHAT? AM I SPEAKING CHINESE? YES!
I'M MARY WILKINSON. I, LIKE, GO TO SCHOOL HERE.
WERE YOU FRIENDS?
LIKE IN THE FOURTH GRADE, BUT NOT NOW.
YOU *USED* TO BE FRIENDS?
YEAH.
SHE -- UH -- SHE KIND OF GOT SICK OF ME OR SOMETHING.
I REALLY DON'T REMEMBER WHAT --
SO HOW DID SHE COME TO TELL YOU SHE WAS A MUTANT IF YOU WEREN'T FRIENDS ANYMORE?
LIZ THE CHEER-LEADER TOLD YOU.
NO. FREDDY THOMPSON TOLD HER AND SHE ASKED REBECCA.
AND REBECCA DIDN'T DENY IT.
FREDDY?
HE'S ON THE FOOTBALL TEAM.
FREDDY THE FOOTBALL PLAYER.
IT'S TRUE.
WHAT KIND OF POWERS DID SHE HAVE?

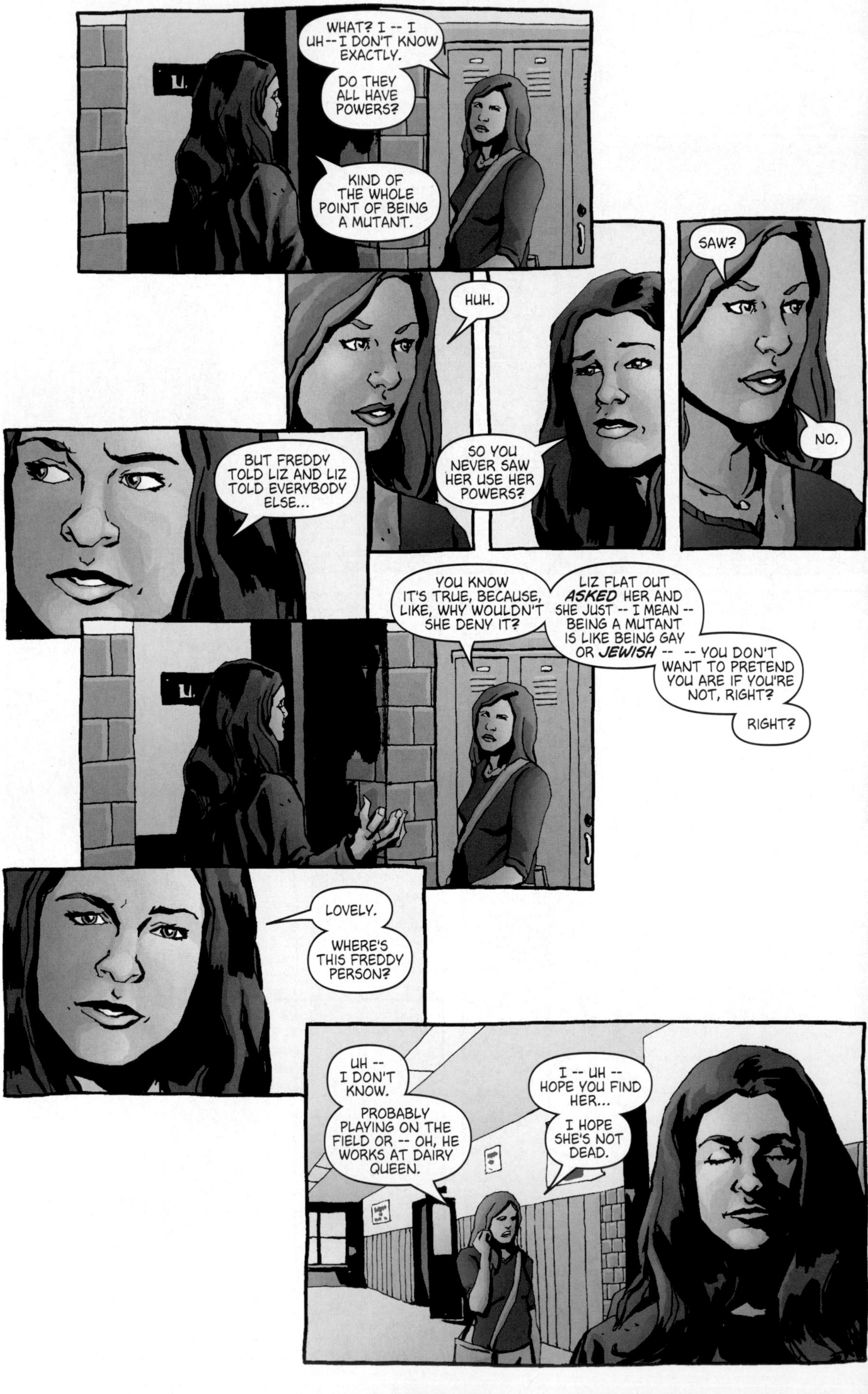
WHAT? I -- I UH -- I DON'T KNOW EXACTLY.
DO THEY ALL HAVE POWERS?
KIND OF THE WHOLE POINT OF BEING A MUTANT.
HUH.
SO YOU NEVER SAW HER USE HER POWERS?
SAW?
NO.
BUT FREDDY TOLD LIZ AND LIZ TOLD EVERYBODY ELSE...
YOU KNOW IT'S TRUE, BECAUSE, LIKE, WHY WOULDN'T SHE DENY IT?
LIZ FLAT OUT ASKED HER AND SHE JUST -- I MEAN -- BEING A MUTANT IS LIKE BEING GAY OR JEWISH --
-- YOU DON'T WANT TO PRETEND YOU ARE IF YOU'RE NOT, RIGHT?
RIGHT?
LOVELY.
WHERE'S THIS FREDDY PERSON?
UH -- I DON'T KNOW.
PROBABLY PLAYING ON THE FIELD OR -- OH, HE WORKS AT DAIRY QUEEN.
I -- UH -- HOPE YOU FIND HER...
I HOPE SHE'S NOT DEAD.

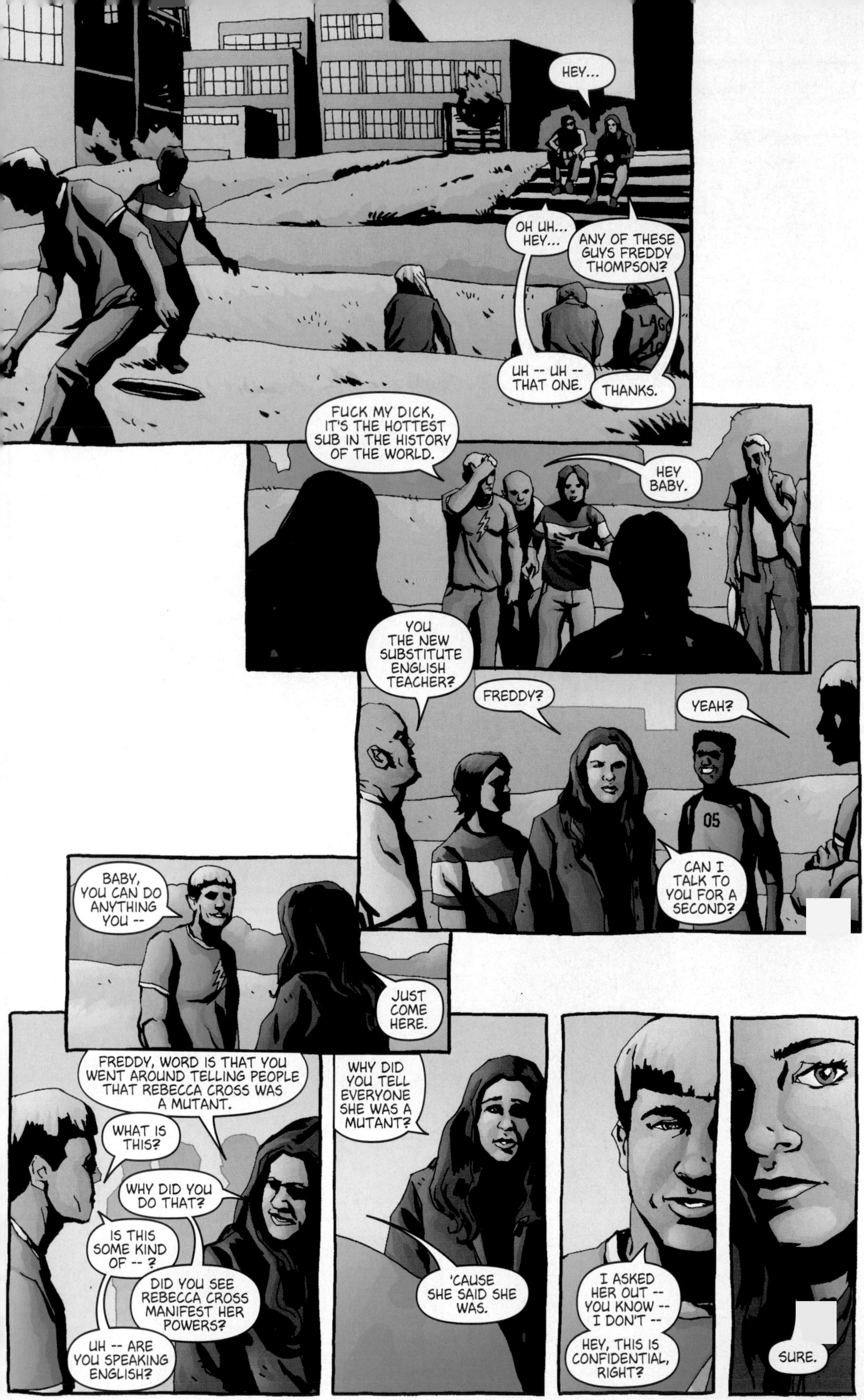
HEY...
OH UH... HEY...
ANY OF THESE GUYS FREDDY THOMPSON?
UH -- UH -- THAT ONE.
THANKS.
FUCK MY DICK, IT'S THE HOTTEST SUB IN THE HISTORY OF THE WORLD.
HEY BABY.
YOU THE NEW SUBSTITUTE ENGLISH TEACHER?
FREDDY?
YEAH?
CAN I TALK TO YOU FOR A SECOND?
BABY, YOU CAN DO ANYTHING YOU --
JUST COME HERE.
FREDDY, WORD IS THAT YOU WENT AROUND TELLING PEOPLE THAT REBECCA CROSS WAS A MUTANT.
WHAT IS THIS?
WHY DID YOU DO THAT?
IS THIS SOME KIND OF -- ?
DID YOU SEE REBECCA CROSS MANIFEST HER POWERS?
UH -- ARE YOU SPEAKING ENGLISH?
WHY DID YOU TELL EVERYONE SHE WAS A MUTANT?
'CAUSE SHE SAID SHE WAS.
I ASKED HER OUT -- YOU KNOW -- I DON'T --
HEY, THIS IS CONFIDENTIAL, RIGHT?
SURE.

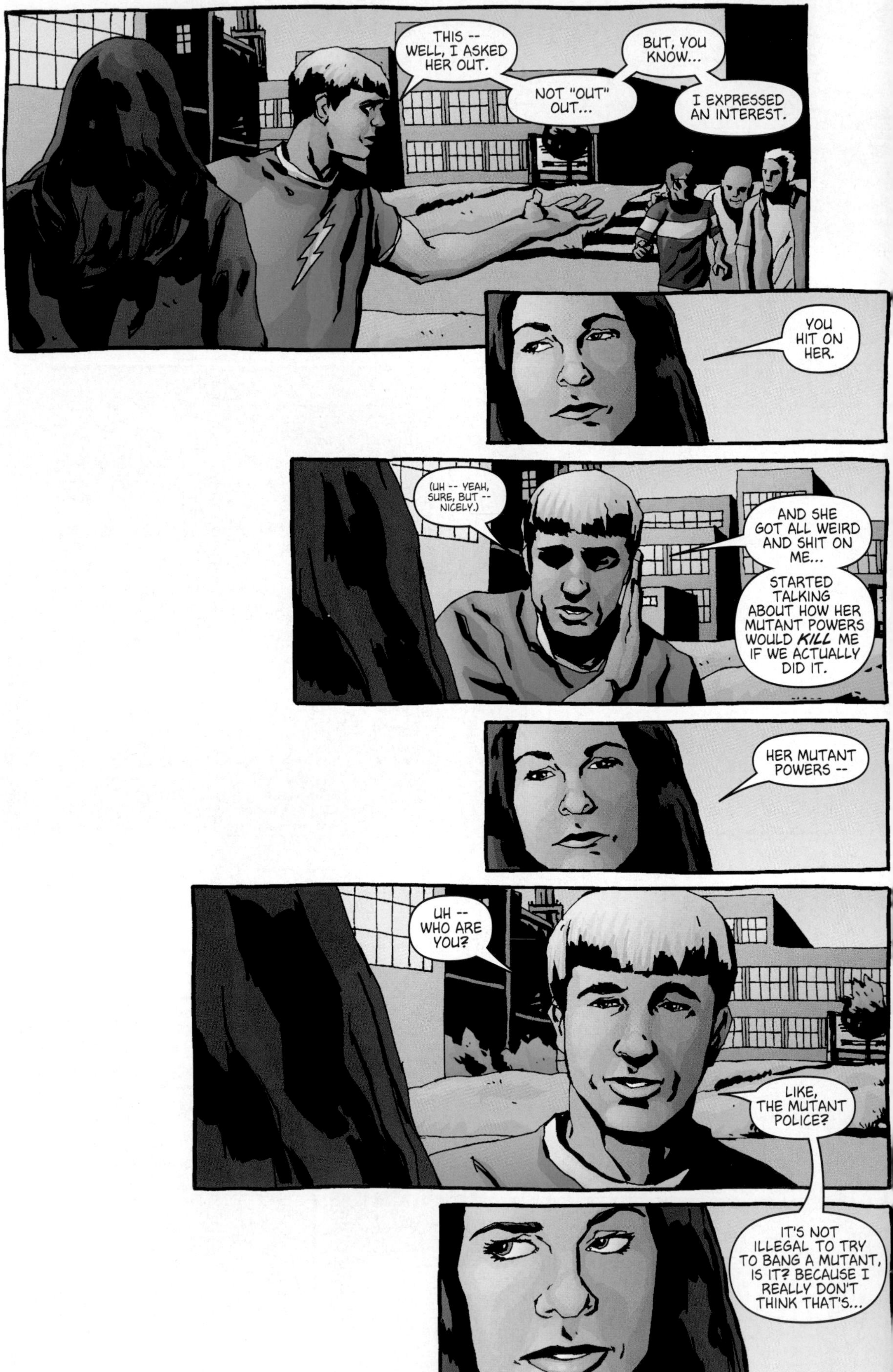
THIS -- WELL, I ASKED HER OUT.
NOT "OUT" OUT...
BUT, YOU KNOW...
I EXPRESSED AN INTEREST.
YOU HIT ON HER.
(UH -- YEAH, SURE, BUT -- NICELY.)
AND SHE GOT ALL WEIRD AND SHIT ON ME...
STARTED TALKING ABOUT HOW HER MUTANT POWERS WOULD KILL ME IF WE ACTUALLY DID IT.
HER MUTANT POWERS --
UH -- WHO ARE YOU?
LIKE, THE MUTANT POLICE?
IT'S NOT ILLEGAL TO TRY TO BANG A MUTANT, IS IT? BECAUSE I REALLY DON'T THINK THAT'S...

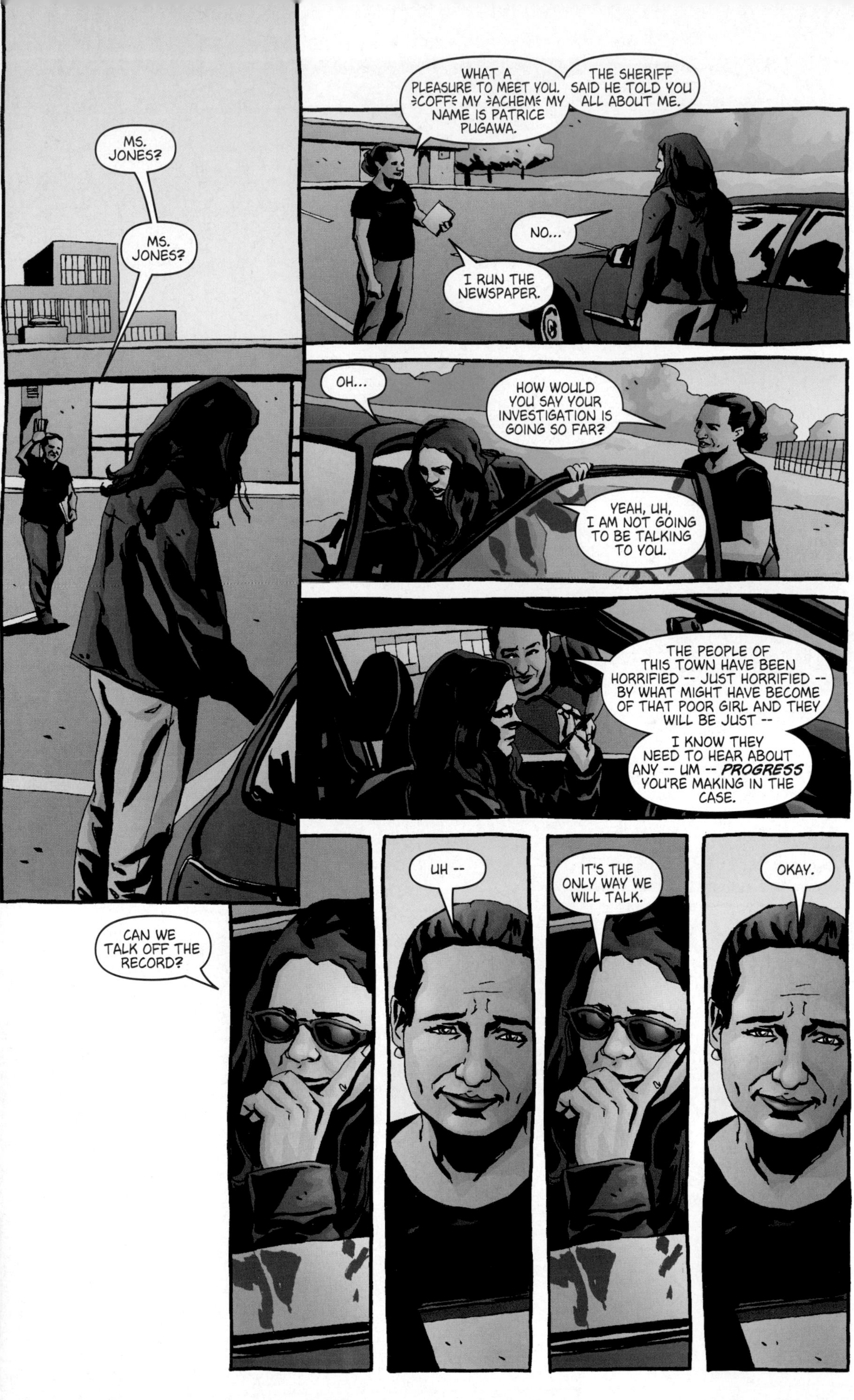
MS. JONES?
MS. JONES?
WHAT A PLEASURE TO MEET YOU. *COFF* MY *ACHEM* MY NAME IS PATRICE PUGAWA.
THE SHERIFF SAID HE TOLD YOU ALL ABOUT ME.
NO...
I RUN THE NEWSPAPER.
OH...
HOW WOULD YOU SAY YOUR INVESTIGATION IS GOING SO FAR?
YEAH, UH, I AM NOT GOING TO BE TALKING TO YOU.
THE PEOPLE OF THIS TOWN HAVE BEEN HORRIFIED -- JUST HORRIFIED -- BY WHAT MIGHT HAVE BECOME OF THAT POOR GIRL AND THEY WILL BE JUST --
I KNOW THEY NEED TO HEAR ABOUT ANY -- UM -- ***PROGRESS*** YOU'RE MAKING IN THE CASE.
CAN WE TALK OFF THE RECORD?
UH --
IT'S THE ONLY WAY WE WILL TALK.
OKAY.

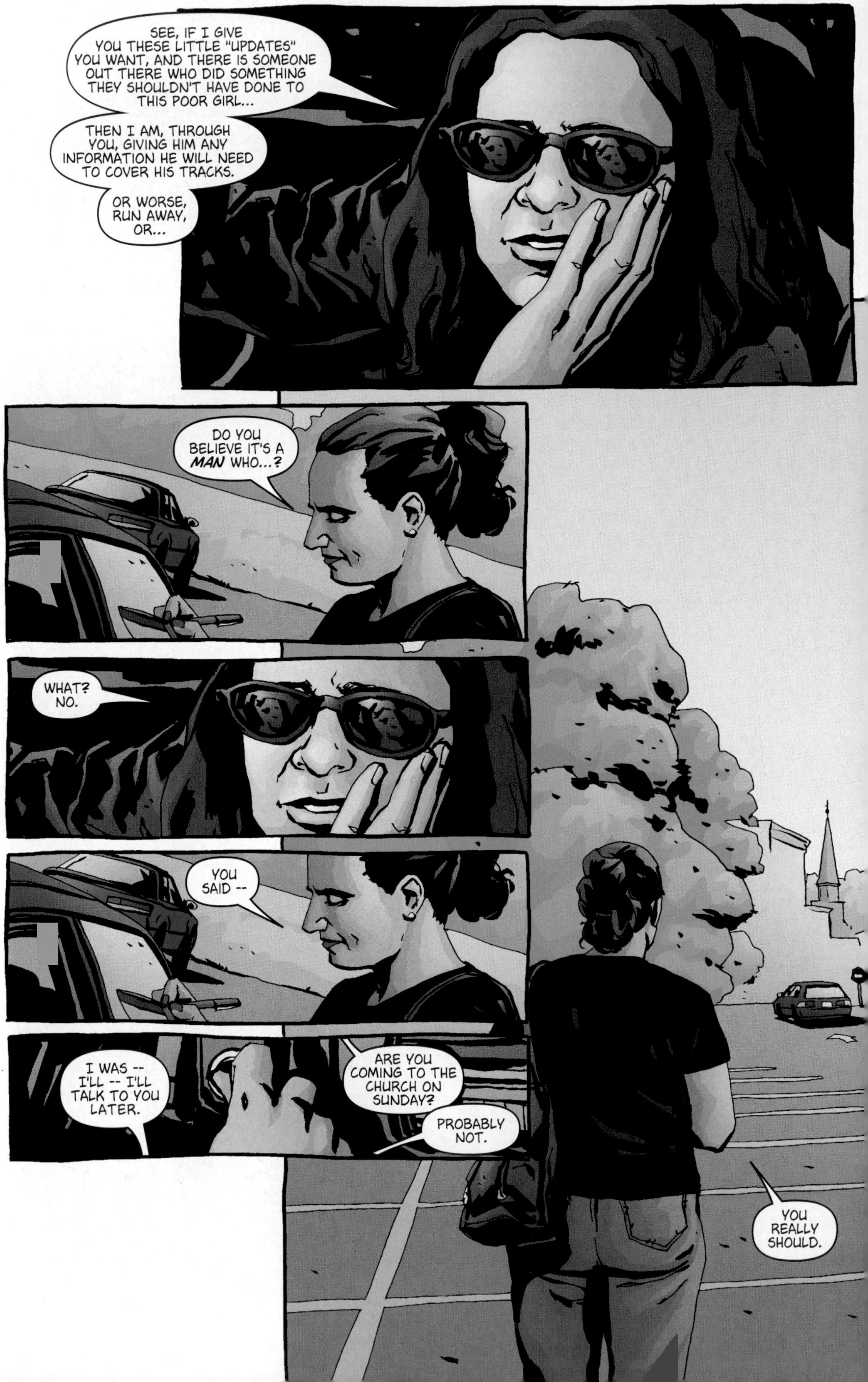
SEE, IF I GIVE YOU THESE LITTLE "UPDATES" YOU WANT, AND THERE IS SOMEONE OUT THERE WHO DID SOMETHING THEY SHOULDN'T HAVE DONE TO THIS POOR GIRL...
THEN I AM, THROUGH YOU, GIVING HIM ANY INFORMATION HE WILL NEED TO COVER HIS TRACKS.
OR WORSE, RUN AWAY, OR...
DO YOU BELIEVE IT'S A *MAN* WHO...?
WHAT? NO.
YOU SAID --
I WAS -- I'LL -- I'LL TALK TO YOU LATER.
ARE YOU COMING TO THE CHURCH ON SUNDAY?
PROBABLY NOT.
YOU REALLY SHOULD.

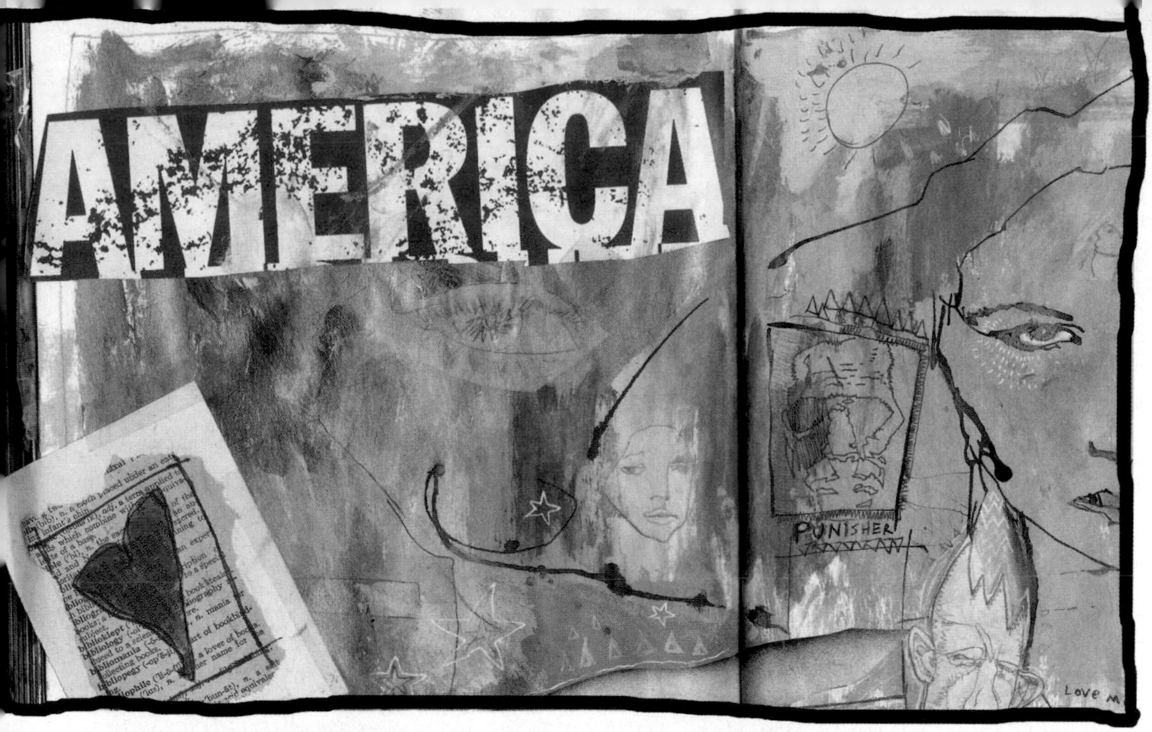
AMERICA
PUNISHER
Love m

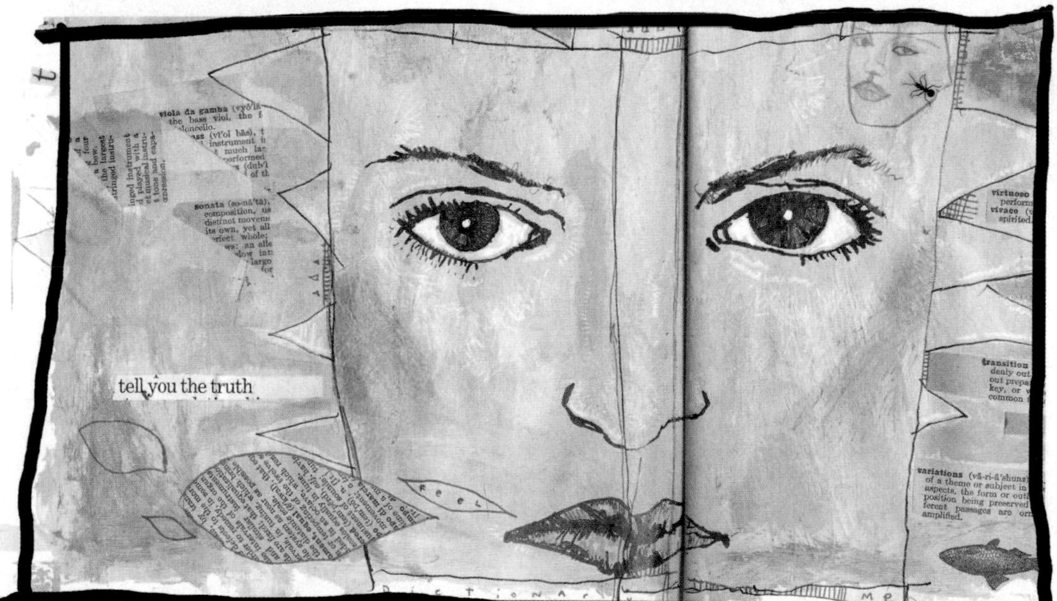
viola da gamba
sonata
tell you the truth
feel
virtuoso
transition
variations (vā-ri-ā'shuns)
of a theme or subject in
aspects, the form or outl
position being preserved
ferent passages are or
amplified.
Dictionary of me

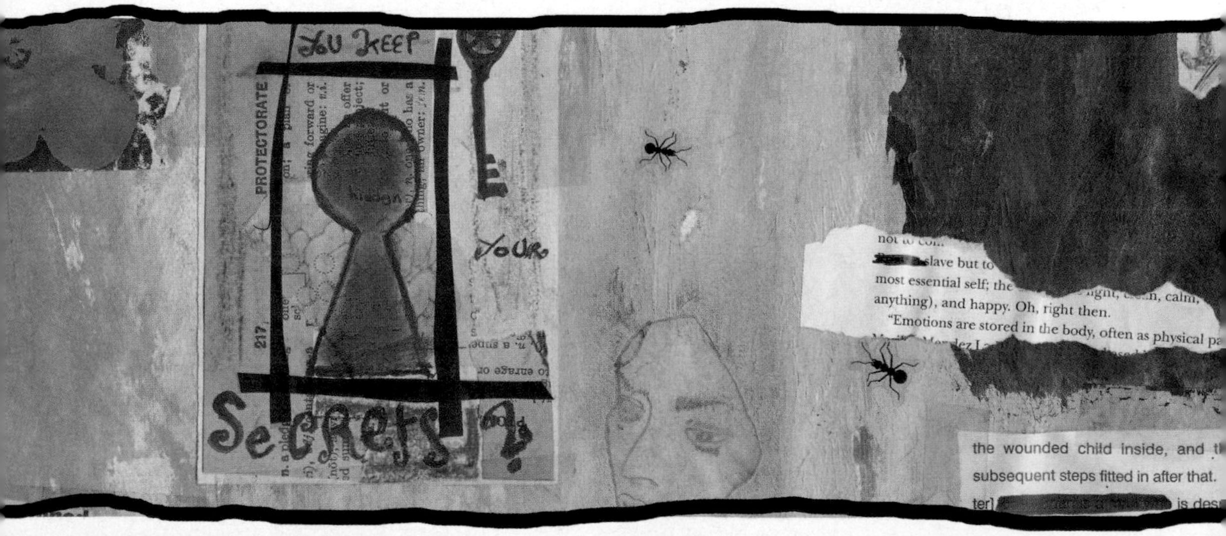
You keep
PROTECTORATE
your
Secrets?
[redacted] slave but to
most essential self; the
anything), and happy. Oh, right then.
“Emotions are stored in the body, often as physical pa
the wounded child inside, and t
subsequent steps fitted in after that.
ter] [redacted] is des

LAST
ENTRY

ΔΔ
ΔΔ ΔΔΔ

ΔΔΔ

frig...ed work...ome of her
tures she has inscribed a text, su... ...
"Do you love me?" or "Do not abandon
me." These are the pieces I underst...
...ecause the words
...of th...

...en you...
...it in qu...

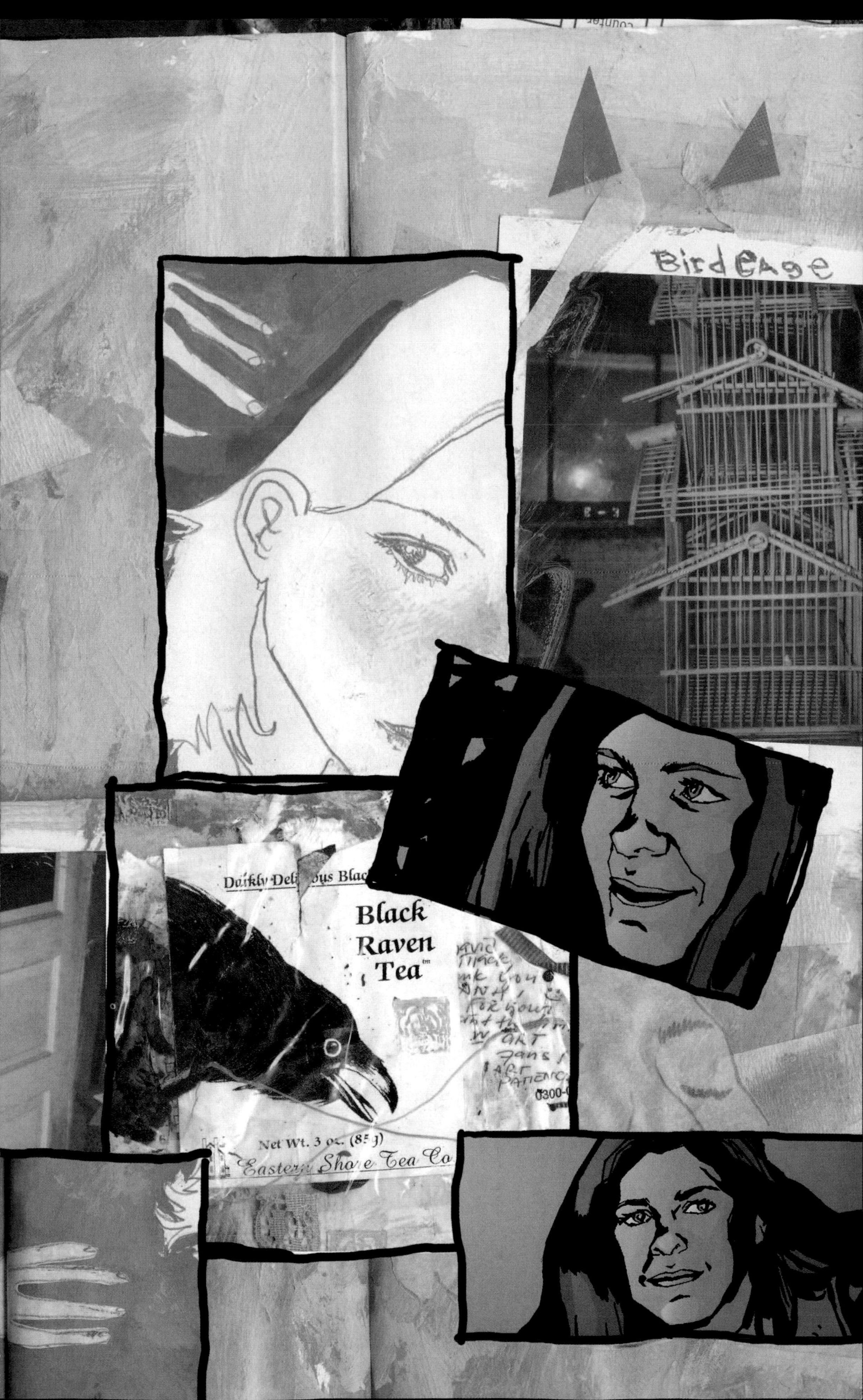
Bird Cage
Black
Raven
Tea
Net Wt. 3 oz. (85g)

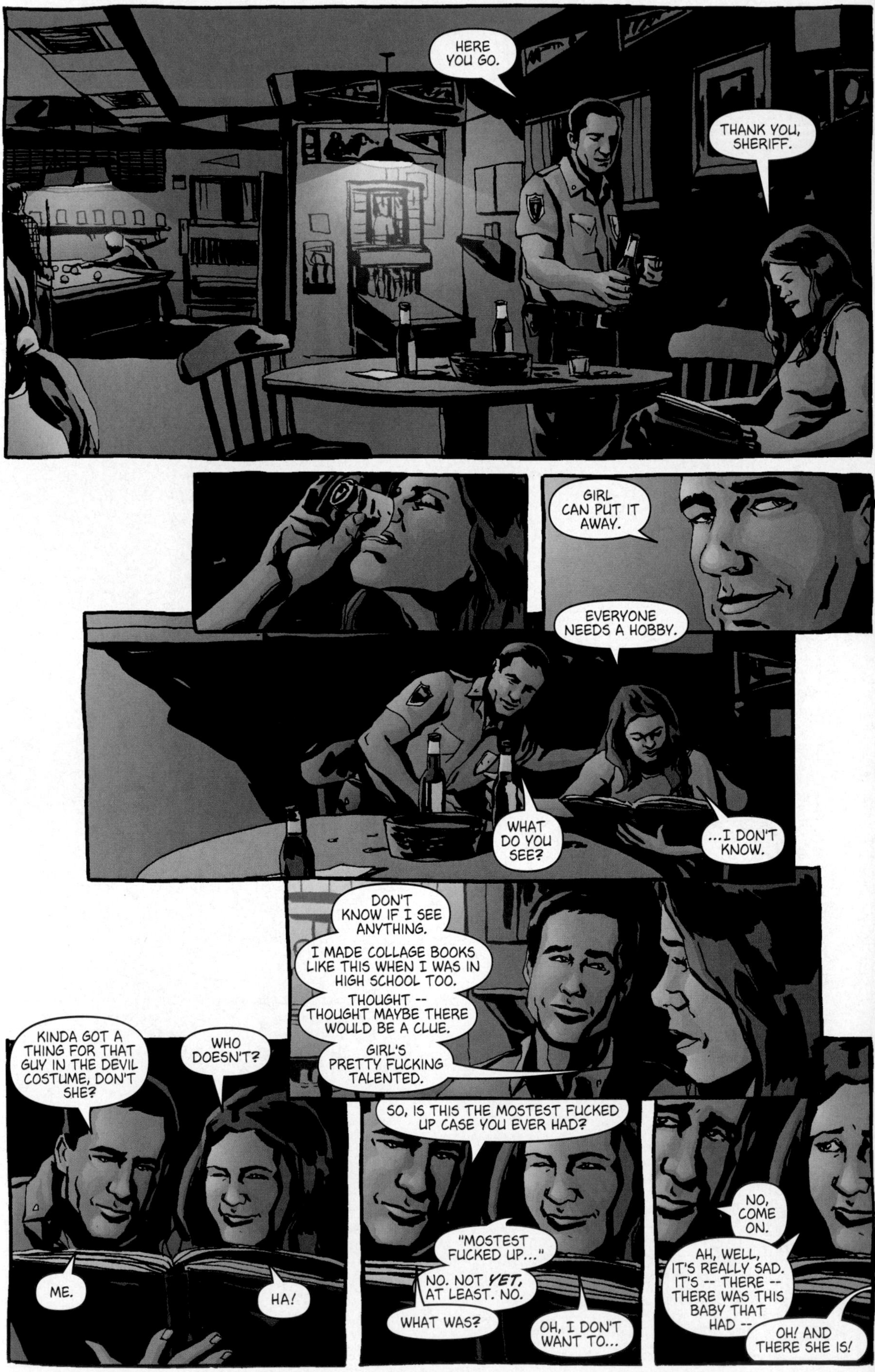
HERE YOU GO.
THANK YOU, SHERIFF.
GIRL CAN PUT IT AWAY.
EVERYONE NEEDS A HOBBY.
WHAT DO YOU SEE?
...I DON'T KNOW.
DON'T KNOW IF I SEE ANYTHING.
I MADE COLLAGE BOOKS LIKE THIS WHEN I WAS IN HIGH SCHOOL TOO.
THOUGHT -- THOUGHT MAYBE THERE WOULD BE A CLUE.
GIRL'S PRETTY FUCKING TALENTED.
KINDA GOT A THING FOR THAT GUY IN THE DEVIL COSTUME, DON'T SHE?
WHO DOESN'T?
ME.
HA!
SO, IS THIS THE MOSTEST FUCKED UP CASE YOU EVER HAD?
"MOSTEST FUCKED UP..."
NO. NOT YET, AT LEAST. NO.
WHAT WAS?
OH, I DON'T WANT TO...
NO, COME ON.
AH, WELL, IT'S REALLY SAD. IT'S -- THERE -- THERE WAS THIS BABY THAT HAD --
OH! AND THERE SHE IS!

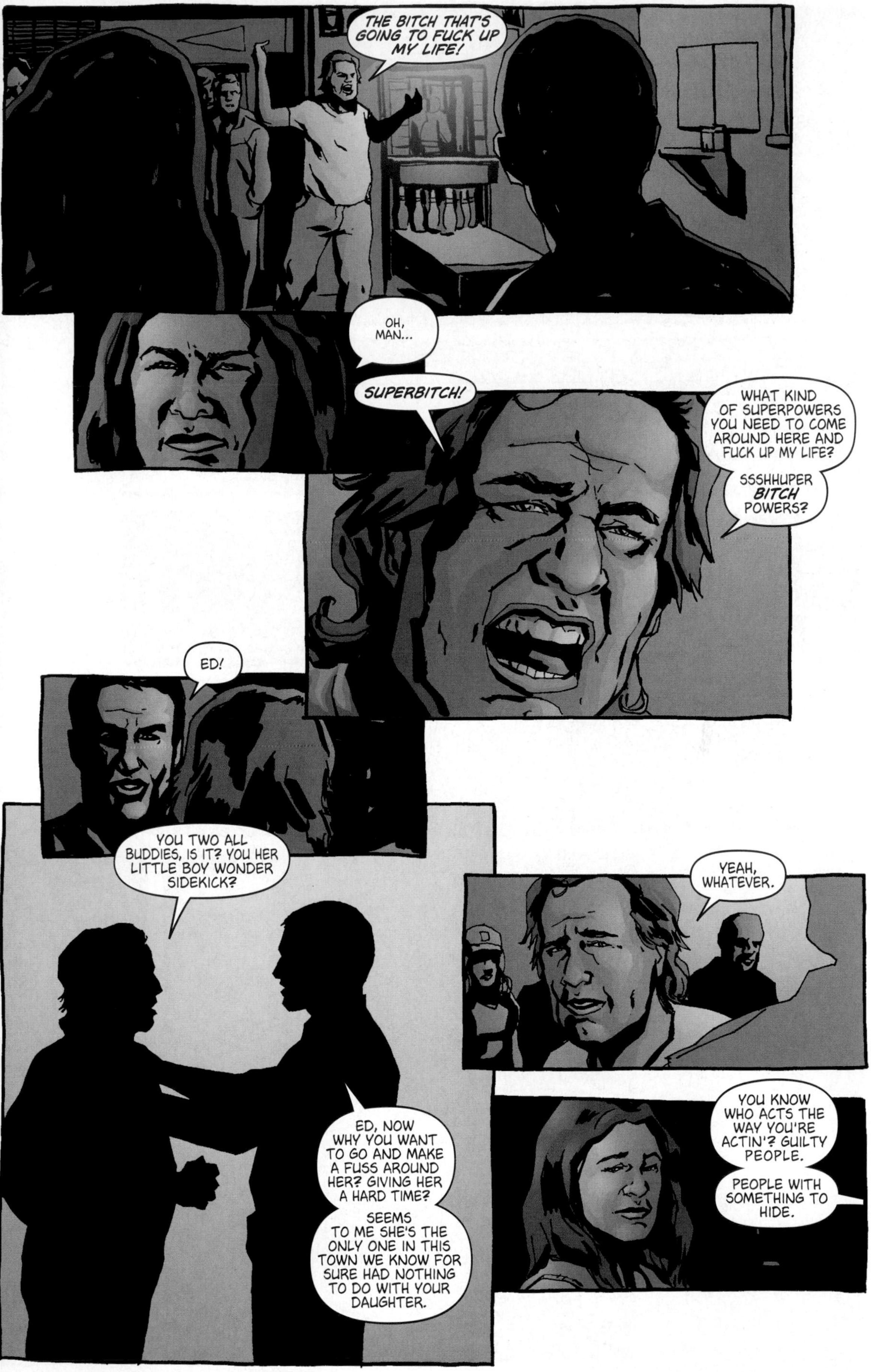
THE BITCH THAT'S GOING TO FUCK UP MY LIFE!
OH, MAN...
SUPERBITCH!
WHAT KIND OF SUPERPOWERS YOU NEED TO COME AROUND HERE AND FUCK UP MY LIFE?
SSSHHUPER BITCH POWERS?
ED!
YOU TWO ALL BUDDIES, IS IT? YOU HER LITTLE BOY WONDER SIDEKICK?
ED, NOW WHY YOU WANT TO GO AND MAKE A FUSS AROUND HER? GIVING HER A HARD TIME?
SEEMS TO ME SHE'S THE ONLY ONE IN THIS TOWN WE KNOW FOR SURE HAD NOTHING TO DO WITH YOUR DAUGHTER.
YEAH, WHATEVER.
YOU KNOW WHO ACTS THE WAY YOU'RE ACTIN'? GUILTY PEOPLE.
PEOPLE WITH SOMETHING TO HIDE.

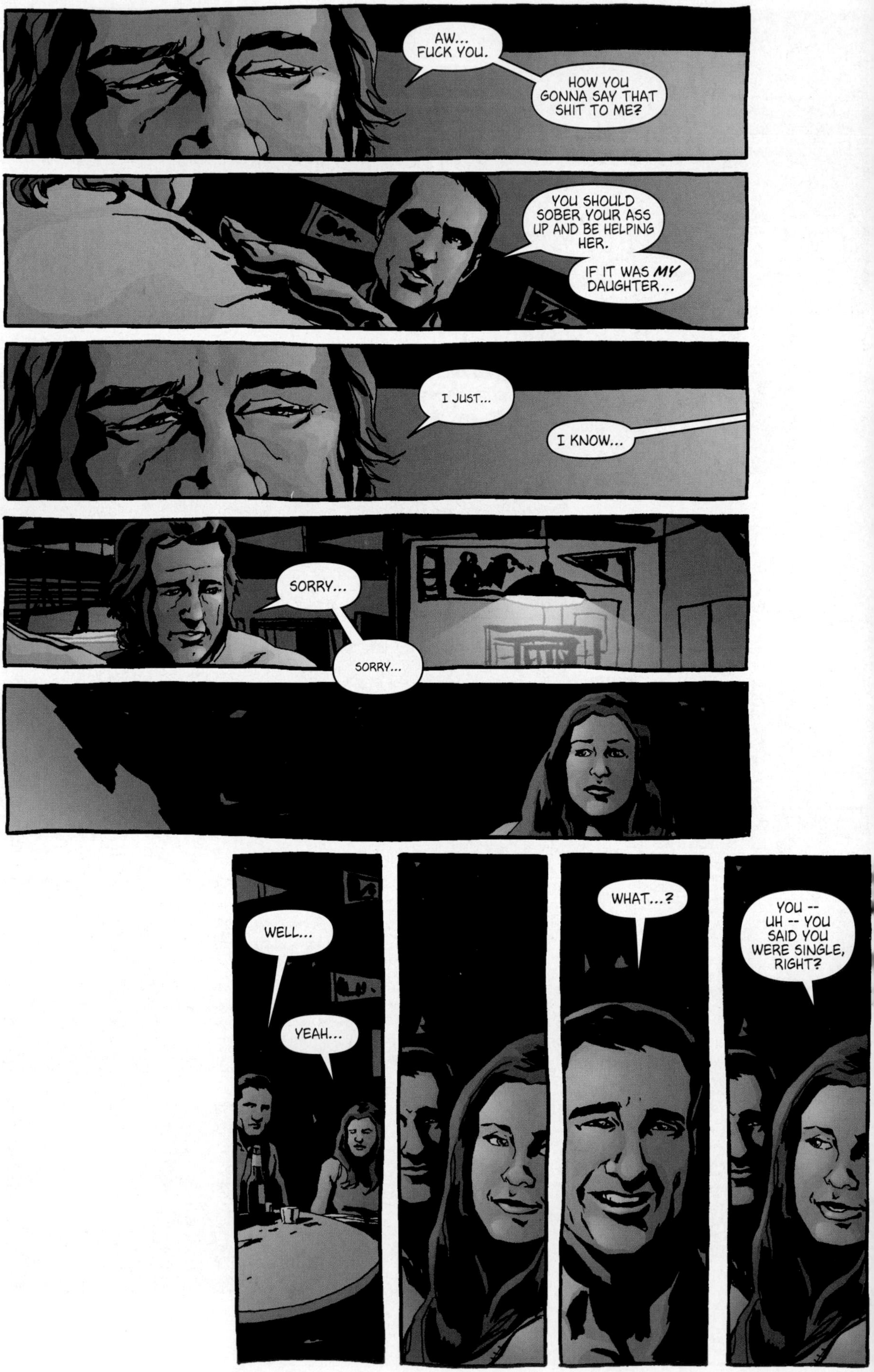
AW... FUCK YOU.
HOW YOU GONNA SAY THAT SHIT TO ME?
YOU SHOULD SOBER YOUR ASS UP AND BE HELPING HER.
IF IT WAS MY DAUGHTER...
I JUST...
I KNOW...
SORRY...
SORRY...
WELL...
YEAH...
WHAT...?
YOU -- UH -- YOU SAID YOU WERE SINGLE, RIGHT?

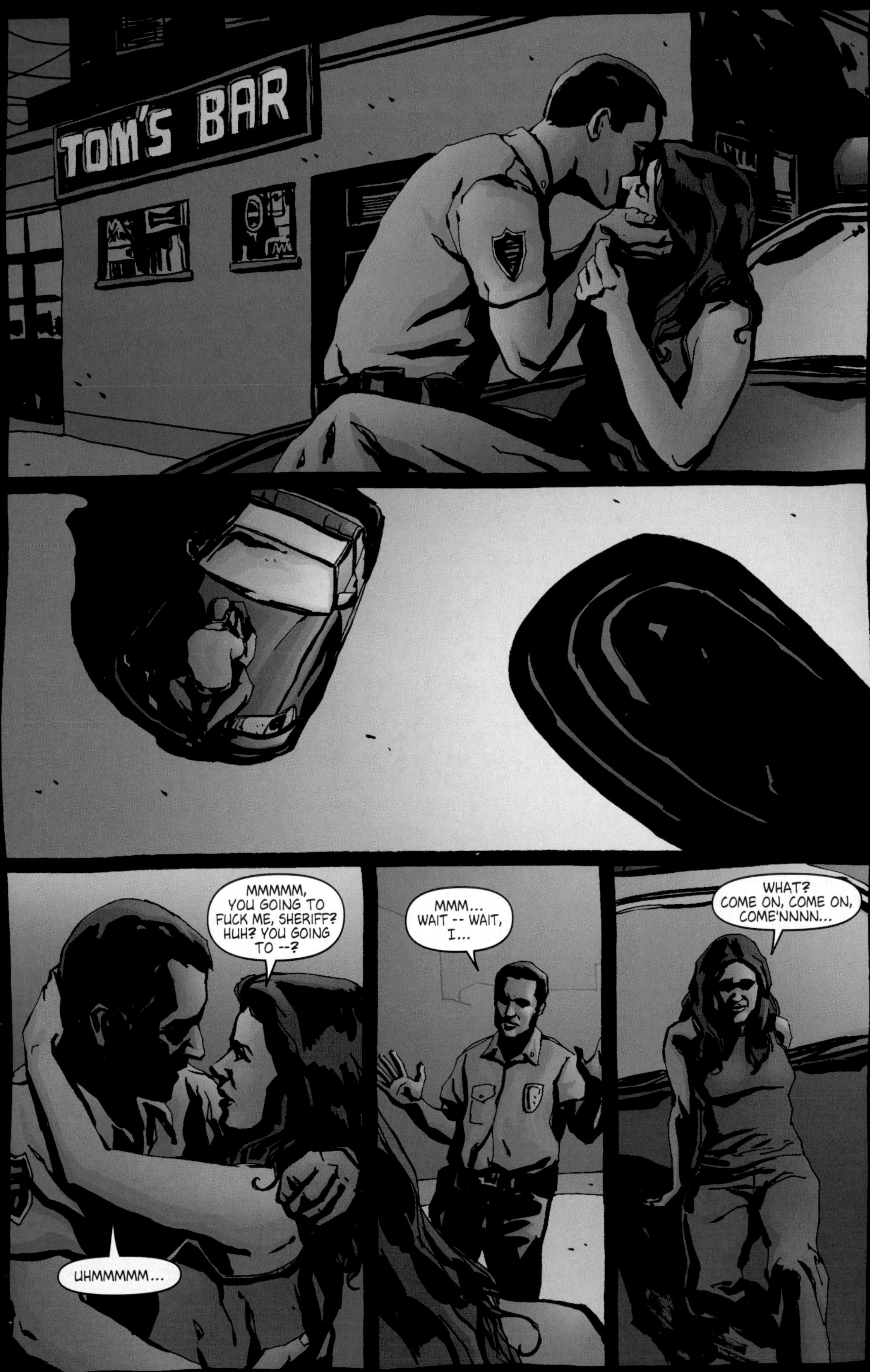
TOM'S BAR
MMMMM, YOU GOING TO FUCK ME, SHERIFF? HUH? YOU GOING TO --?
UHMMMMM...
MMM... WAIT -- WAIT, I...
WHAT? COME ON, COME ON, COME'NNNN...

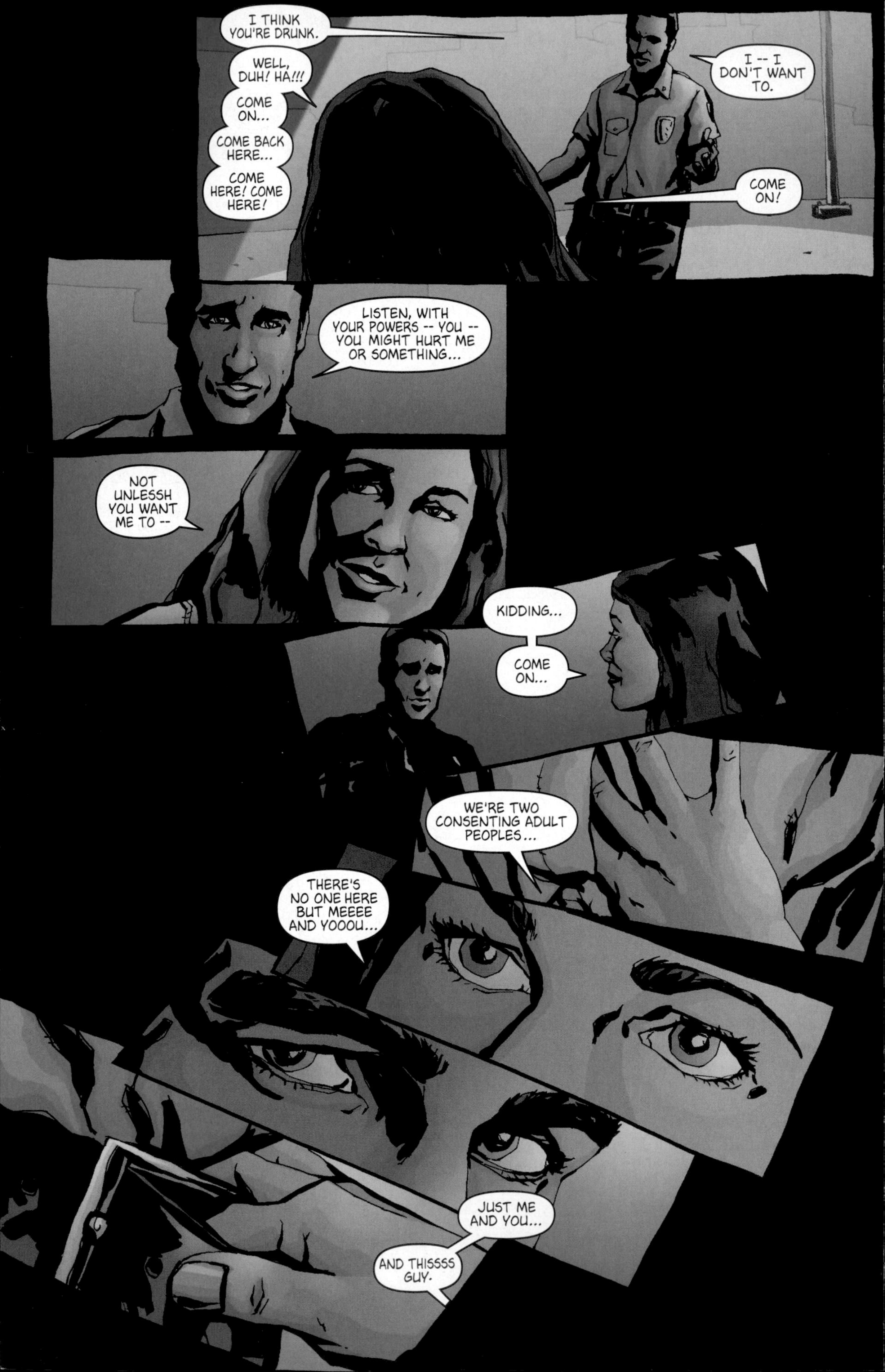
I THINK YOU'RE DRUNK.
WELL, DUH! HA!!!
COME ON...
COME BACK HERE...
COME HERE! COME HERE!
I -- I DON'T WANT TO.
COME ON!
LISTEN, WITH YOUR POWERS -- YOU -- YOU MIGHT HURT ME OR SOMETHING...
NOT UNLESSH YOU WANT ME TO --
KIDDING...
COME ON...
WE'RE TWO CONSENTING ADULT PEOPLES...
THERE'S NO ONE HERE BUT MEEEE AND YOOOU...
JUST ME AND YOU...
AND THISSSS GUY.

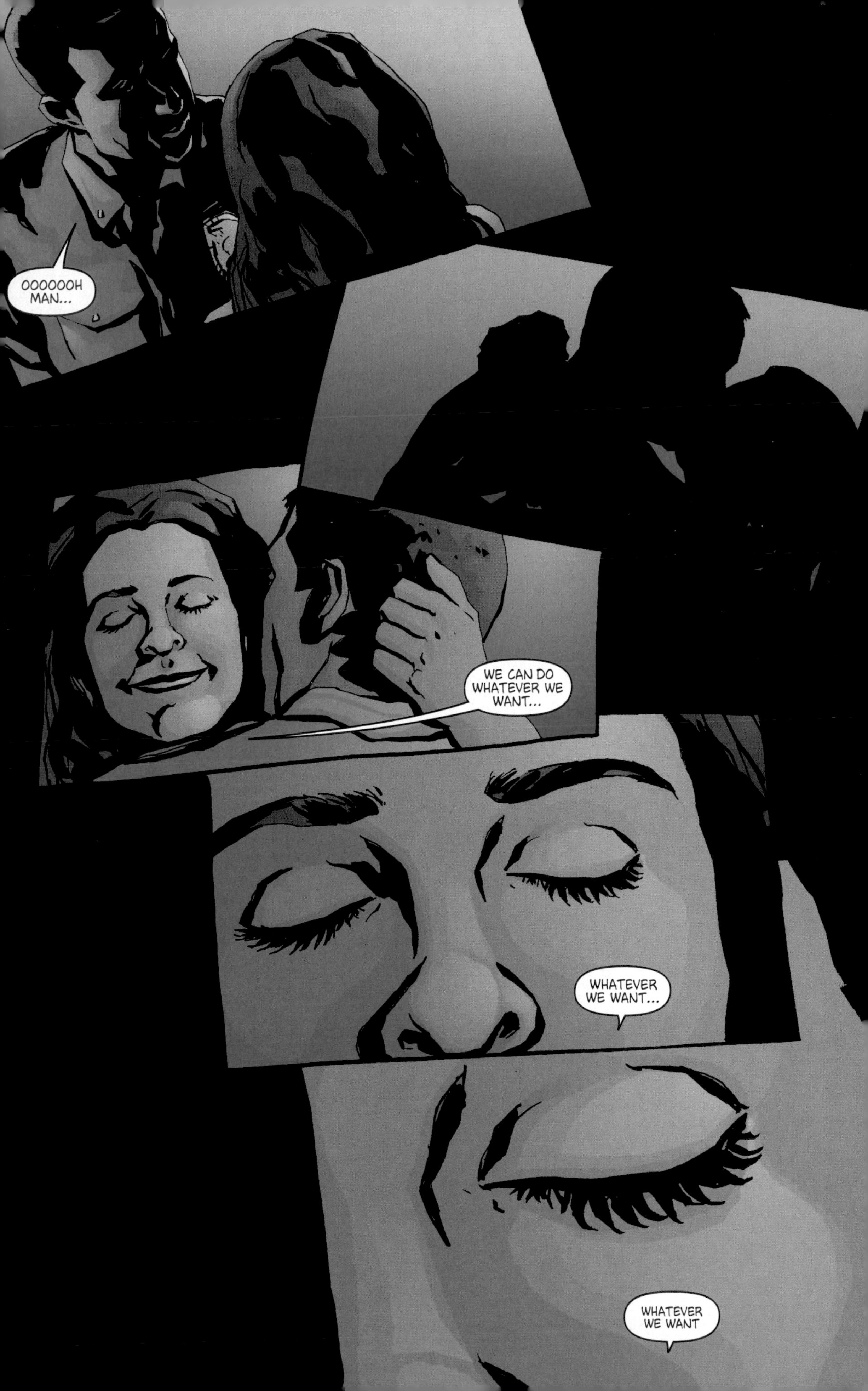
OOOOOOH MAN...
WE CAN DO WHATEVER WE WANT...
WHATEVER WE WANT...
WHATEVER WE WANT

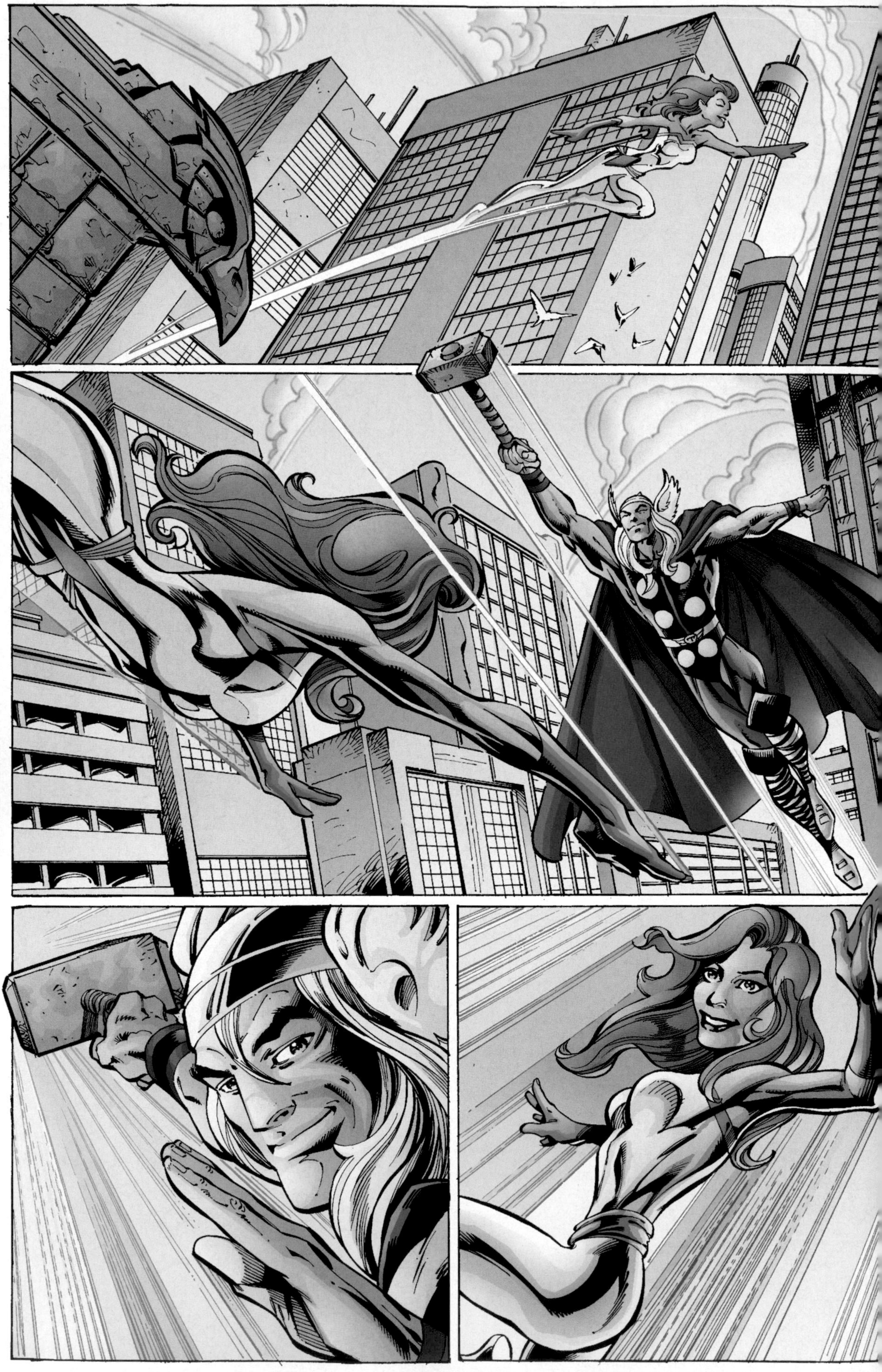

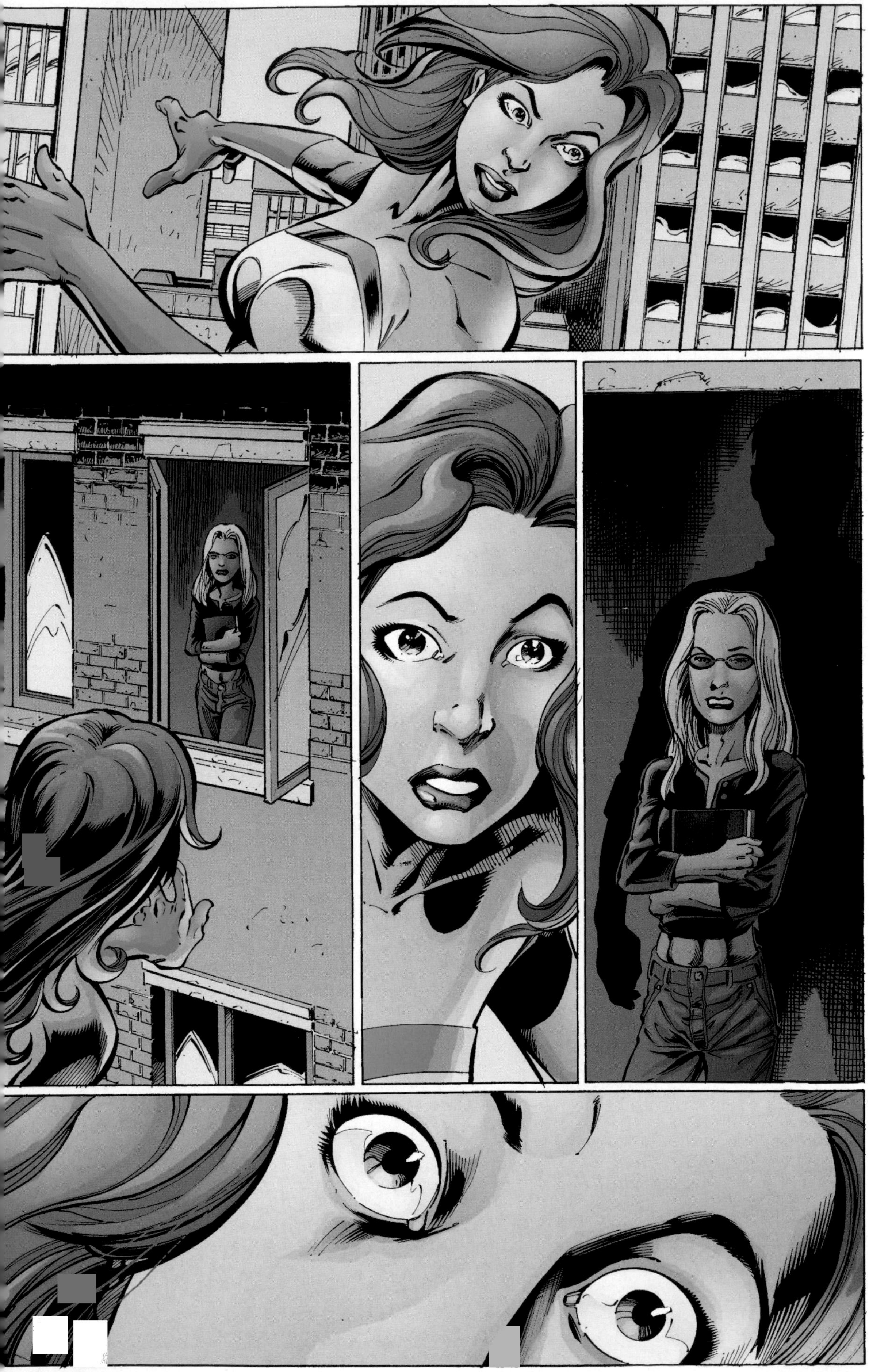

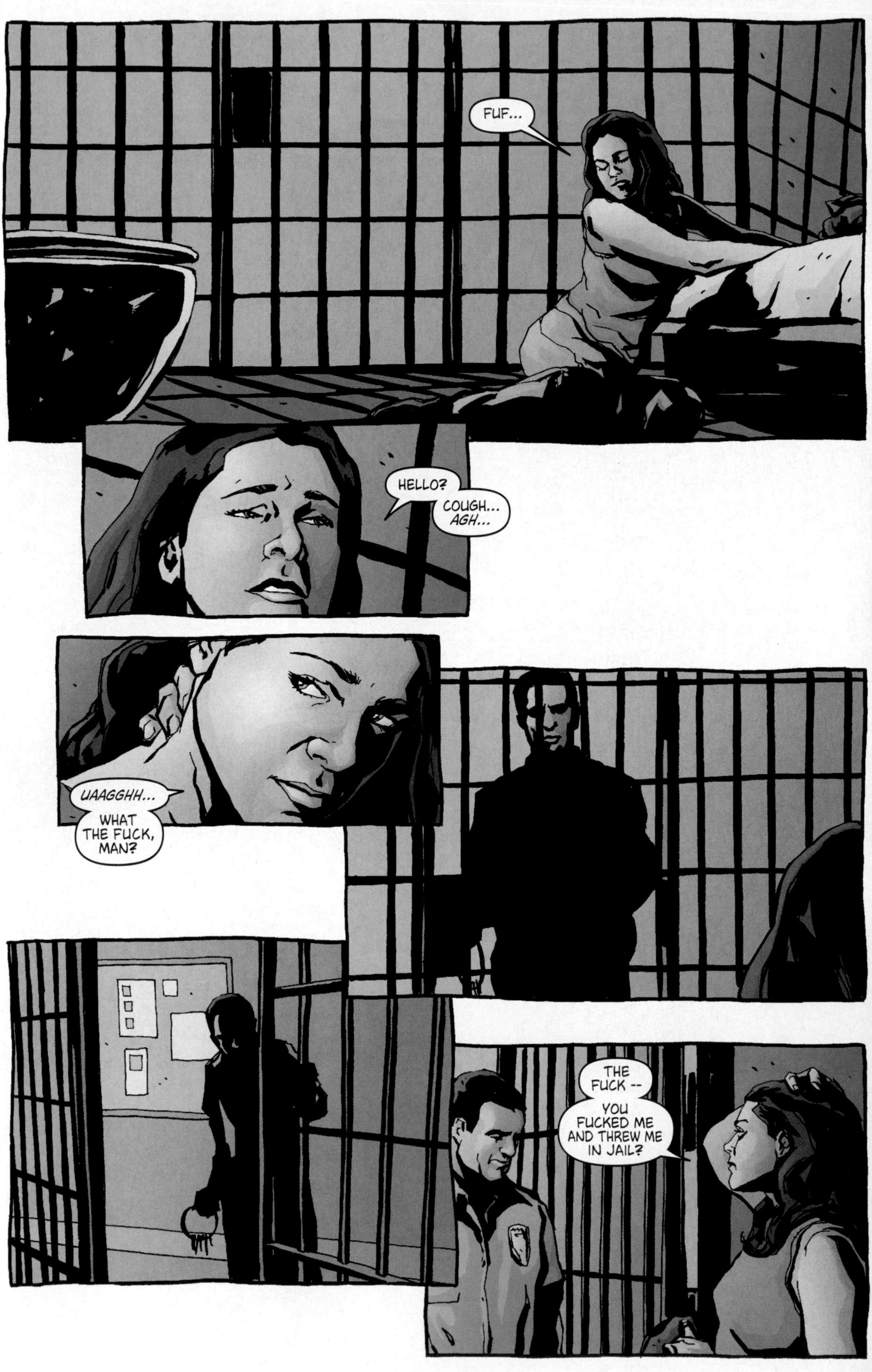
FUF...
HELLO?
COUGH... AGH...
UAAGGHH...
WHAT THE FUCK, MAN?
THE FUCK --
YOU FUCKED ME AND THREW ME IN JAIL?

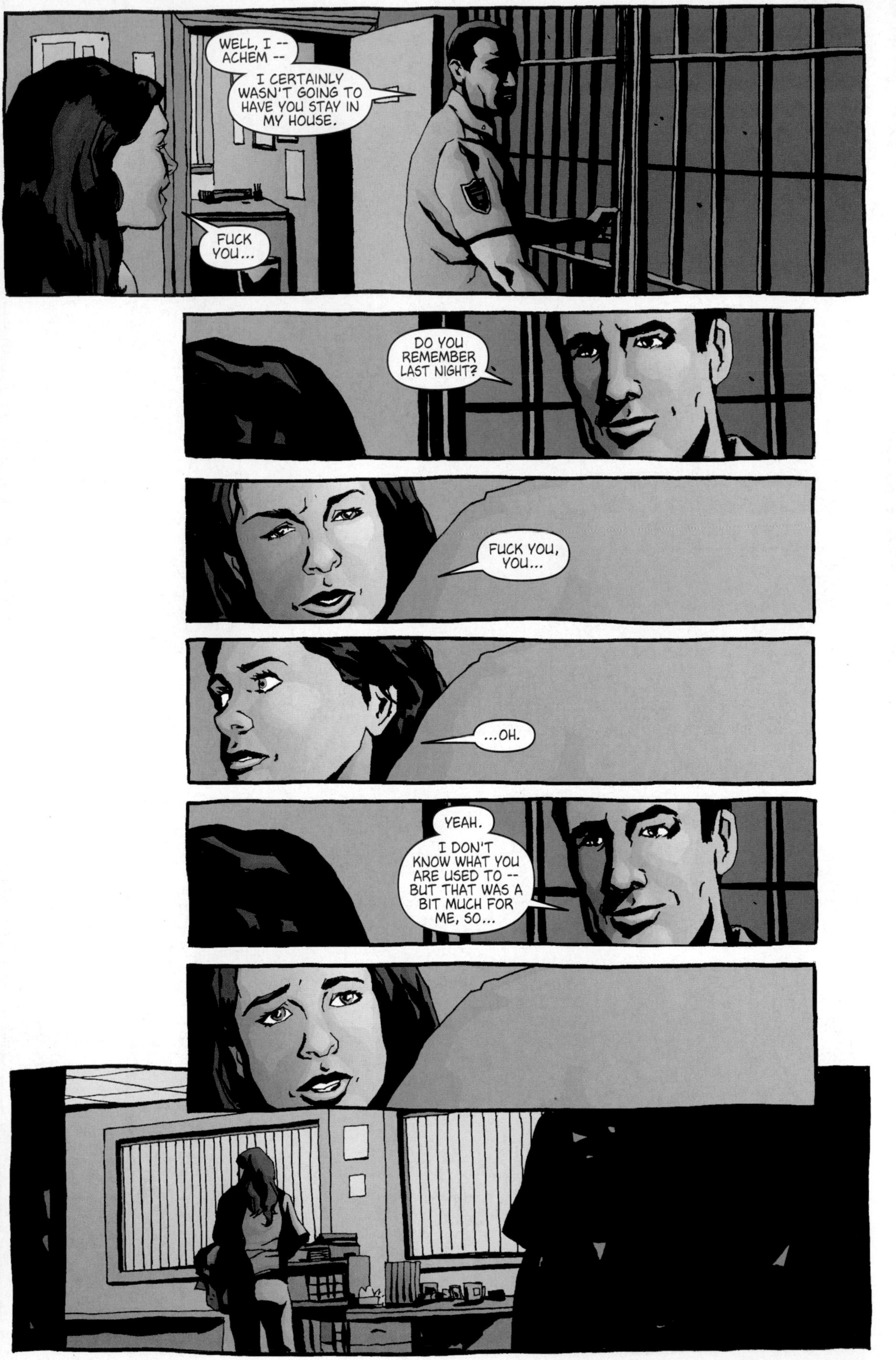
WELL, I -- ACHEM --
I CERTAINLY WASN'T GOING TO HAVE YOU STAY IN MY HOUSE.
FUCK YOU...
DO YOU REMEMBER LAST NIGHT?
FUCK YOU, YOU...
...OH.
YEAH.
I DON'T KNOW WHAT YOU ARE USED TO -- BUT THAT WAS A BIT MUCH FOR ME, SO...

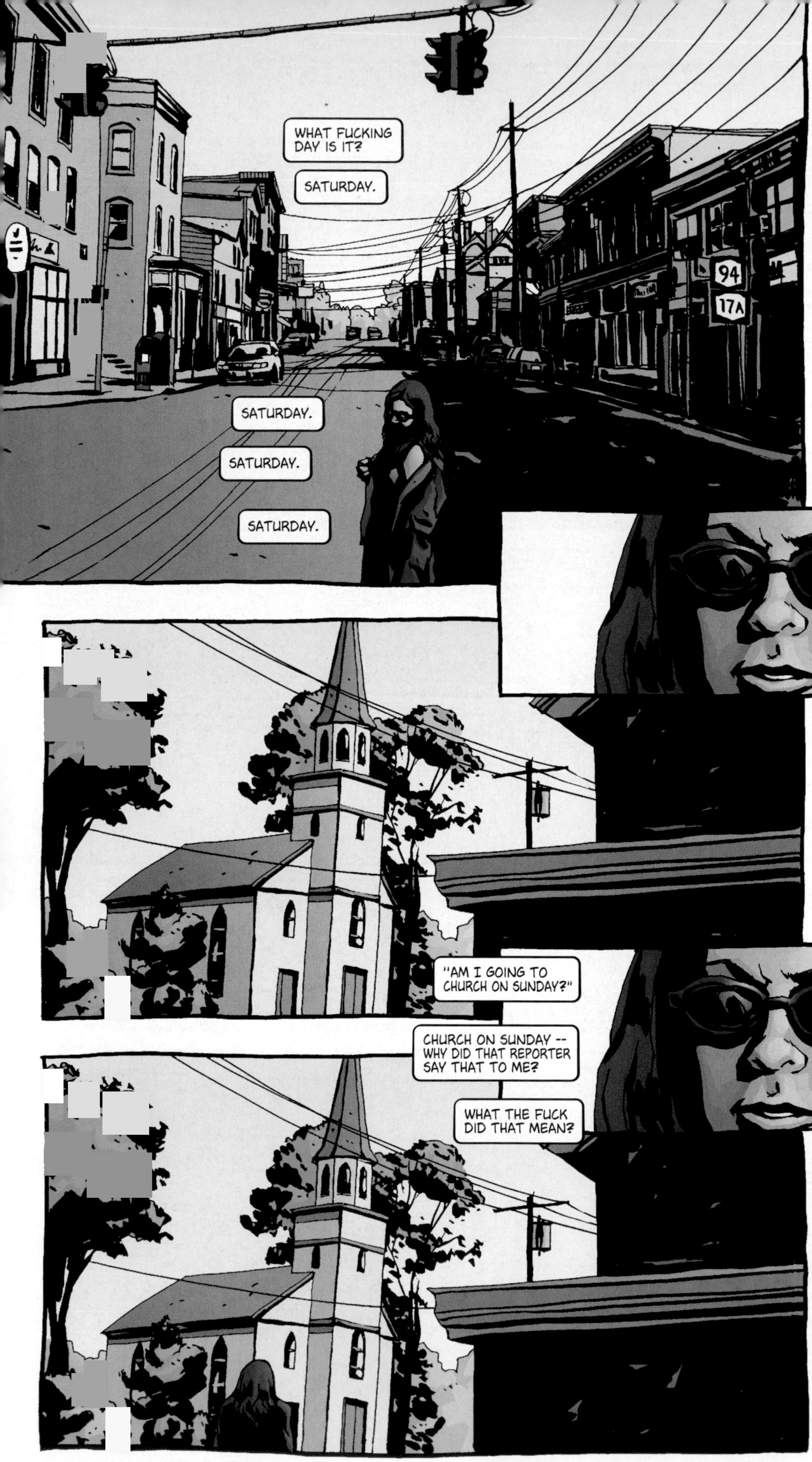
WHAT FUCKING DAY IS IT?
SATURDAY.
SATURDAY.
SATURDAY.
SATURDAY.
94
17A
"AM I GOING TO CHURCH ON SUNDAY?"
CHURCH ON SUNDAY -- WHY DID THAT REPORTER SAY THAT TO ME?
WHAT THE FUCK DID THAT MEAN?

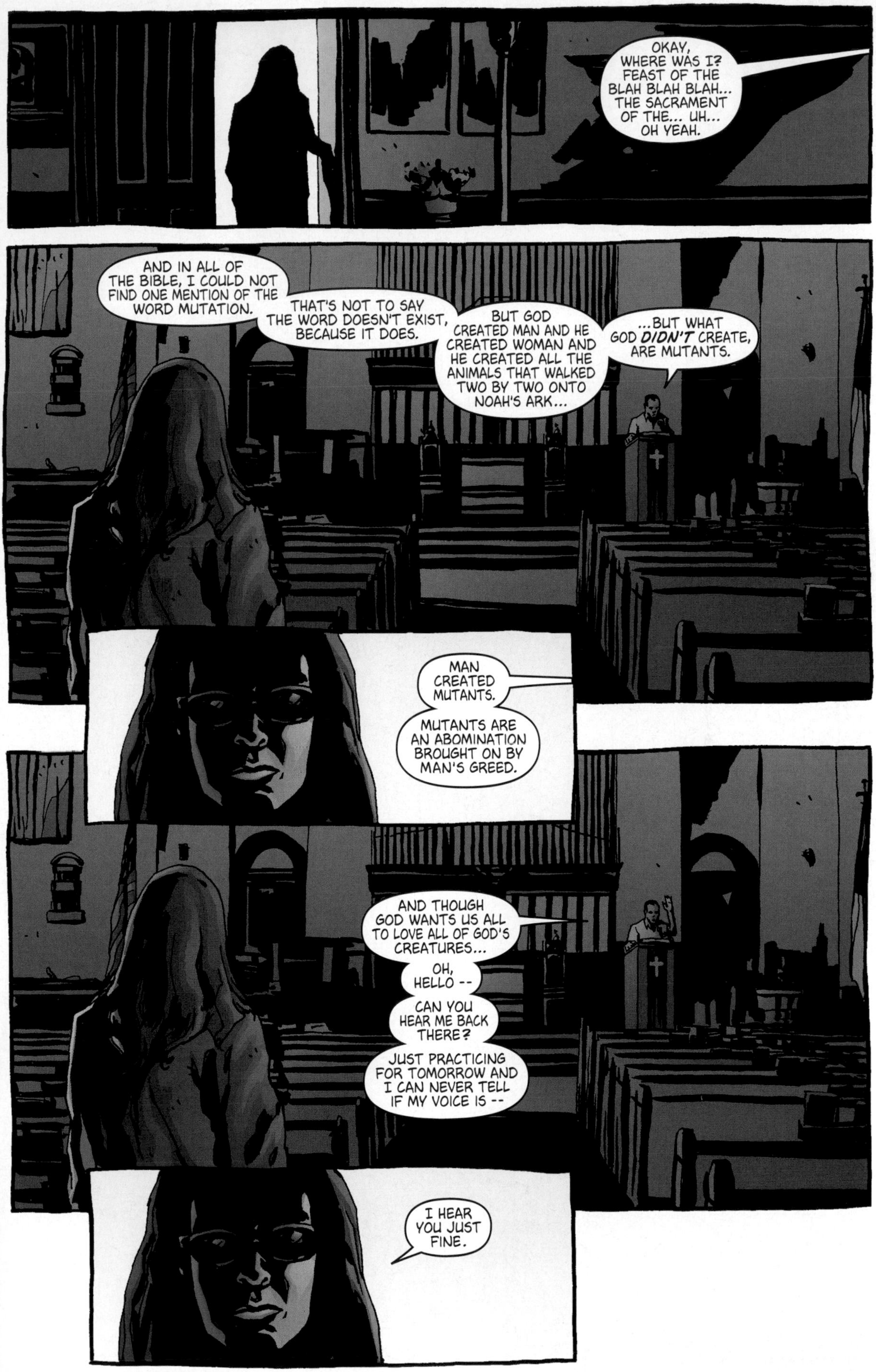
OKAY, WHERE WAS I? FEAST OF THE BLAH BLAH BLAH... THE SACRAMENT OF THE... UH... OH YEAH.
AND IN ALL OF THE BIBLE, I COULD NOT FIND ONE MENTION OF THE WORD MUTATION.
THAT'S NOT TO SAY THE WORD DOESN'T EXIST, BECAUSE IT DOES.
BUT GOD CREATED MAN AND HE CREATED WOMAN AND HE CREATED ALL THE ANIMALS THAT WALKED TWO BY TWO ONTO NOAH'S ARK...
...BUT WHAT GOD *DIDN'T* CREATE, ARE MUTANTS.
MAN CREATED MUTANTS.
MUTANTS ARE AN ABOMINATION BROUGHT ON BY MAN'S GREED.
AND THOUGH GOD WANTS US ALL TO LOVE ALL OF GOD'S CREATURES...
OH, HELLO --
CAN YOU HEAR ME BACK THERE?
JUST PRACTICING FOR TOMORROW AND I CAN NEVER TELL IF MY VOICE IS --
I HEAR YOU JUST FINE.

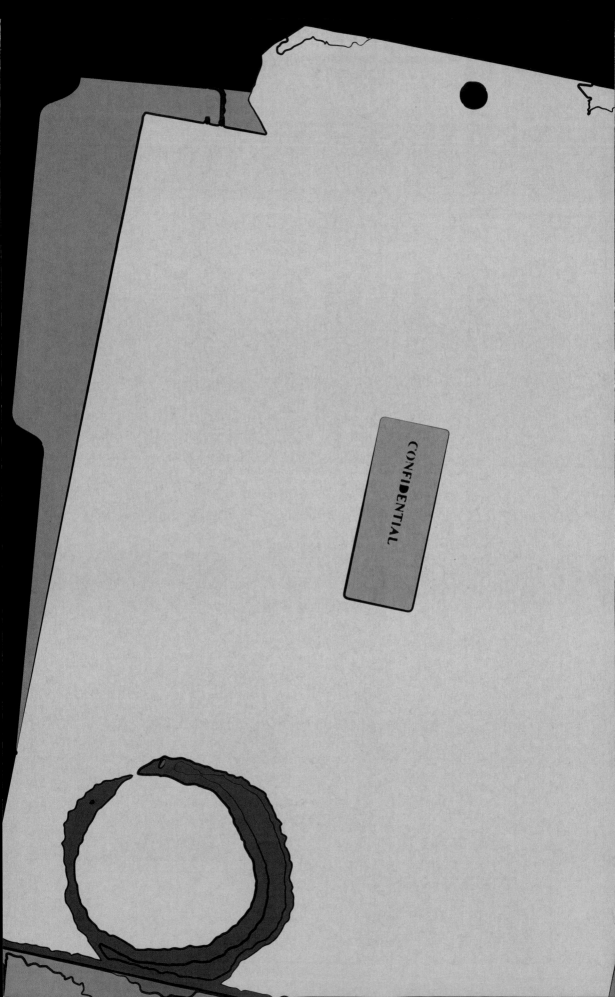

CONFIDENTIAL

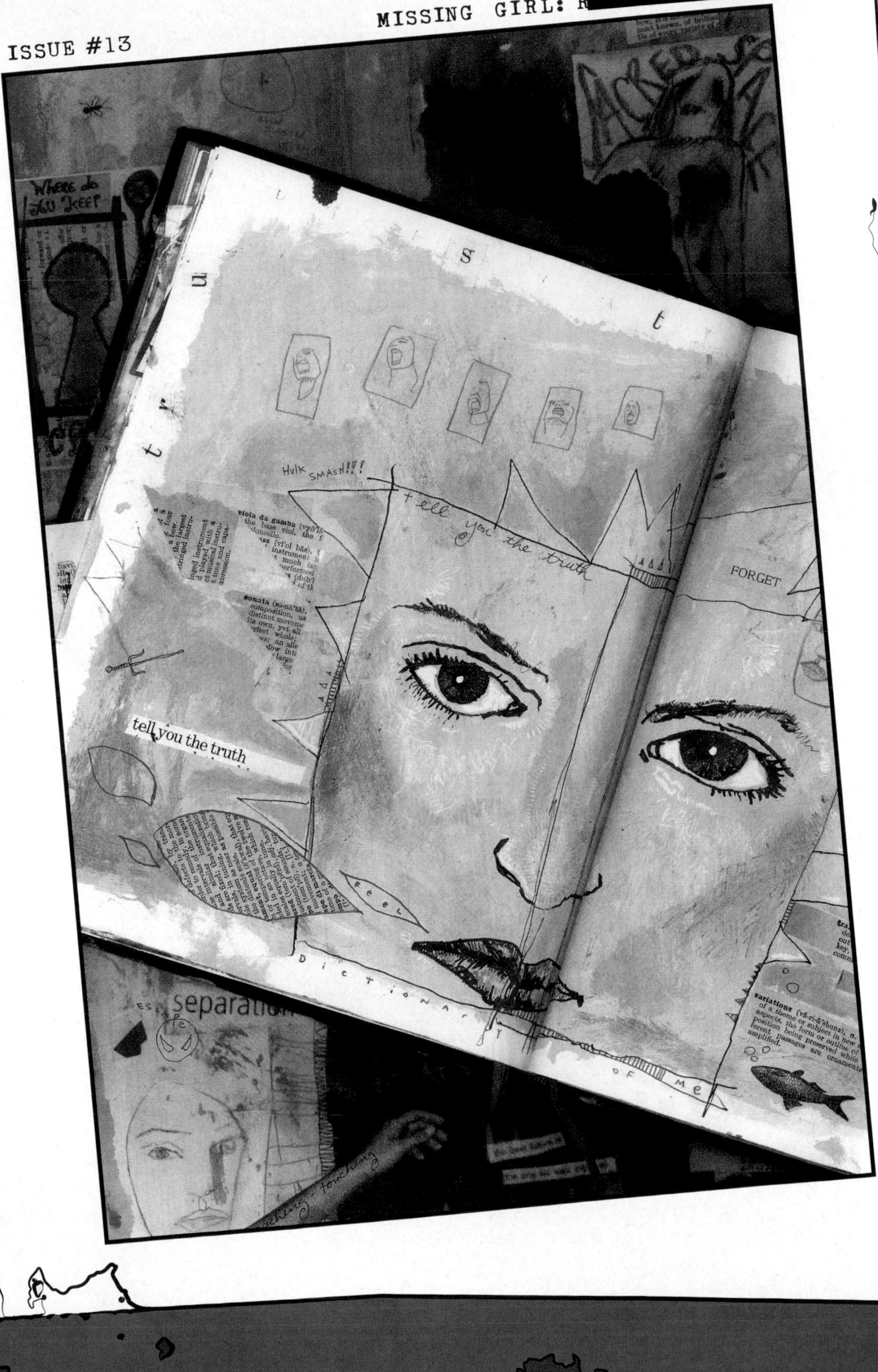
Hulk SMASH!!!
tell you the truth
FORGET
tell you the truth
feel
DICTIONARY
OF ME
separation

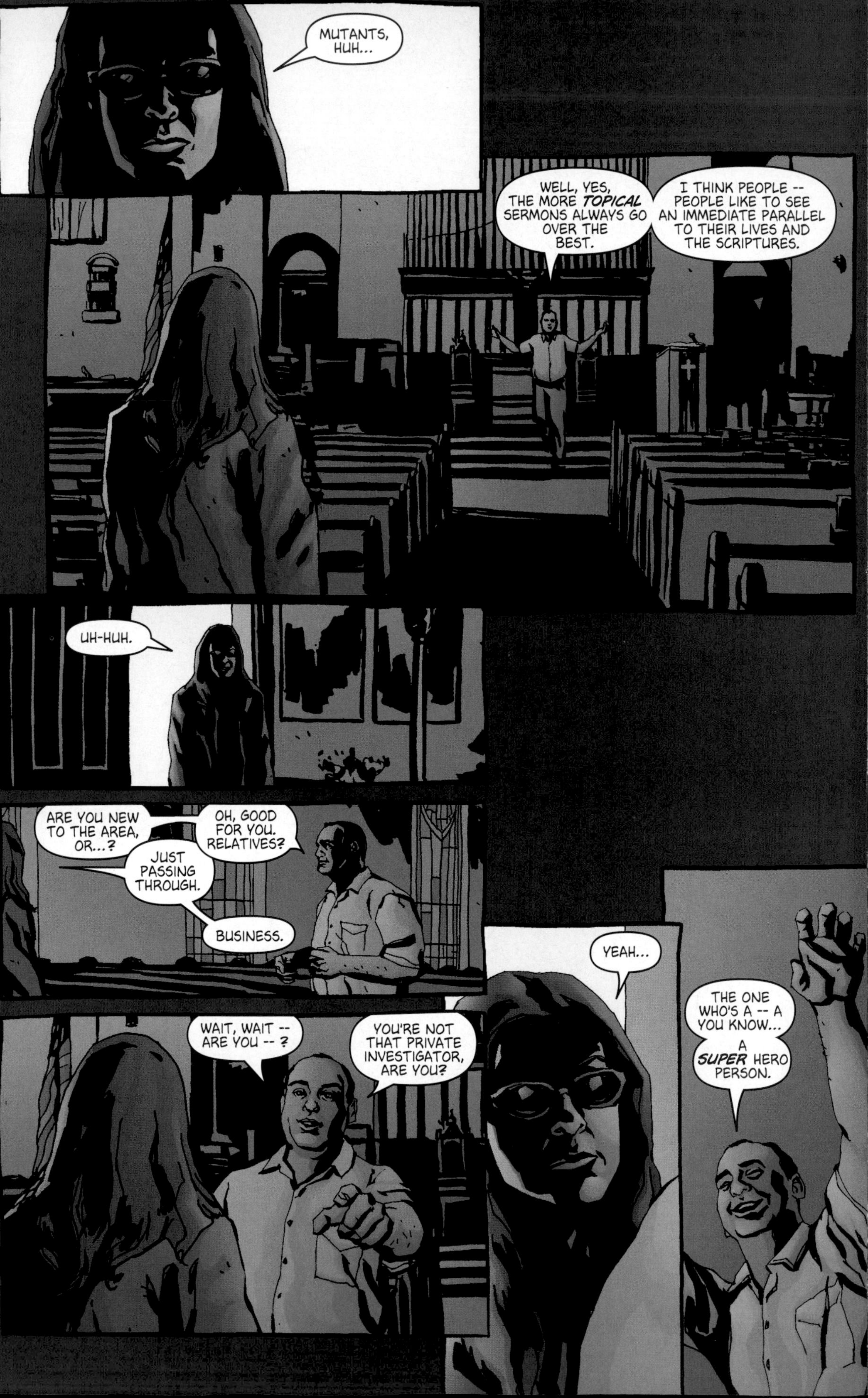
MUTANTS, HUH...
WELL, YES, THE MORE TOPICAL SERMONS ALWAYS GO OVER THE BEST.
I THINK PEOPLE -- PEOPLE LIKE TO SEE AN IMMEDIATE PARALLEL TO THEIR LIVES AND THE SCRIPTURES.
UH-HUH.
ARE YOU NEW TO THE AREA, OR...?
JUST PASSING THROUGH.
OH, GOOD FOR YOU. RELATIVES?
BUSINESS.
WAIT, WAIT -- ARE YOU -- ?
YOU'RE NOT THAT PRIVATE INVESTIGATOR, ARE YOU?
YEAH...
THE ONE WHO'S A -- A YOU KNOW... A SUPER HERO PERSON.

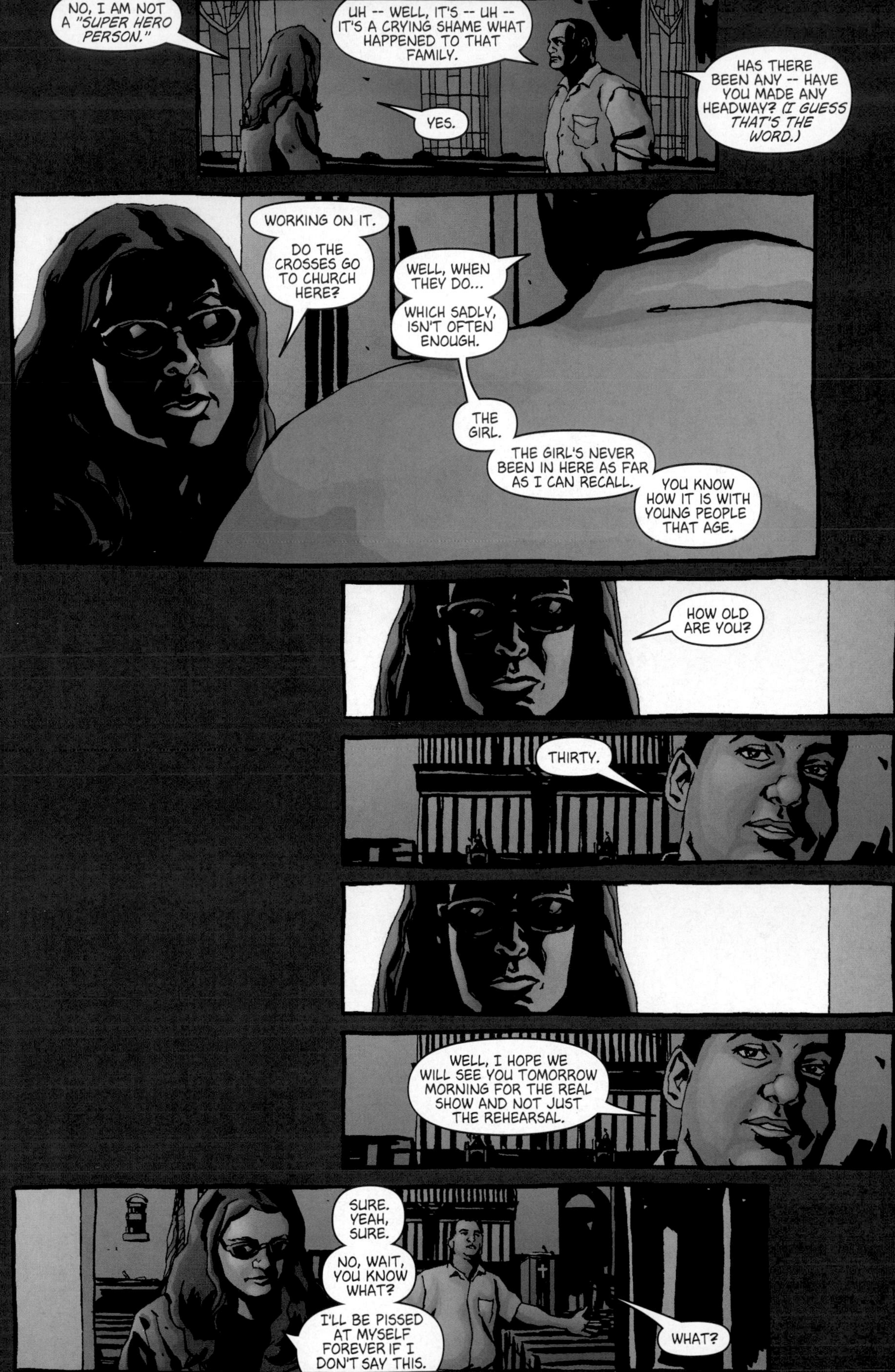
NO, I AM NOT A "SUPER HERO PERSON."
UH -- WELL, IT'S -- UH -- IT'S A CRYING SHAME WHAT HAPPENED TO THAT FAMILY.
YES.
HAS THERE BEEN ANY -- HAVE YOU MADE ANY HEADWAY? *(I GUESS THAT'S THE WORD.)*
WORKING ON IT.
DO THE CROSSES GO TO CHURCH HERE?
WELL, WHEN THEY DO...
WHICH SADLY, ISN'T OFTEN ENOUGH.
THE GIRL.
THE GIRL'S NEVER BEEN IN HERE AS FAR AS I CAN RECALL.
YOU KNOW HOW IT IS WITH YOUNG PEOPLE THAT AGE.
HOW OLD ARE YOU?
THIRTY.
WELL, I HOPE WE WILL SEE YOU TOMORROW MORNING FOR THE REAL SHOW AND NOT JUST THE REHEARSAL.
SURE. YEAH, SURE.
NO, WAIT, YOU KNOW WHAT?
I'LL BE PISSED AT MYSELF FOREVER IF I DON'T SAY THIS.
WHAT?

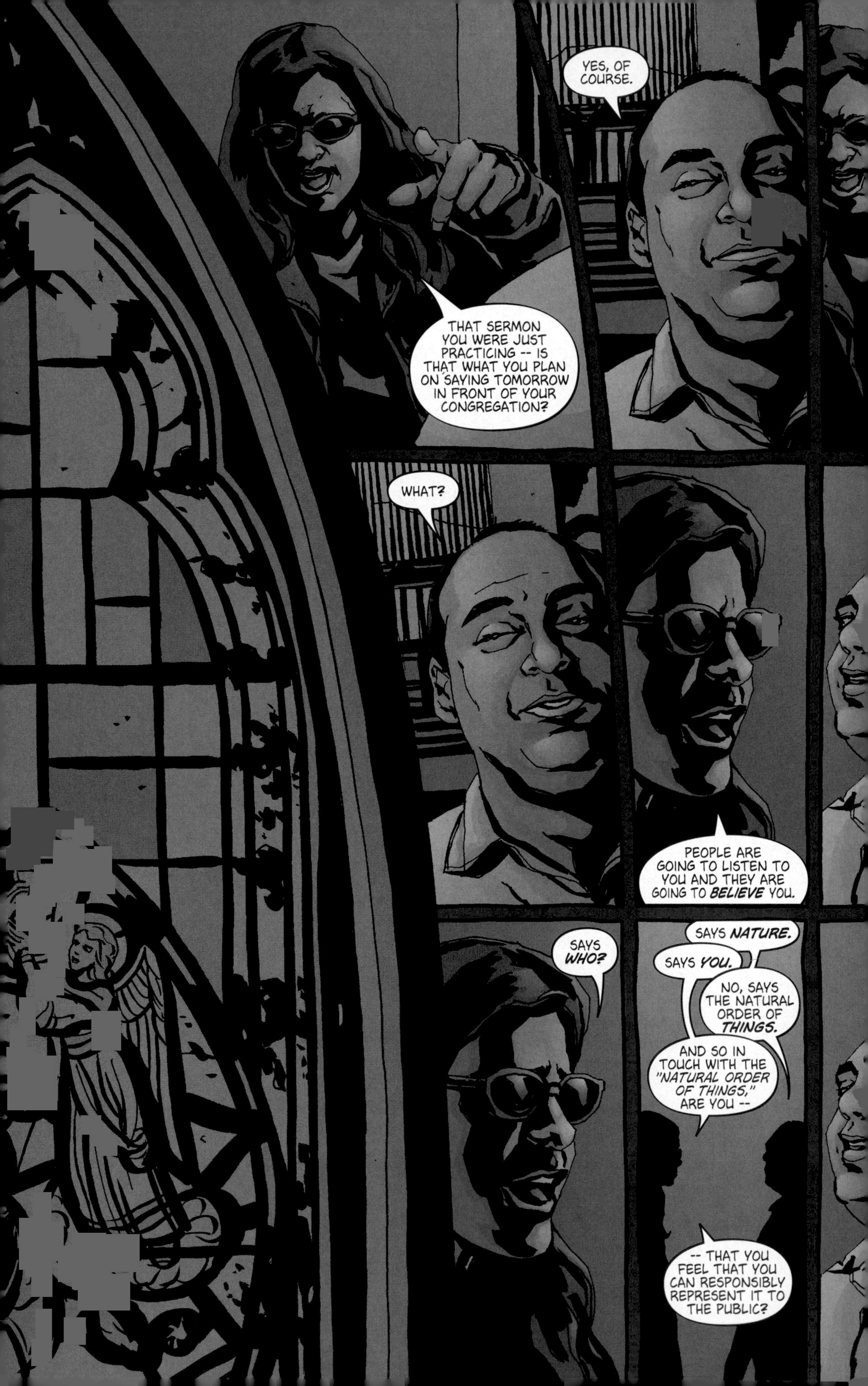
YES, OF COURSE.
THAT SERMON YOU WERE JUST PRACTICING -- IS THAT WHAT YOU PLAN ON SAYING TOMORROW IN FRONT OF YOUR CONGREGATION?
WHAT?
PEOPLE ARE GOING TO LISTEN TO YOU AND THEY ARE GOING TO BELIEVE YOU.
SAYS WHO?
SAYS NATURE.
SAYS YOU.
NO, SAYS THE NATURAL ORDER OF THINGS.
AND SO IN TOUCH WITH THE "NATURAL ORDER OF THINGS," ARE YOU --
-- THAT YOU FEEL THAT YOU CAN RESPONSIBLY REPRESENT IT TO THE PUBLIC?

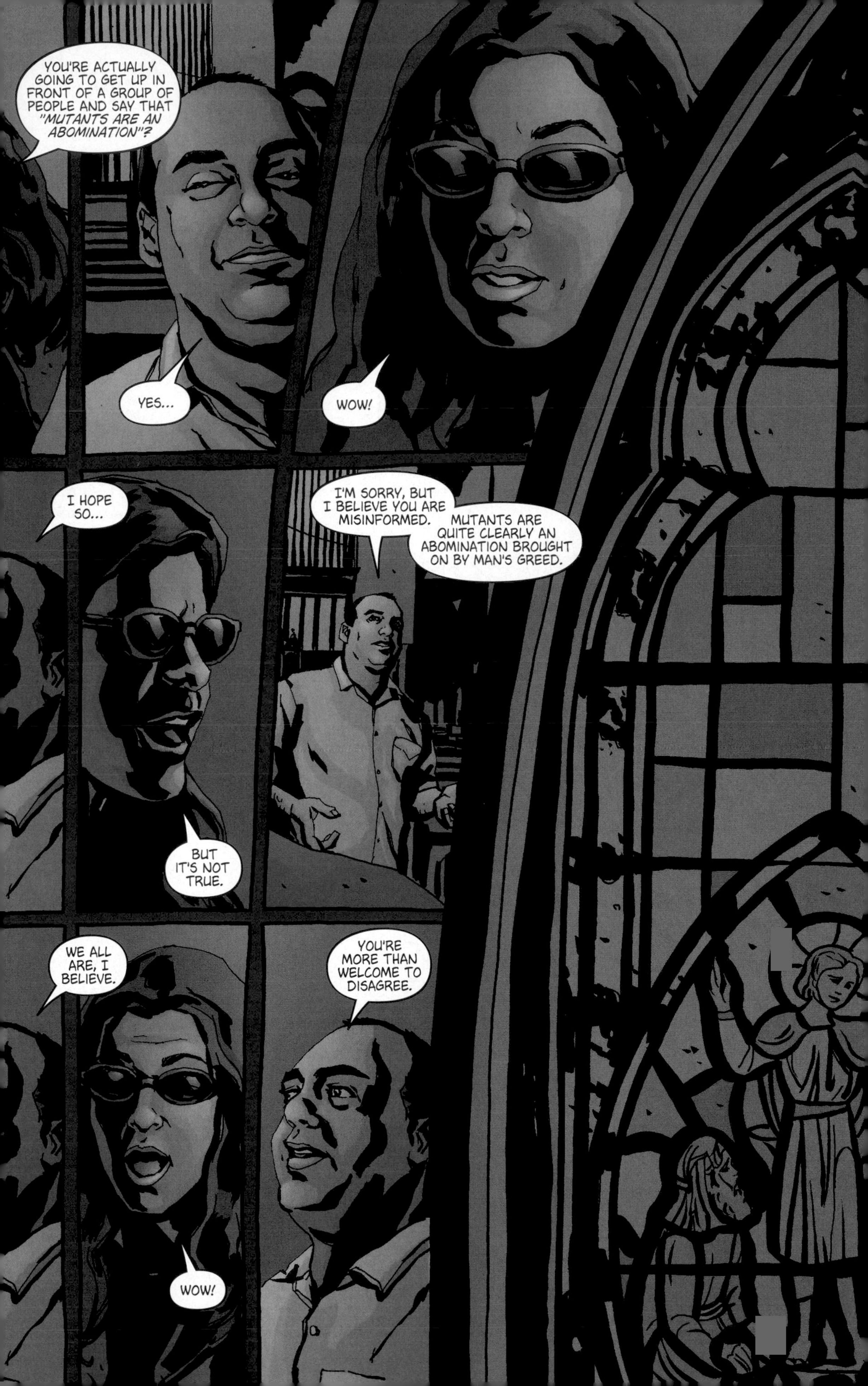
YOU'RE ACTUALLY GOING TO GET UP IN FRONT OF A GROUP OF PEOPLE AND SAY THAT "MUTANTS ARE AN ABOMINATION"?
YES...
WOW!
I HOPE SO...
BUT IT'S NOT TRUE.
I'M SORRY, BUT I BELIEVE YOU ARE MISINFORMED.
MUTANTS ARE QUITE CLEARLY AN ABOMINATION BROUGHT ON BY MAN'S GREED.
WE ALL ARE, I BELIEVE.
WOW!
YOU'RE MORE THAN WELCOME TO DISAGREE.

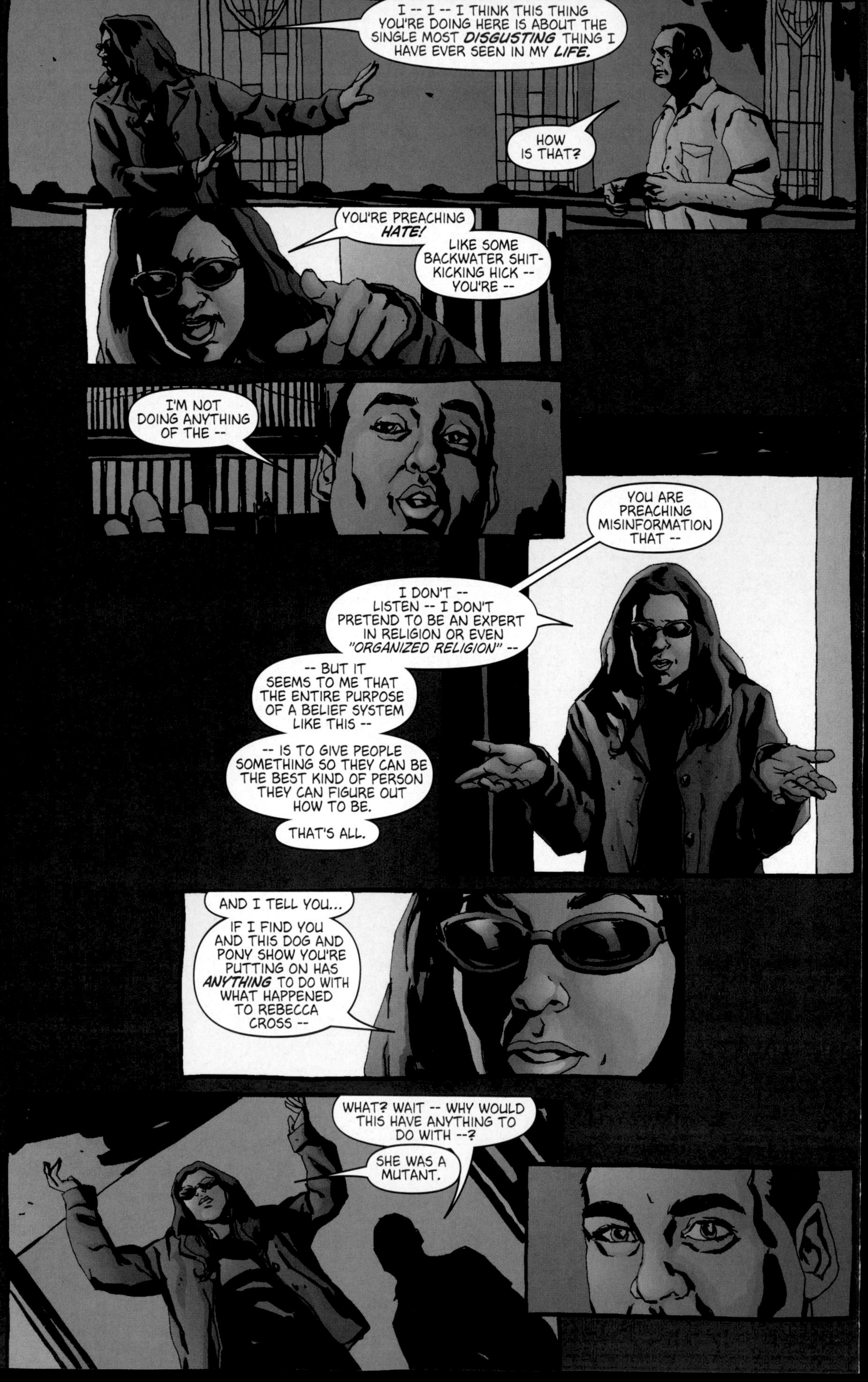
I -- I -- I THINK THIS THING YOU'RE DOING HERE IS ABOUT THE SINGLE MOST *DISGUSTING* THING I HAVE EVER SEEN IN MY *LIFE.*
HOW IS THAT?
YOU'RE PREACHING *HATE!*
LIKE SOME BACKWATER SHIT-KICKING HICK -- YOU'RE --
I'M NOT DOING ANYTHING OF THE --
YOU ARE PREACHING MISINFORMATION THAT --
I DON'T -- LISTEN -- I DON'T PRETEND TO BE AN EXPERT IN RELIGION OR EVEN *"ORGANIZED RELIGION"* --
-- BUT IT SEEMS TO ME THAT THE ENTIRE PURPOSE OF A BELIEF SYSTEM LIKE THIS --
-- IS TO GIVE PEOPLE SOMETHING SO THEY CAN BE THE BEST KIND OF PERSON THEY CAN FIGURE OUT HOW TO BE.
THAT'S ALL.
AND I TELL YOU...
IF I FIND YOU AND THIS DOG AND PONY SHOW YOU'RE PUTTING ON HAS *ANYTHING* TO DO WITH WHAT HAPPENED TO REBECCA CROSS --
WHAT? WAIT -- WHY WOULD THIS HAVE ANYTHING TO DO WITH --?
SHE WAS A MUTANT.

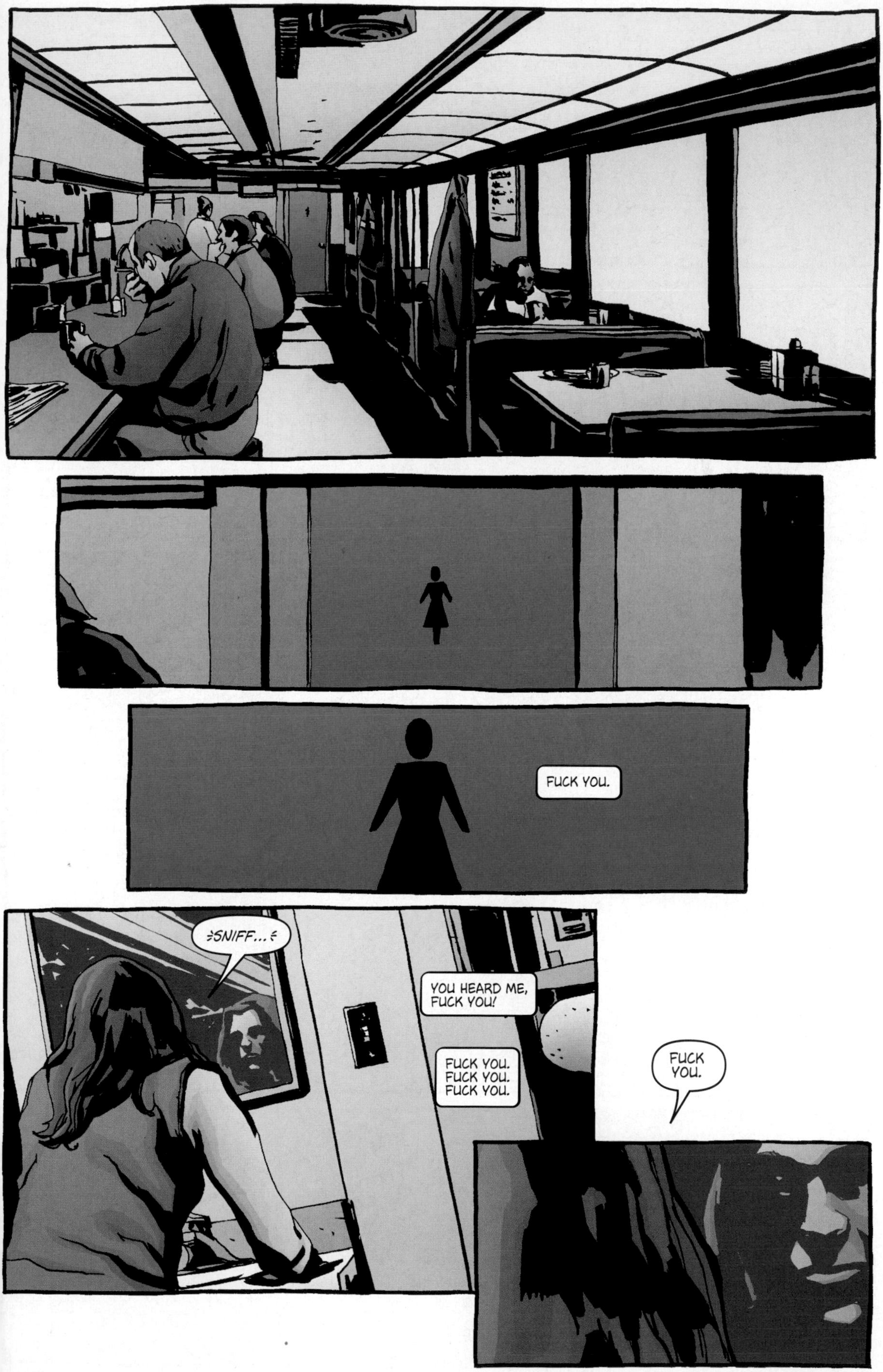
FUCK YOU.
SNIFF...
YOU HEARD ME, FUCK YOU!
FUCK YOU. FUCK YOU. FUCK YOU.
FUCK YOU.

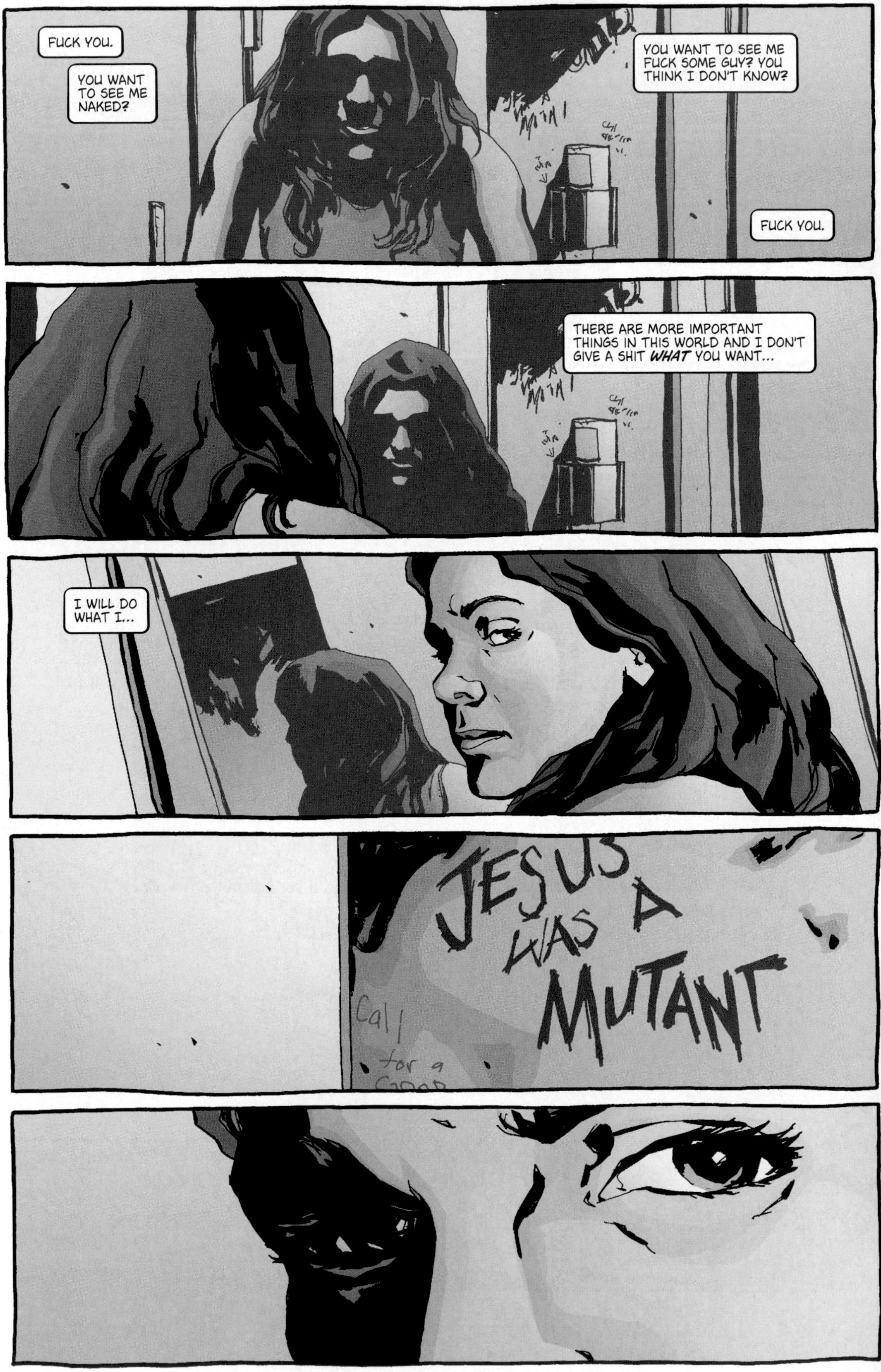

FUCK YOU.
YOU WANT TO SEE ME NAKED?
YOU WANT TO SEE ME FUCK SOME GUY? YOU THINK I DON'T KNOW?
FUCK YOU.
THERE ARE MORE IMPORTANT THINGS IN THIS WORLD AND I DON'T GIVE A SHIT *WHAT* YOU WANT...
I WILL DO WHAT I...
JESUS WAS A MUTANT
Call for a

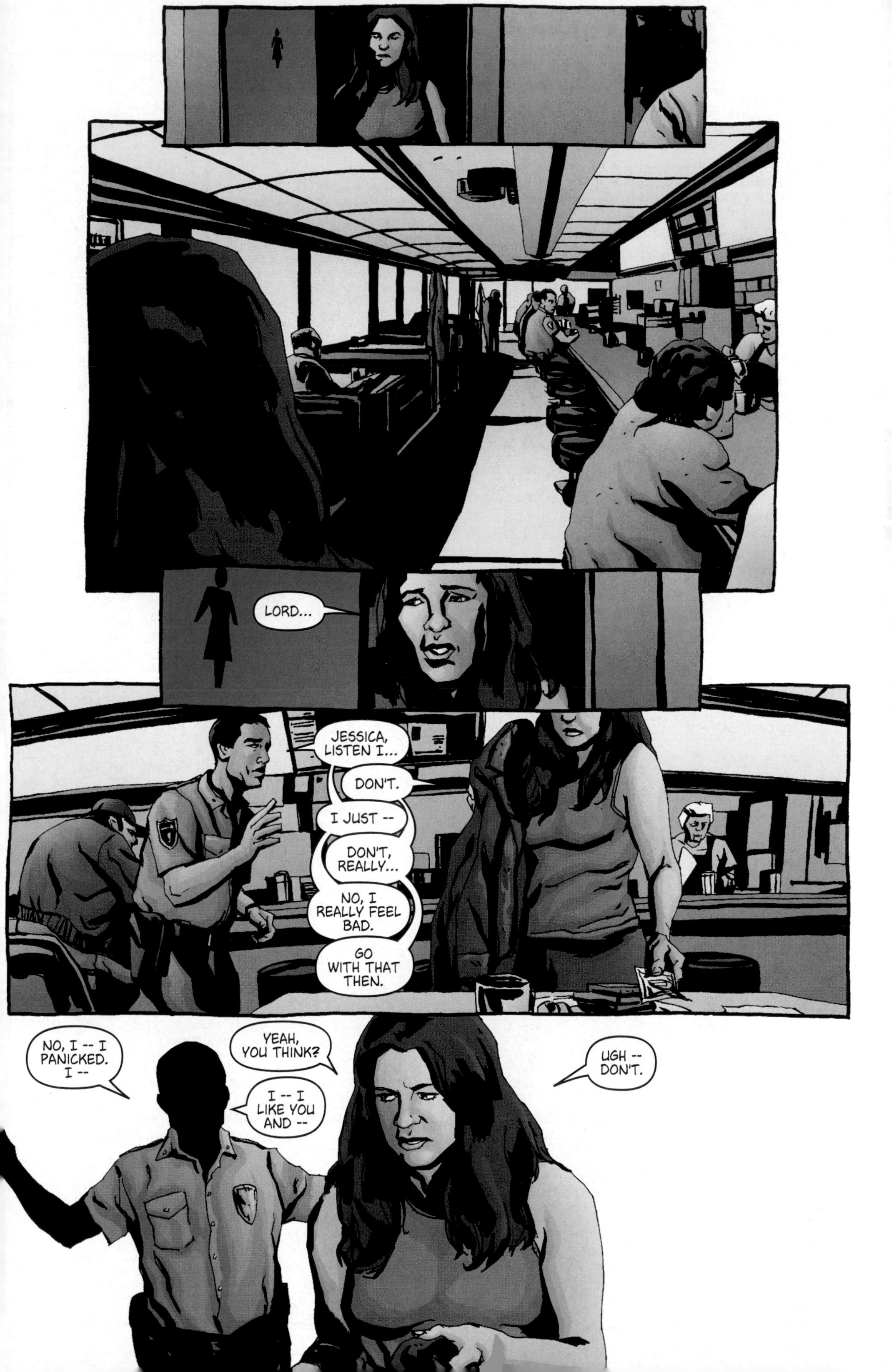
LORD...
JESSICA, LISTEN I...
DON'T.
I JUST --
DON'T, REALLY...
NO, I REALLY FEEL BAD.
GO WITH THAT THEN.
NO, I -- I PANICKED. I --
YEAH, YOU THINK?
I -- I LIKE YOU AND --
UGH -- DON'T.

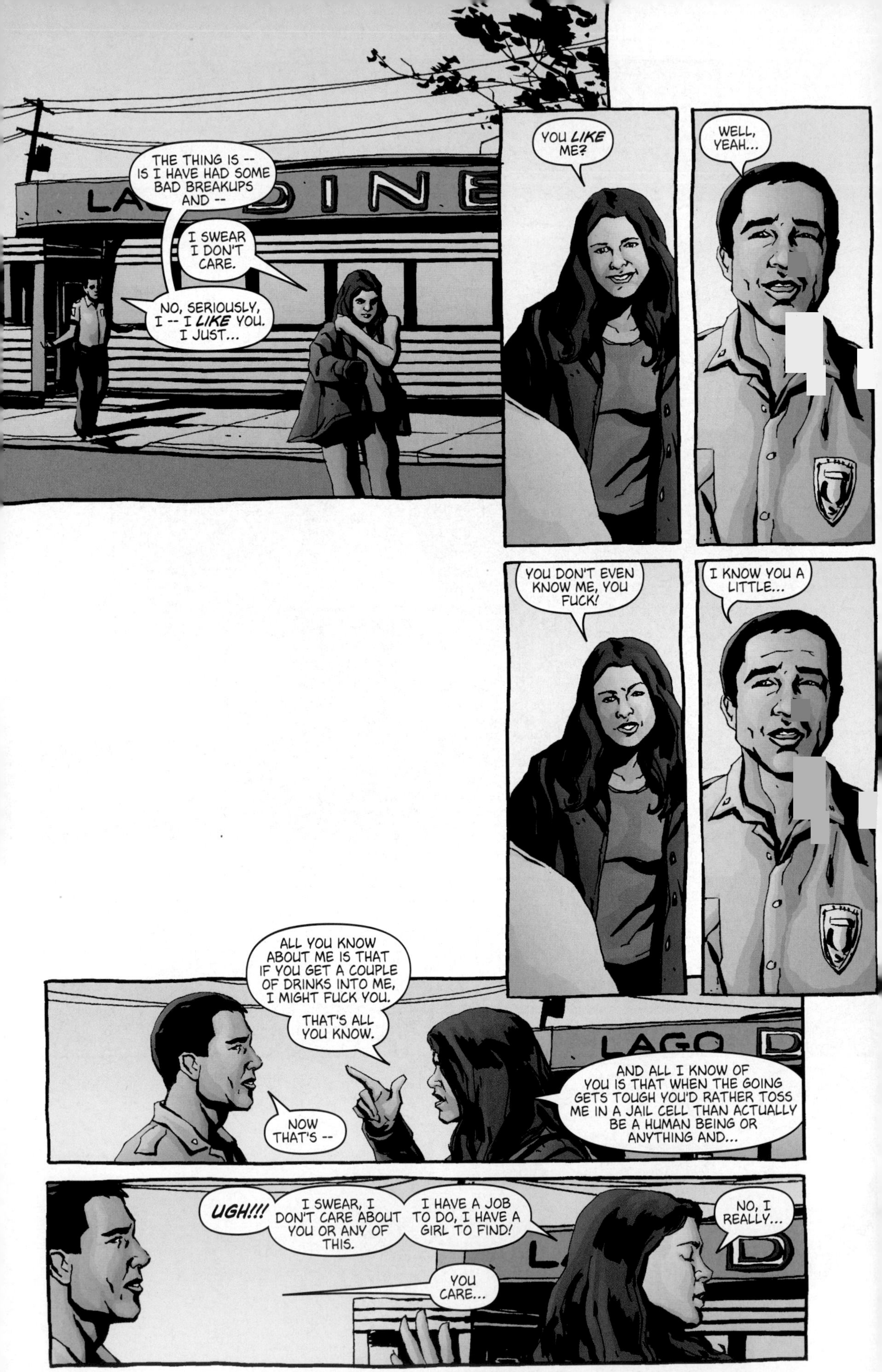
THE THING IS -- IS I HAVE HAD SOME BAD BREAKUPS AND --
I SWEAR I DON'T CARE.
NO, SERIOUSLY, I -- I *LIKE* YOU. I JUST...
YOU *LIKE* ME?
WELL, YEAH...
YOU DON'T EVEN KNOW ME, YOU FUCK!
I KNOW YOU A LITTLE...
ALL YOU KNOW ABOUT ME IS THAT IF YOU GET A COUPLE OF DRINKS INTO ME, I MIGHT FUCK YOU.
THAT'S ALL YOU KNOW.
NOW THAT'S --
AND ALL I KNOW OF YOU IS THAT WHEN THE GOING GETS TOUGH YOU'D RATHER TOSS ME IN A JAIL CELL THAN ACTUALLY BE A HUMAN BEING OR ANYTHING AND...
UGH!!!
I SWEAR, I DON'T CARE ABOUT YOU OR ANY OF THIS.
I HAVE A JOB TO DO, I HAVE A GIRL TO FIND!
YOU CARE...
NO, I REALLY...

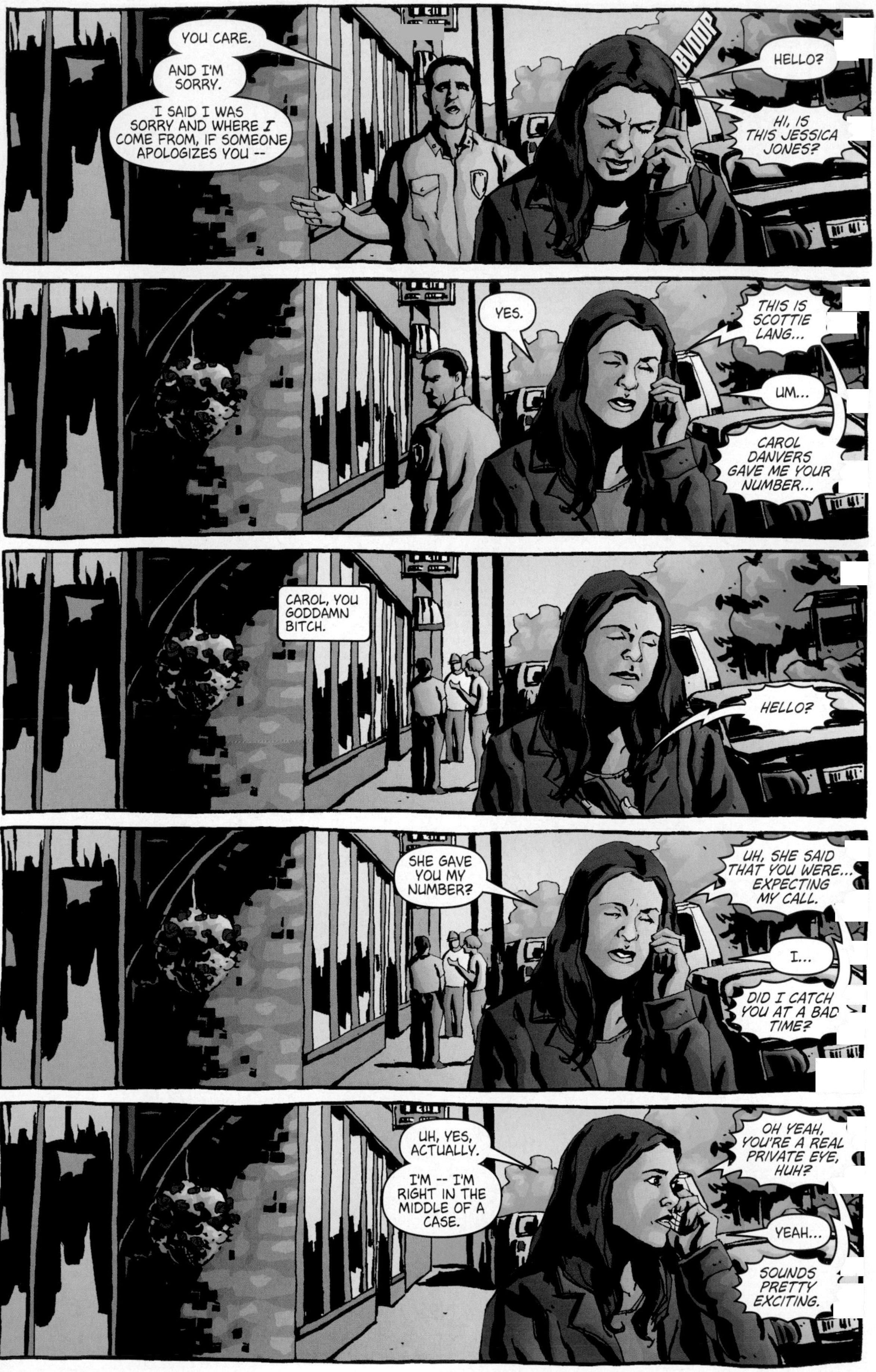
YOU CARE.
AND I'M SORRY.
I SAID I WAS SORRY AND WHERE I COME FROM, IF SOMEONE APOLOGIZES YOU --
BVDDP
HELLO?
HI, IS THIS JESSICA JONES?
YES.
THIS IS SCOTTIE LANG...
UM...
CAROL DANVERS GAVE ME YOUR NUMBER...
CAROL, YOU GODDAMN BITCH.
HELLO?
SHE GAVE YOU MY NUMBER?
UH, SHE SAID THAT YOU WERE... EXPECTING MY CALL.
I...
DID I CATCH YOU AT A BAD TIME?
UH, YES, ACTUALLY.
I'M -- I'M RIGHT IN THE MIDDLE OF A CASE.
OH YEAH, YOU'RE A REAL PRIVATE EYE, HUH?
YEAH...
SOUNDS PRETTY EXCITING.

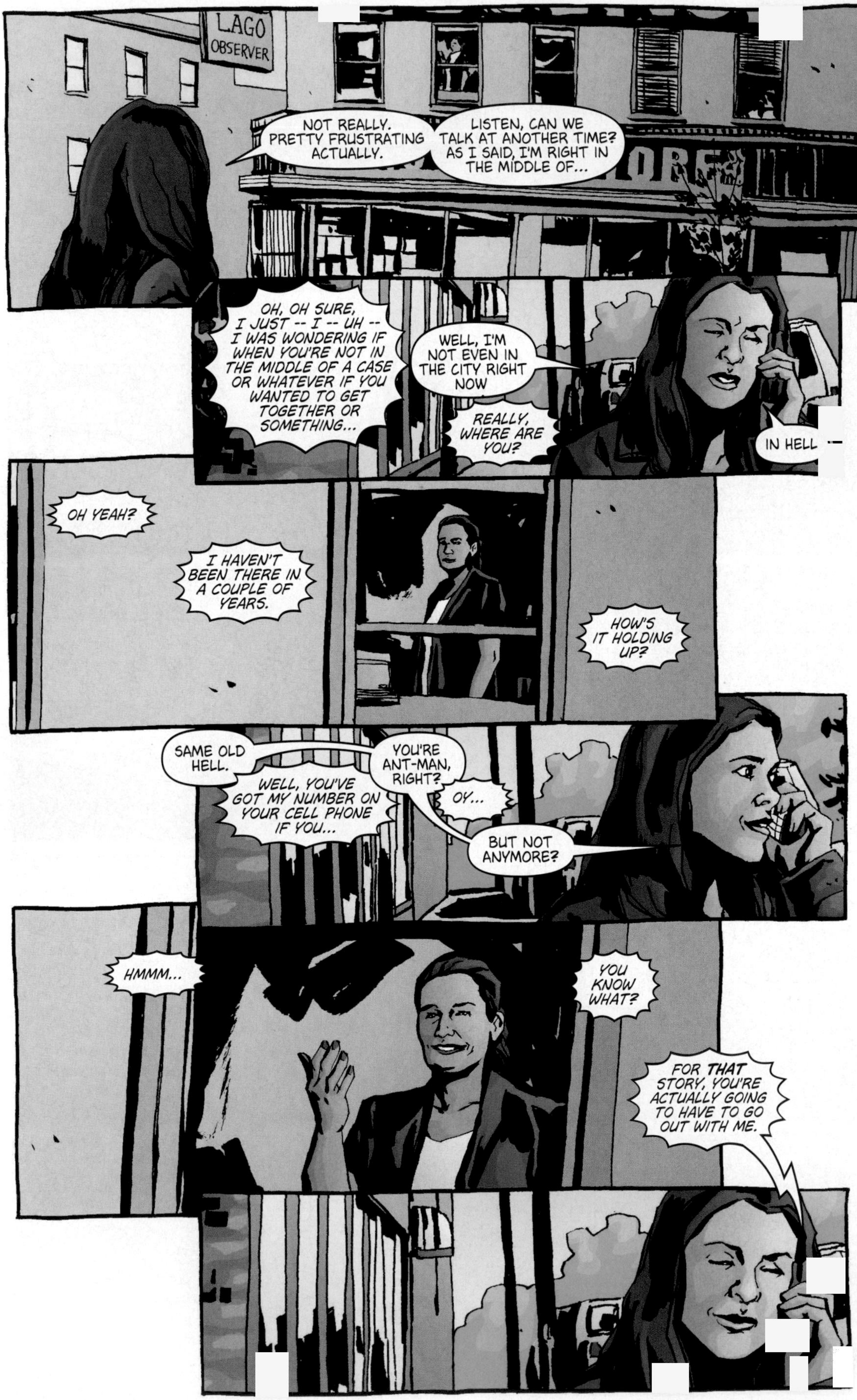
LAGO OBSERVER
NOT REALLY. PRETTY FRUSTRATING ACTUALLY.
LISTEN, CAN WE TALK AT ANOTHER TIME? AS I SAID, I'M RIGHT IN THE MIDDLE OF...
OH, OH SURE, I JUST -- I -- UH -- I WAS WONDERING IF WHEN YOU'RE NOT IN THE MIDDLE OF A CASE OR WHATEVER IF YOU WANTED TO GET TOGETHER OR SOMETHING...
WELL, I'M NOT EVEN IN THE CITY RIGHT NOW
REALLY, WHERE ARE YOU?
IN HELL
OH YEAH?
I HAVEN'T BEEN THERE IN A COUPLE OF YEARS.
HOW'S IT HOLDING UP?
SAME OLD HELL.
YOU'RE ANT-MAN, RIGHT?
WELL, YOU'VE GOT MY NUMBER ON YOUR CELL PHONE IF YOU...
OY...
BUT NOT ANYMORE?
HMMM...
YOU KNOW WHAT?
FOR THAT STORY, YOU'RE ACTUALLY GOING TO HAVE TO GO OUT WITH ME.

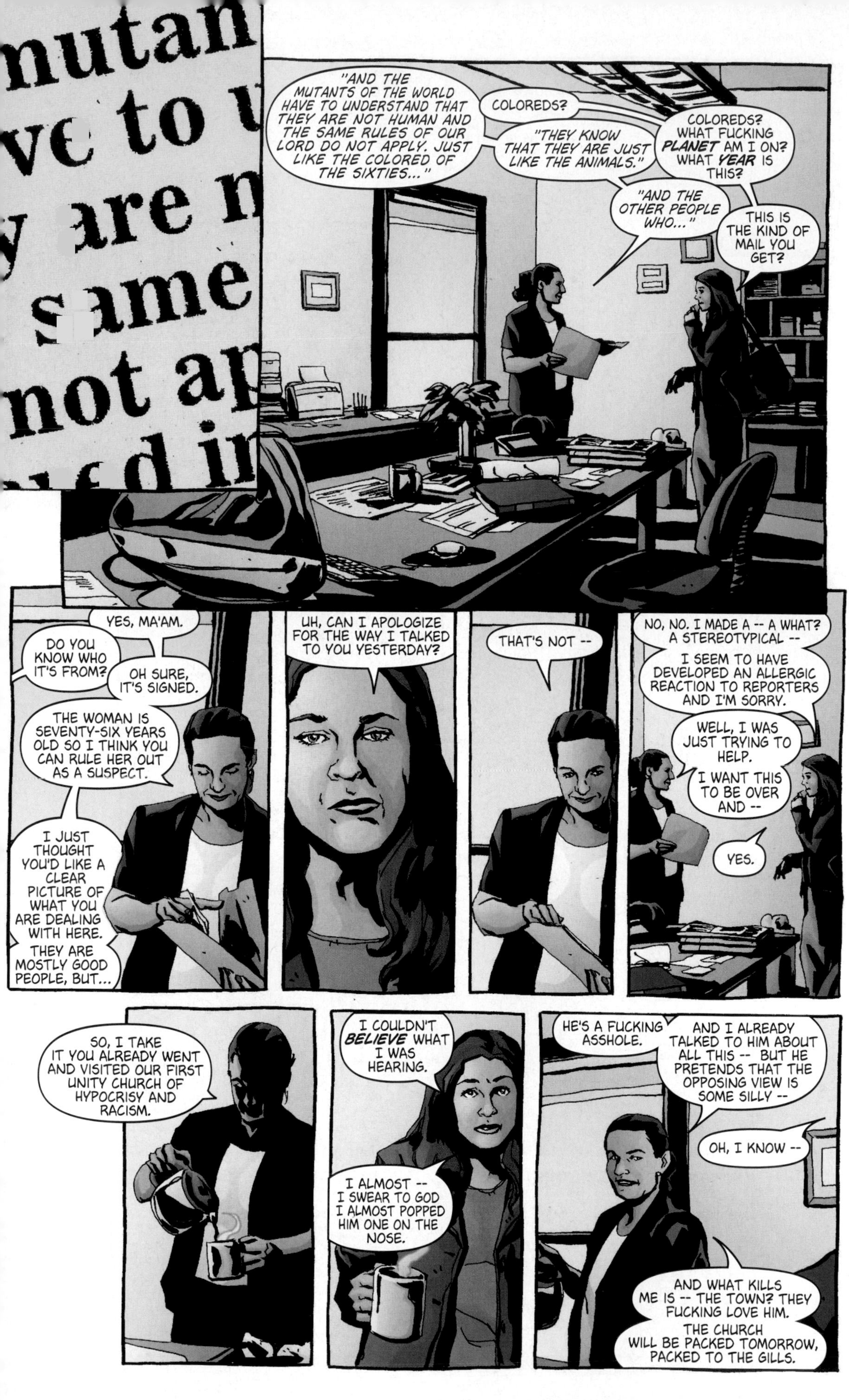
mutan
ve to u
y are n
same
not ap
ufd in
"AND THE MUTANTS OF THE WORLD HAVE TO UNDERSTAND THAT THEY ARE NOT HUMAN AND THE SAME RULES OF OUR LORD DO NOT APPLY. JUST LIKE THE COLORED OF THE SIXTIES..."
COLOREDS?
"THEY KNOW THAT THEY ARE JUST LIKE THE ANIMALS."
COLOREDS? WHAT FUCKING PLANET AM I ON? WHAT YEAR IS THIS?
"AND THE OTHER PEOPLE WHO..."
THIS IS THE KIND OF MAIL YOU GET?
YES, MA'AM.
DO YOU KNOW WHO IT'S FROM?
OH SURE, IT'S SIGNED.
THE WOMAN IS SEVENTY-SIX YEARS OLD SO I THINK YOU CAN RULE HER OUT AS A SUSPECT.
I JUST THOUGHT YOU'D LIKE A CLEAR PICTURE OF WHAT YOU ARE DEALING WITH HERE.
THEY ARE MOSTLY GOOD PEOPLE, BUT...
UH, CAN I APOLOGIZE FOR THE WAY I TALKED TO YOU YESTERDAY?
THAT'S NOT --
NO, NO. I MADE A -- A WHAT? A STEREOTYPICAL --
I SEEM TO HAVE DEVELOPED AN ALLERGIC REACTION TO REPORTERS AND I'M SORRY.
WELL, I WAS JUST TRYING TO HELP.
I WANT THIS TO BE OVER AND --
YES.
SO, I TAKE IT YOU ALREADY WENT AND VISITED OUR FIRST UNITY CHURCH OF HYPOCRISY AND RACISM.
I COULDN'T BELIEVE WHAT I WAS HEARING.
I ALMOST -- I SWEAR TO GOD I ALMOST POPPED HIM ONE ON THE NOSE.
HE'S A FUCKING ASSHOLE.
AND I ALREADY TALKED TO HIM ABOUT ALL THIS -- BUT HE PRETENDS THAT THE OPPOSING VIEW IS SOME SILLY --
OH, I KNOW --
AND WHAT KILLS ME IS -- THE TOWN? THEY FUCKING LOVE HIM.
THE CHURCH WILL BE PACKED TOMORROW, PACKED TO THE GILLS.

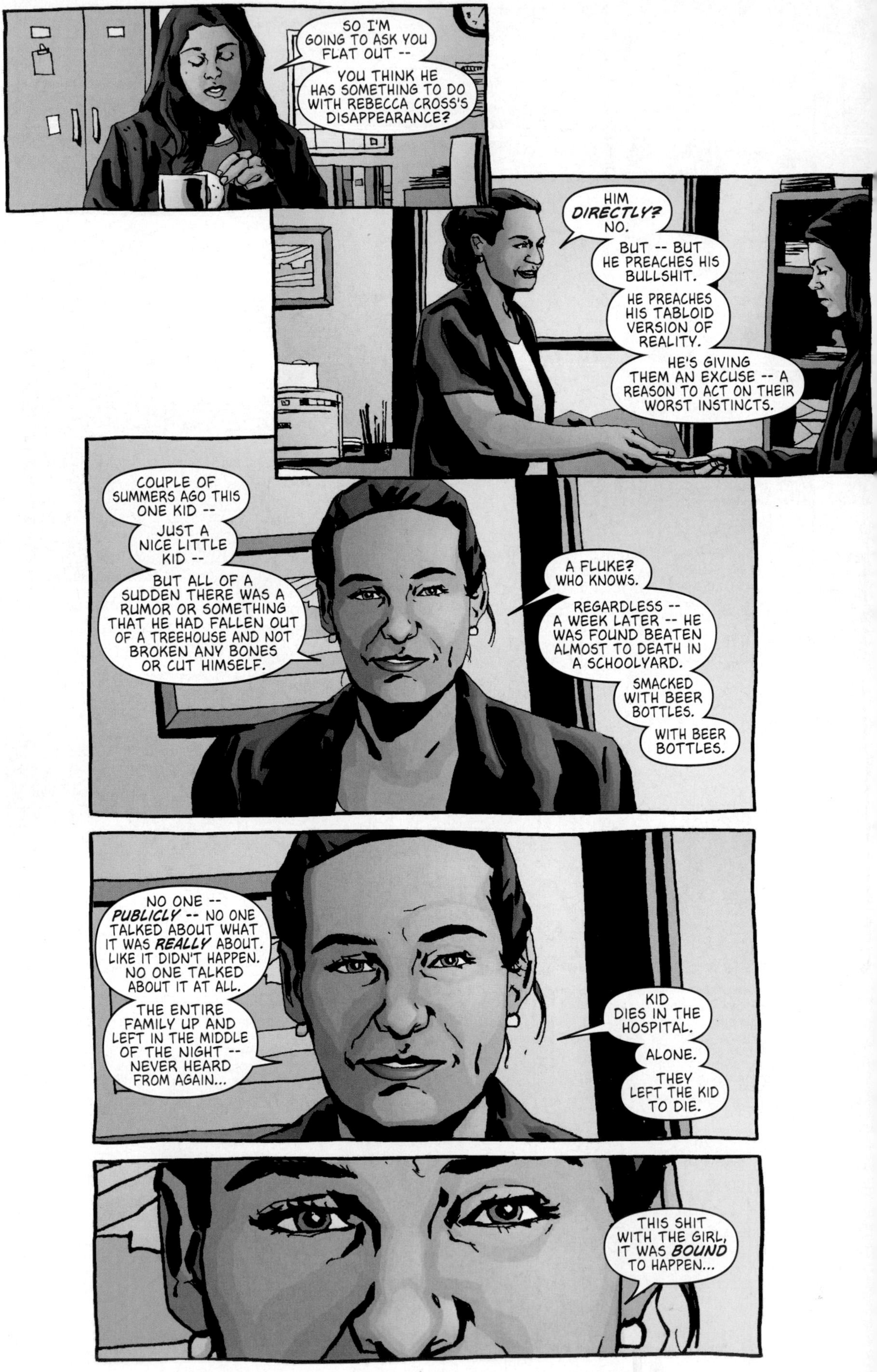
SO I'M GOING TO ASK YOU FLAT OUT --
YOU THINK HE HAS SOMETHING TO DO WITH REBECCA CROSS'S DISAPPEARANCE?
HIM *DIRECTLY?* NO.
BUT -- BUT HE PREACHES HIS BULLSHIT.
HE PREACHES HIS TABLOID VERSION OF REALITY.
HE'S GIVING THEM AN EXCUSE -- A REASON TO ACT ON THEIR WORST INSTINCTS.
COUPLE OF SUMMERS AGO THIS ONE KID --
JUST A NICE LITTLE KID --
BUT ALL OF A SUDDEN THERE WAS A RUMOR OR SOMETHING THAT HE HAD FALLEN OUT OF A TREEHOUSE AND NOT BROKEN ANY BONES OR CUT HIMSELF.
A FLUKE? WHO KNOWS.
REGARDLESS -- A WEEK LATER -- HE WAS FOUND BEATEN ALMOST TO DEATH IN A SCHOOLYARD.
SMACKED WITH BEER BOTTLES.
WITH BEER BOTTLES.
NO ONE -- *PUBLICLY* -- NO ONE TALKED ABOUT WHAT IT WAS *REALLY* ABOUT. LIKE IT DIDN'T HAPPEN. NO ONE TALKED ABOUT IT AT ALL.
THE ENTIRE FAMILY UP AND LEFT IN THE MIDDLE OF THE NIGHT -- NEVER HEARD FROM AGAIN...
KID DIES IN THE HOSPITAL.
ALONE.
THEY LEFT THE KID TO DIE.
THIS SHIT WITH THE GIRL, IT WAS *BOUND* TO HAPPEN...

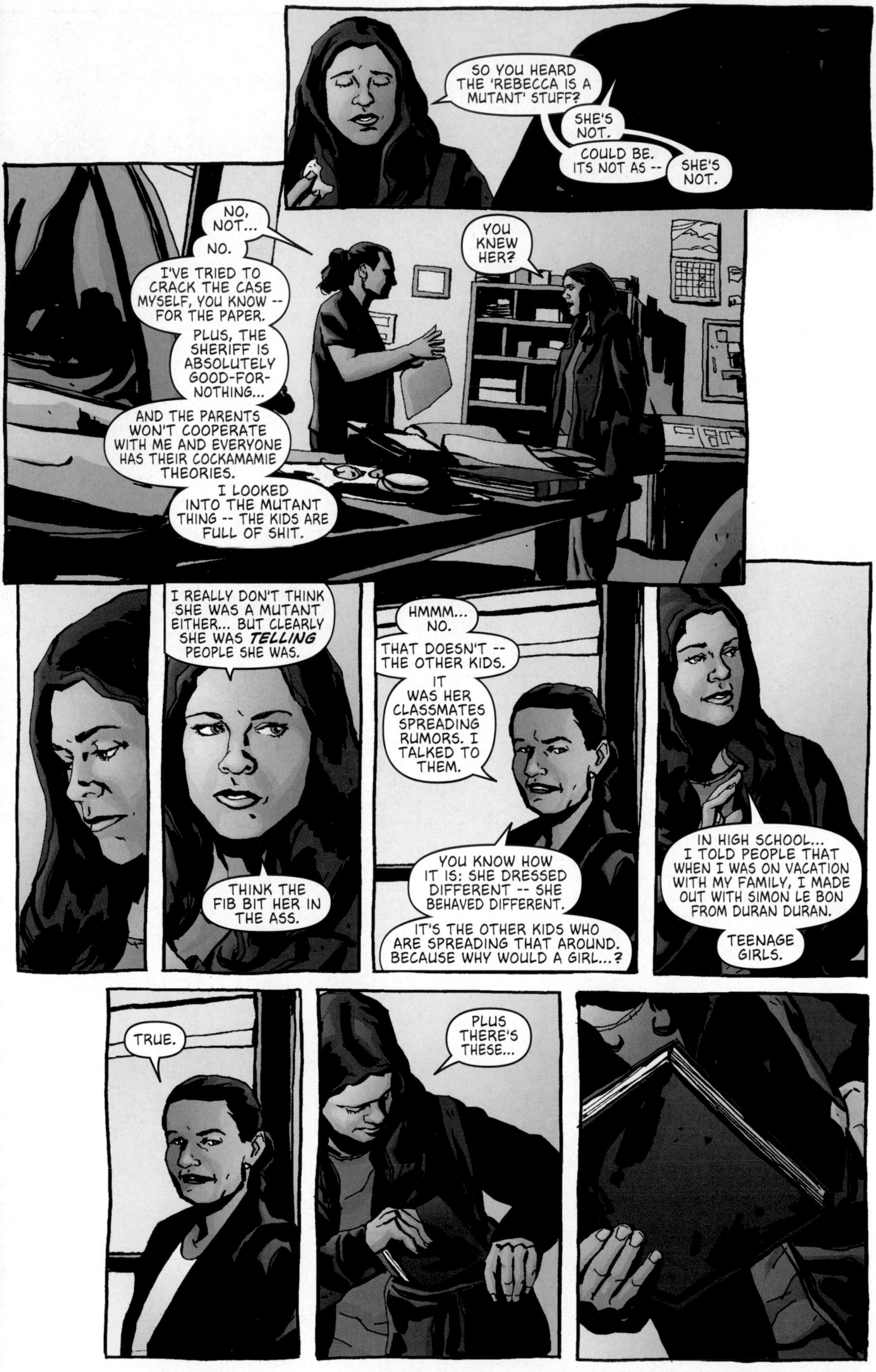
SO YOU HEARD THE 'REBECCA IS A MUTANT' STUFF?
SHE'S NOT.
COULD BE. ITS NOT AS --
SHE'S NOT.
NO, NOT...
NO.
YOU KNEW HER?
I'VE TRIED TO CRACK THE CASE MYSELF, YOU KNOW -- FOR THE PAPER.
PLUS, THE SHERIFF IS ABSOLUTELY GOOD-FOR-NOTHING...
AND THE PARENTS WON'T COOPERATE WITH ME AND EVERYONE HAS THEIR COCKAMAMIE THEORIES.
I LOOKED INTO THE MUTANT THING -- THE KIDS ARE FULL OF SHIT.
I REALLY DON'T THINK SHE WAS A MUTANT EITHER... BUT CLEARLY SHE WAS *TELLING* PEOPLE SHE WAS.
THINK THE FIB BIT HER IN THE ASS.
HMMM... NO.
THAT DOESN'T -- THE OTHER KIDS.
IT WAS HER CLASSMATES SPREADING RUMORS. I TALKED TO THEM.
YOU KNOW HOW IT IS: SHE DRESSED DIFFERENT -- SHE BEHAVED DIFFERENT.
IT'S THE OTHER KIDS WHO ARE SPREADING THAT AROUND. BECAUSE WHY WOULD A GIRL...?
IN HIGH SCHOOL... I TOLD PEOPLE THAT WHEN I WAS ON VACATION WITH MY FAMILY, I MADE OUT WITH SIMON LE BON FROM DURAN DURAN.
TEENAGE GIRLS.
TRUE.
PLUS THERE'S THESE...

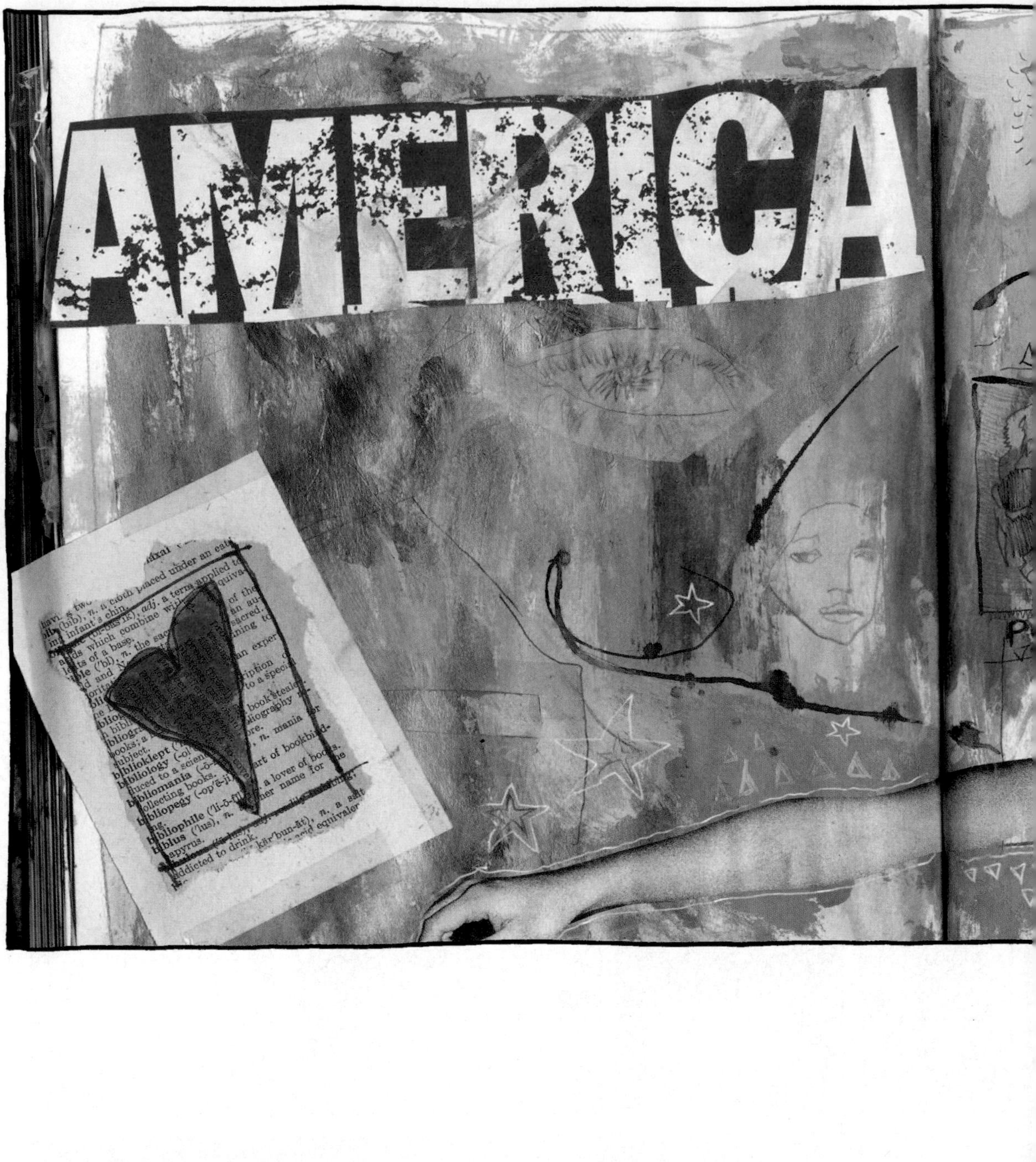
AMERICA

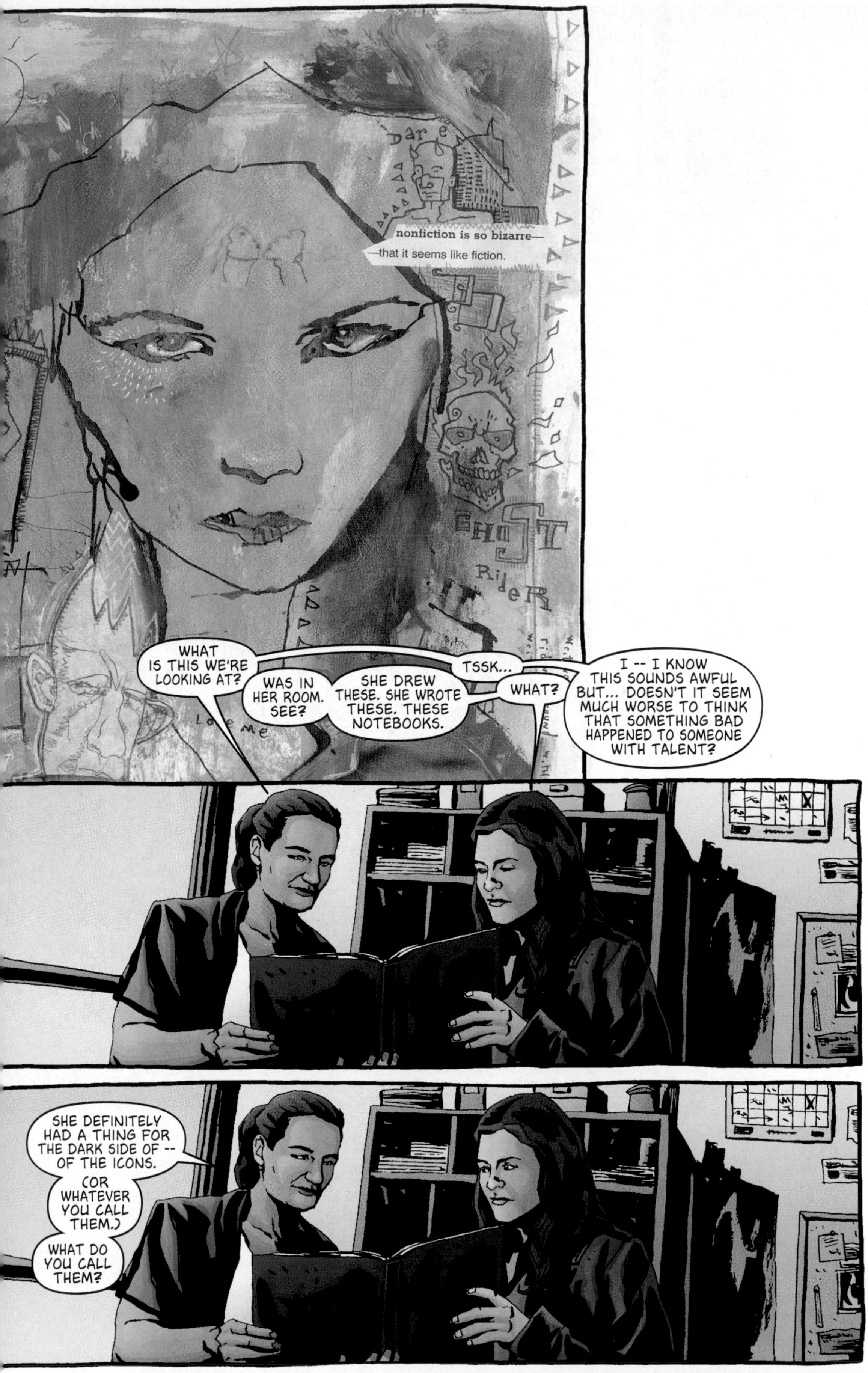
nonfiction is so bizarre—
—that it seems like fiction.
WHAT IS THIS WE'RE LOOKING AT?
WAS IN HER ROOM. SEE?
SHE DREW THESE. SHE WROTE THESE. THESE NOTEBOOKS.
TSSK...
WHAT?
I -- I KNOW THIS SOUNDS AWFUL BUT... DOESN'T IT SEEM MUCH WORSE TO THINK THAT SOMETHING BAD HAPPENED TO SOMEONE WITH TALENT?
SHE DEFINITELY HAD A THING FOR THE DARK SIDE OF -- OF THE ICONS.
(OR WHATEVER YOU CALL THEM.)
WHAT DO YOU CALL THEM?

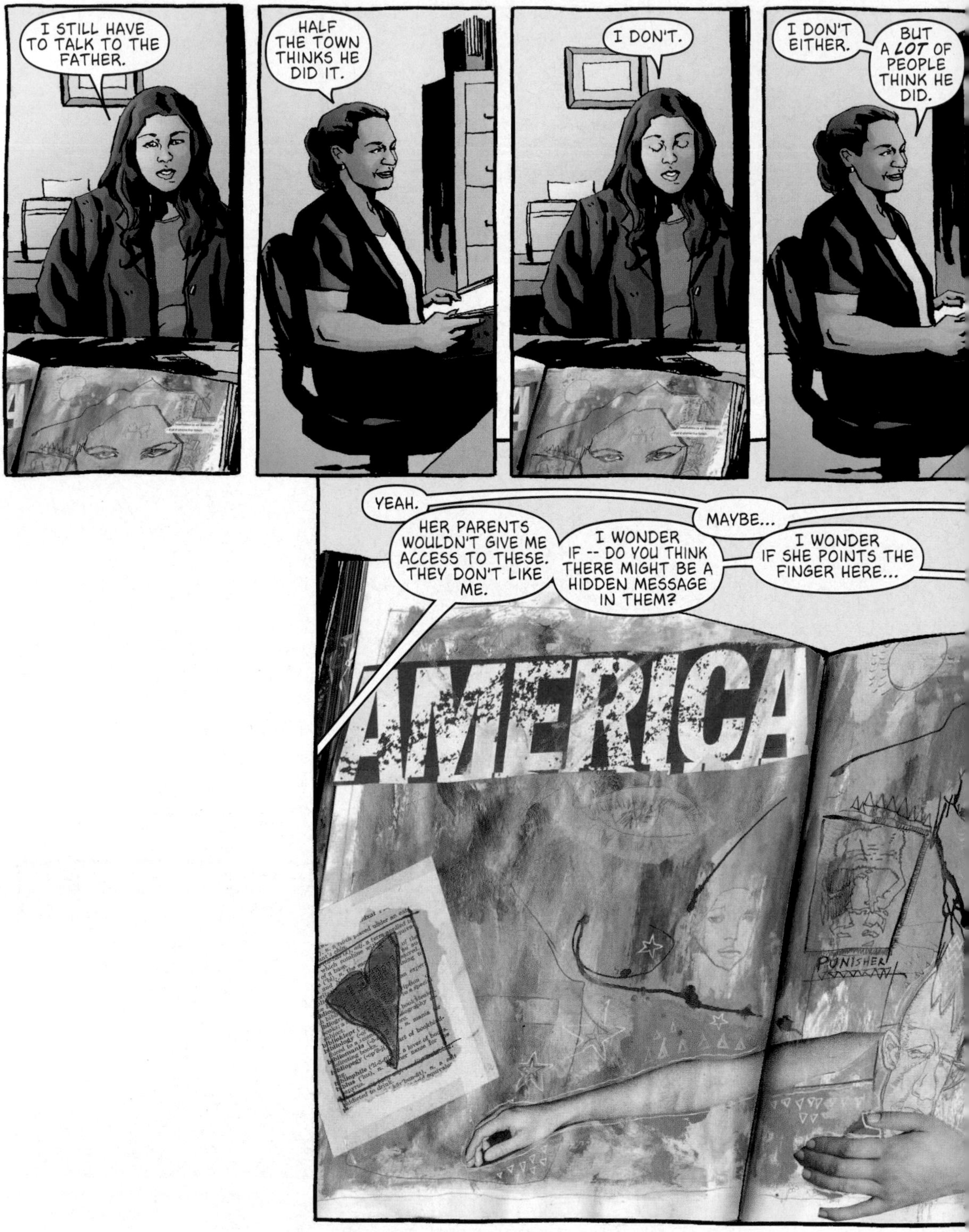
I STILL HAVE TO TALK TO THE FATHER.
HALF THE TOWN THINKS HE DID IT.
I DON'T.
I DON'T EITHER.
BUT A LOT OF PEOPLE THINK HE DID.
YEAH.
HER PARENTS WOULDN'T GIVE ME ACCESS TO THESE. THEY DON'T LIKE ME.
MAYBE...
I WONDER IF -- DO YOU THINK THERE MIGHT BE A HIDDEN MESSAGE IN THEM?
I WONDER IF SHE POINTS THE FINGER HERE...
AMERICA
PUNISHER

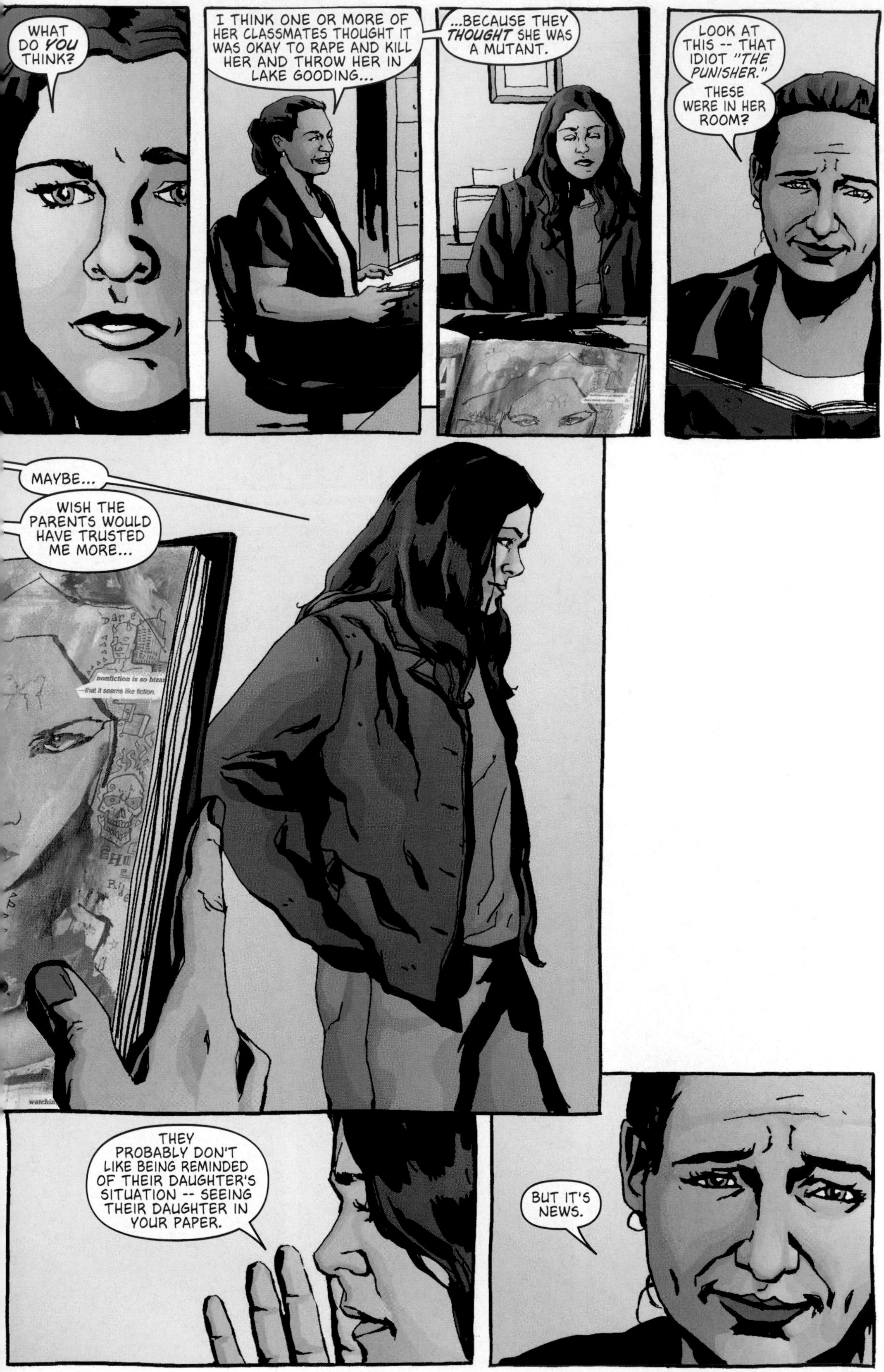
WHAT DO *YOU* THINK?
I THINK ONE OR MORE OF HER CLASSMATES THOUGHT IT WAS OKAY TO RAPE AND KILL HER AND THROW HER IN LAKE GOODING...
...BECAUSE THEY *THOUGHT* SHE WAS A MUTANT.
LOOK AT THIS -- THAT IDIOT *"THE PUNISHER."*
THESE WERE IN HER ROOM?
MAYBE...
WISH THE PARENTS WOULD HAVE TRUSTED ME MORE...
—that it seems like fiction.
THEY PROBABLY DON'T LIKE BEING REMINDED OF THEIR DAUGHTER'S SITUATION -- SEEING THEIR DAUGHTER IN YOUR PAPER.
BUT IT'S NEWS.

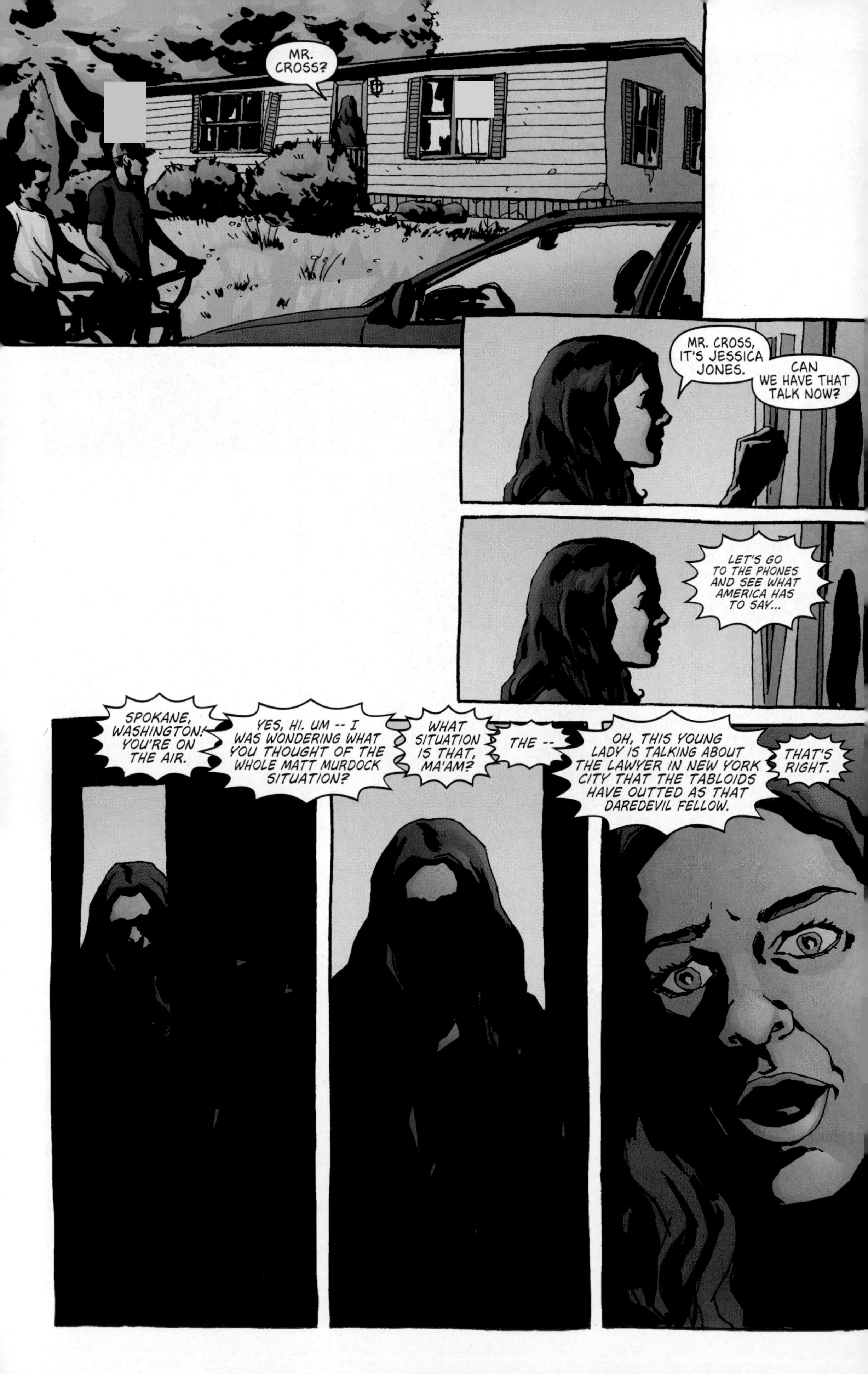
MR. CROSS?
MR. CROSS, IT'S JESSICA JONES.
CAN WE HAVE THAT TALK NOW?
LET'S GO TO THE PHONES AND SEE WHAT AMERICA HAS TO SAY...
SPOKANE, WASHINGTON! YOU'RE ON THE AIR.
YES, HI. UM -- I WAS WONDERING WHAT YOU THOUGHT OF THE WHOLE MATT MURDOCK SITUATION?
WHAT SITUATION IS THAT, MA'AM?
THE --
OH, THIS YOUNG LADY IS TALKING ABOUT THE LAWYER IN NEW YORK CITY THAT THE TABLOIDS HAVE OUTTED AS THAT DAREDEVIL FELLOW.
THAT'S RIGHT.

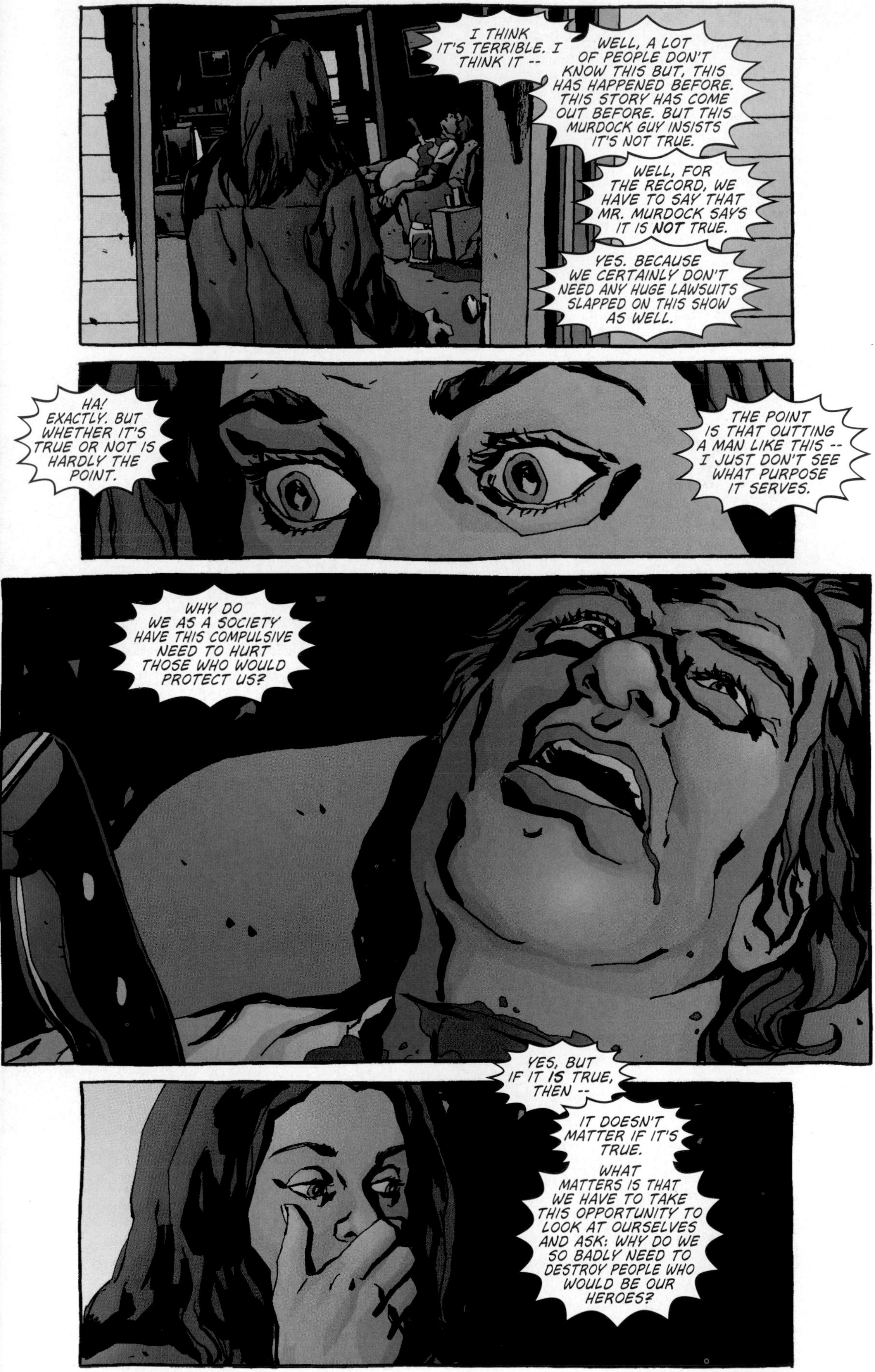
I THINK IT'S TERRIBLE. I THINK IT --
WELL, A LOT OF PEOPLE DON'T KNOW THIS BUT, THIS HAS HAPPENED BEFORE. THIS STORY HAS COME OUT BEFORE. BUT THIS MURDOCK GUY INSISTS IT'S NOT TRUE.
WELL, FOR THE RECORD, WE HAVE TO SAY THAT MR. MURDOCK SAYS IT IS **NOT** TRUE.
YES. BECAUSE WE CERTAINLY DON'T NEED ANY HUGE LAWSUITS SLAPPED ON THIS SHOW AS WELL.
HA! EXACTLY. BUT WHETHER IT'S TRUE OR NOT IS HARDLY THE POINT.
THE POINT IS THAT OUTTING A MAN LIKE THIS -- I JUST DON'T SEE WHAT PURPOSE IT SERVES.
WHY DO WE AS A SOCIETY HAVE THIS COMPULSIVE NEED TO HURT THOSE WHO WOULD PROTECT US?
YES, BUT IF IT **IS** TRUE, THEN --
IT DOESN'T MATTER IF IT'S TRUE.
WHAT MATTERS IS THAT WE HAVE TO TAKE THIS OPPORTUNITY TO LOOK AT OURSELVES AND ASK: WHY DO WE SO BADLY NEED TO DESTROY PEOPLE WHO WOULD BE OUR HEROES?

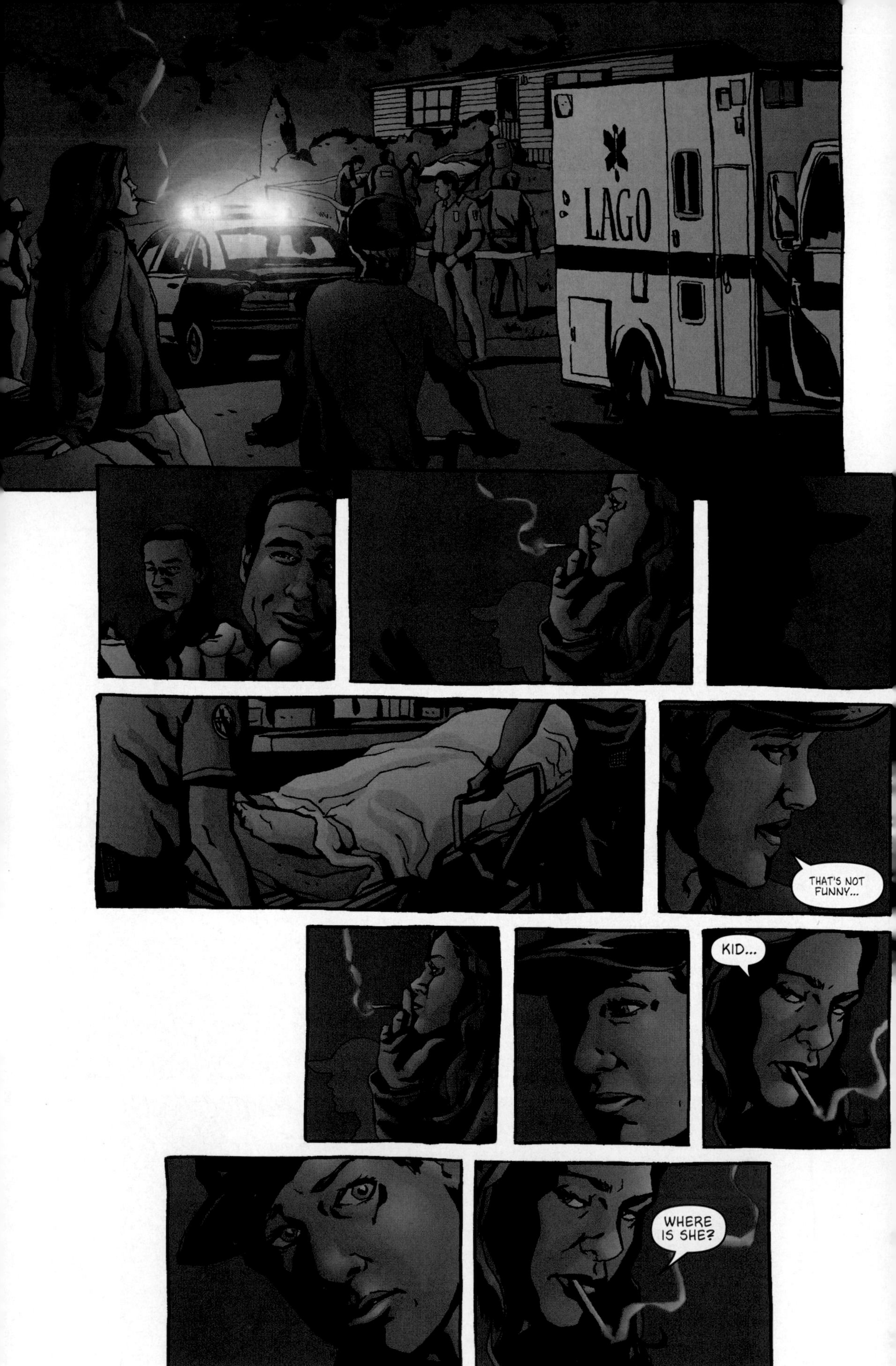
LAGO
THAT'S NOT FUNNY...
KID...
WHERE IS SHE?

INVOICE NUMBER: [redacted]

ISSUE #14

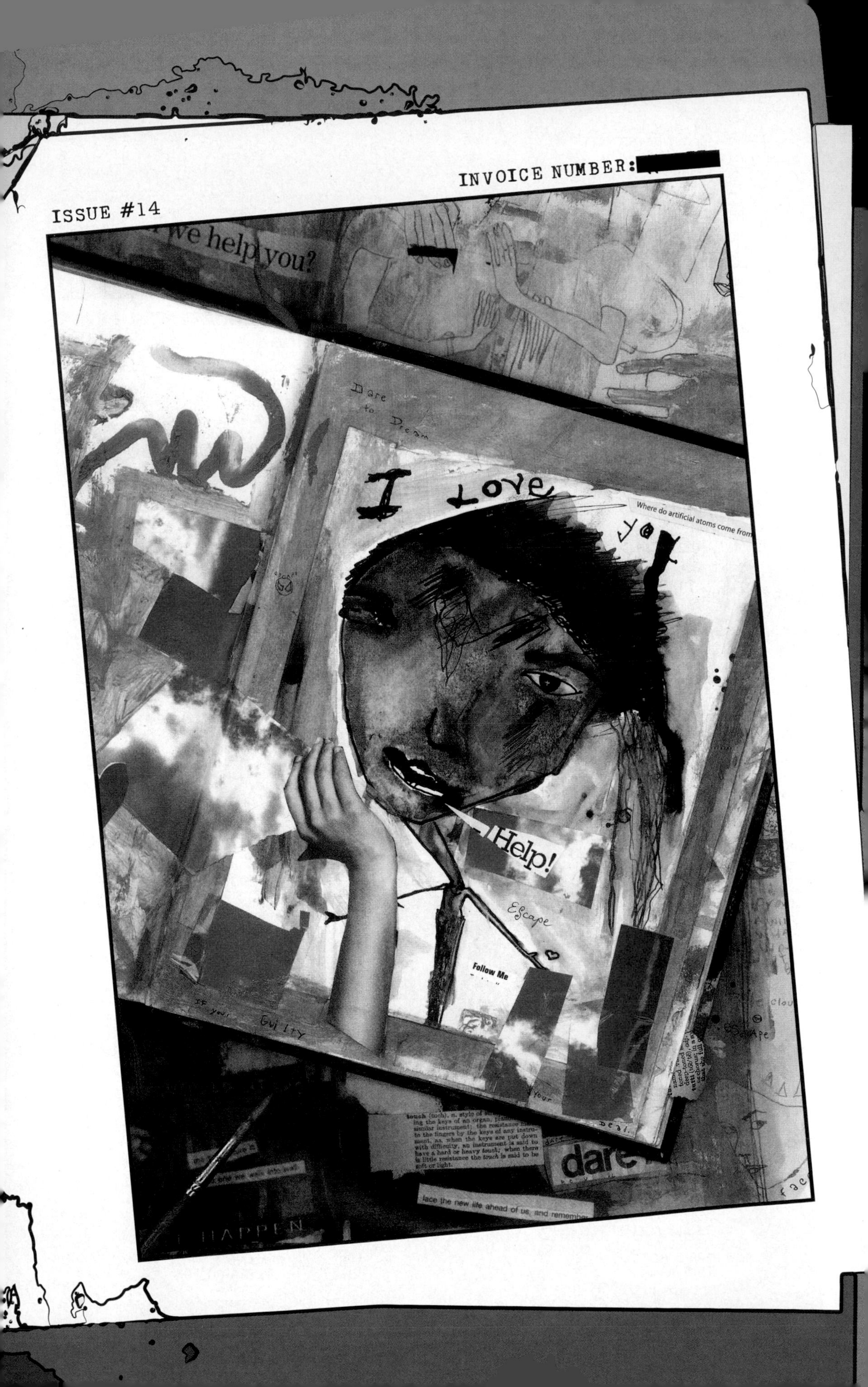
we help you?
Dare to Dream
I Love you
Where do artificial atoms come from
Help!
Escape
Follow Me
If your
Guilty
dare
lace the new life ahead of us, and remember
HAPPEN

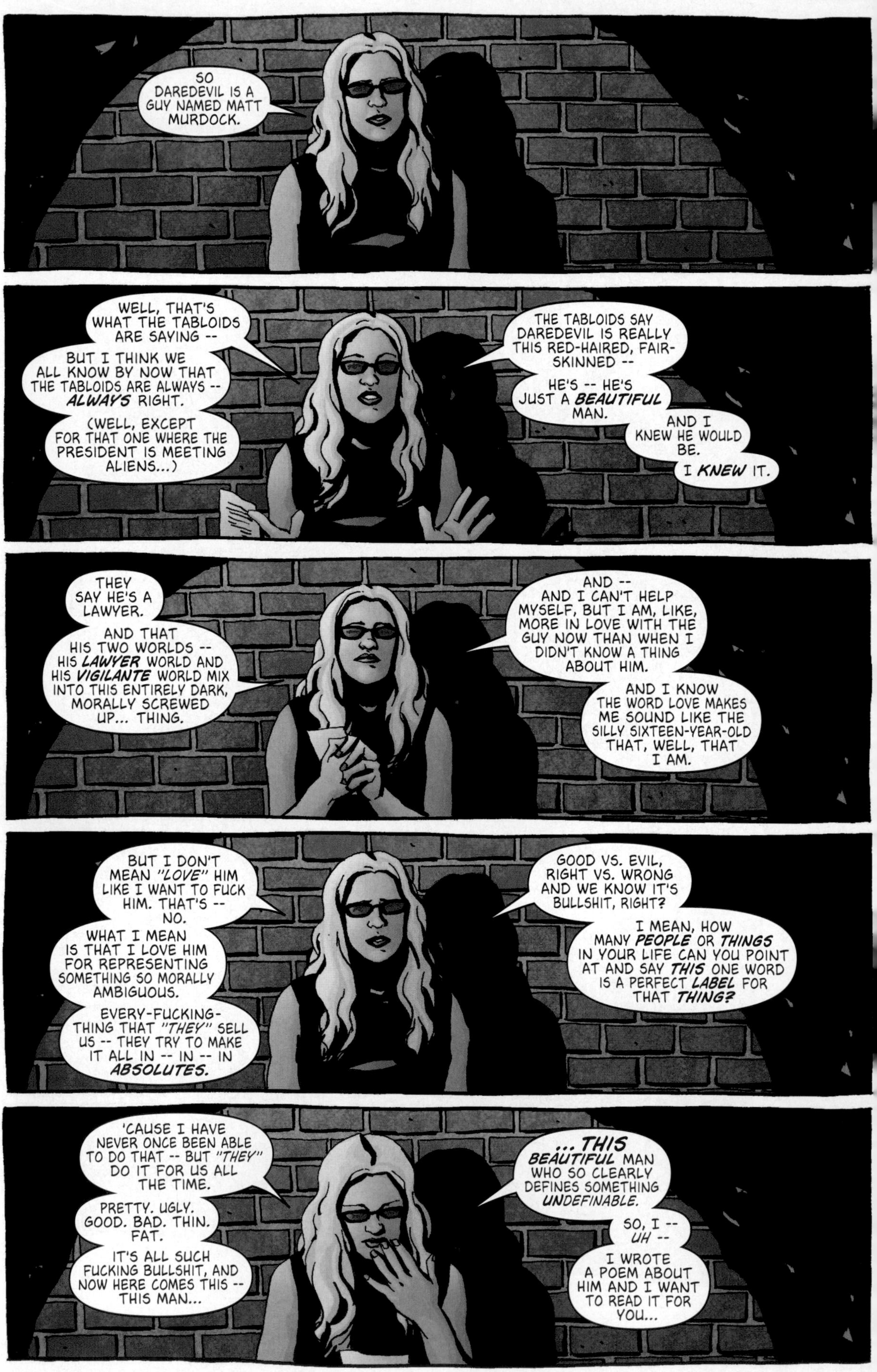
SO DAREDEVIL IS A GUY NAMED MATT MURDOCK.
WELL, THAT'S WHAT THE TABLOIDS ARE SAYING --
BUT I THINK WE ALL KNOW BY NOW THAT THE TABLOIDS ARE ALWAYS -- ALWAYS RIGHT.
(WELL, EXCEPT FOR THAT ONE WHERE THE PRESIDENT IS MEETING ALIENS...)
THE TABLOIDS SAY DAREDEVIL IS REALLY THIS RED-HAIRED, FAIR-SKINNED --
HE'S -- HE'S JUST A BEAUTIFUL MAN.
AND I KNEW HE WOULD BE.
I KNEW IT.
THEY SAY HE'S A LAWYER.
AND THAT HIS TWO WORLDS -- HIS LAWYER WORLD AND HIS VIGILANTE WORLD MIX INTO THIS ENTIRELY DARK, MORALLY SCREWED UP... THING.
AND -- AND I CAN'T HELP MYSELF, BUT I AM, LIKE, MORE IN LOVE WITH THE GUY NOW THAN WHEN I DIDN'T KNOW A THING ABOUT HIM.
AND I KNOW THE WORD LOVE MAKES ME SOUND LIKE THE SILLY SIXTEEN-YEAR-OLD THAT, WELL, THAT I AM.
BUT I DON'T MEAN "LOVE" HIM LIKE I WANT TO FUCK HIM. THAT'S -- NO.
WHAT I MEAN IS THAT I LOVE HIM FOR REPRESENTING SOMETHING SO MORALLY AMBIGUOUS.
EVERY-FUCKING-THING THAT "THEY" SELL US -- THEY TRY TO MAKE IT ALL IN -- IN -- IN ABSOLUTES.
GOOD VS. EVIL, RIGHT VS. WRONG AND WE KNOW IT'S BULLSHIT, RIGHT?
I MEAN, HOW MANY PEOPLE OR THINGS IN YOUR LIFE CAN YOU POINT AT AND SAY THIS ONE WORD IS A PERFECT LABEL FOR THAT THING?
'CAUSE I HAVE NEVER ONCE BEEN ABLE TO DO THAT -- BUT "THEY" DO IT FOR US ALL THE TIME.
PRETTY. UGLY. GOOD. BAD. THIN. FAT.
IT'S ALL SUCH FUCKING BULLSHIT, AND NOW HERE COMES THIS -- THIS MAN...
...THIS BEAUTIFUL MAN WHO SO CLEARLY DEFINES SOMETHING UNDEFINABLE.
SO, I -- UH --
I WROTE A POEM ABOUT HIM AND I WANT TO READ IT FOR YOU...

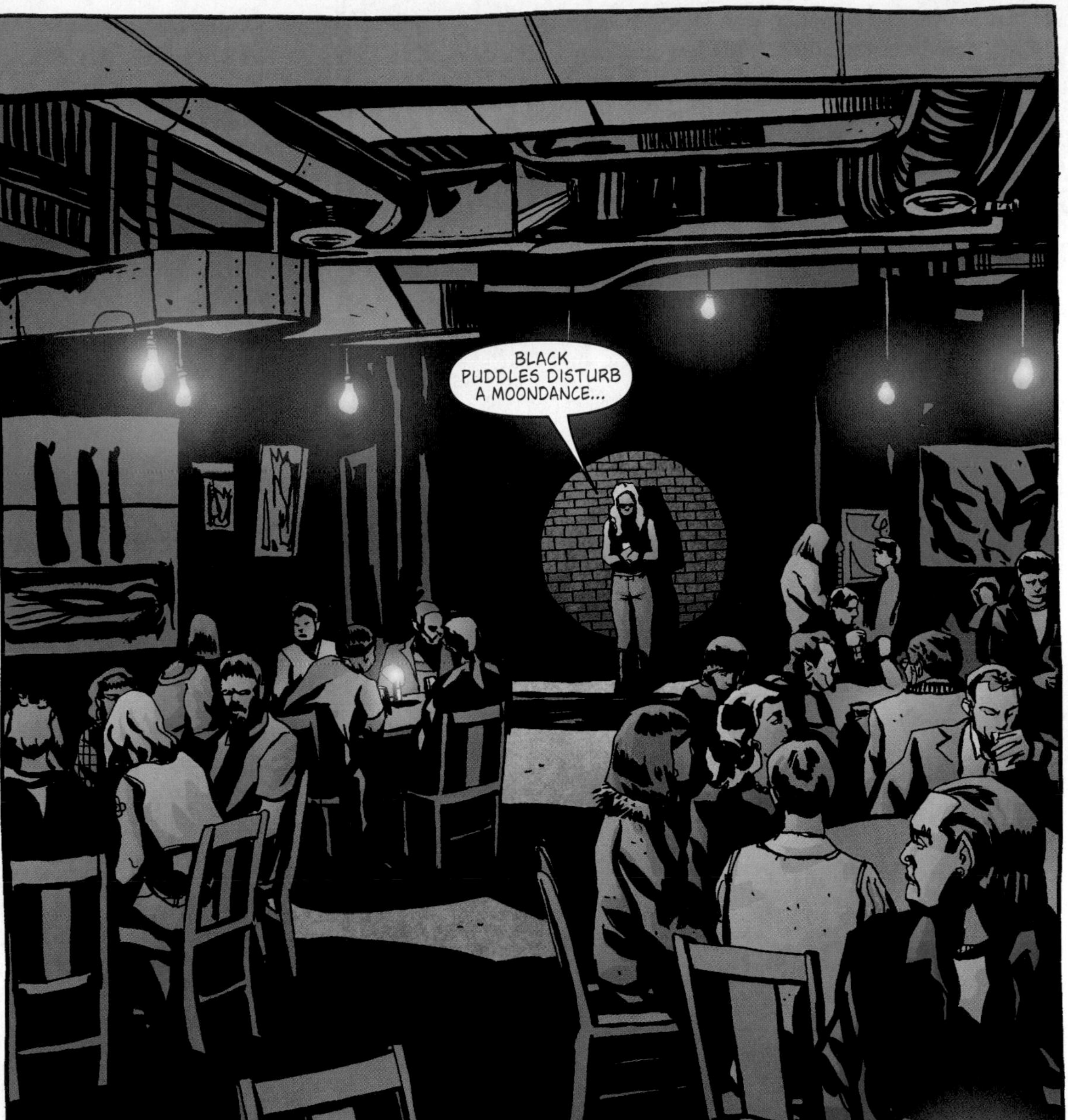
BLACK PUDDLES DISTURB A MOONDANCE...

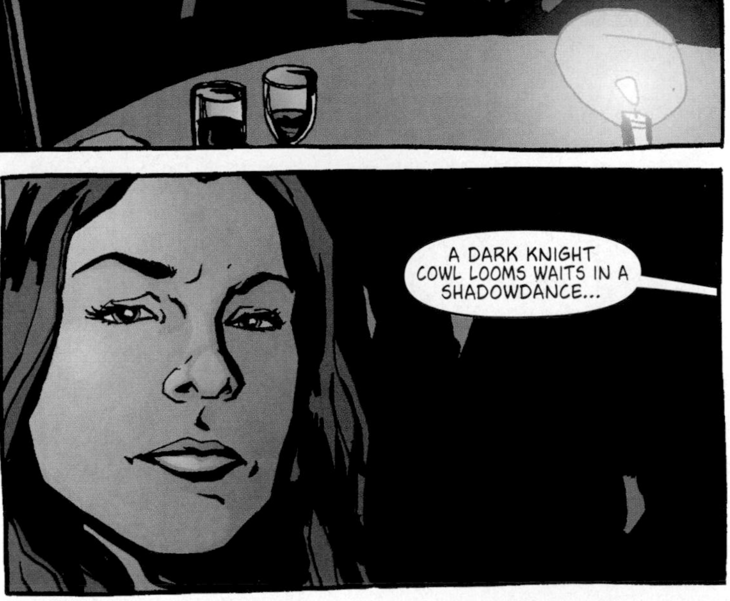
A DARK KNIGHT COWL LOOMS WAITS IN A SHADOWDANCE...

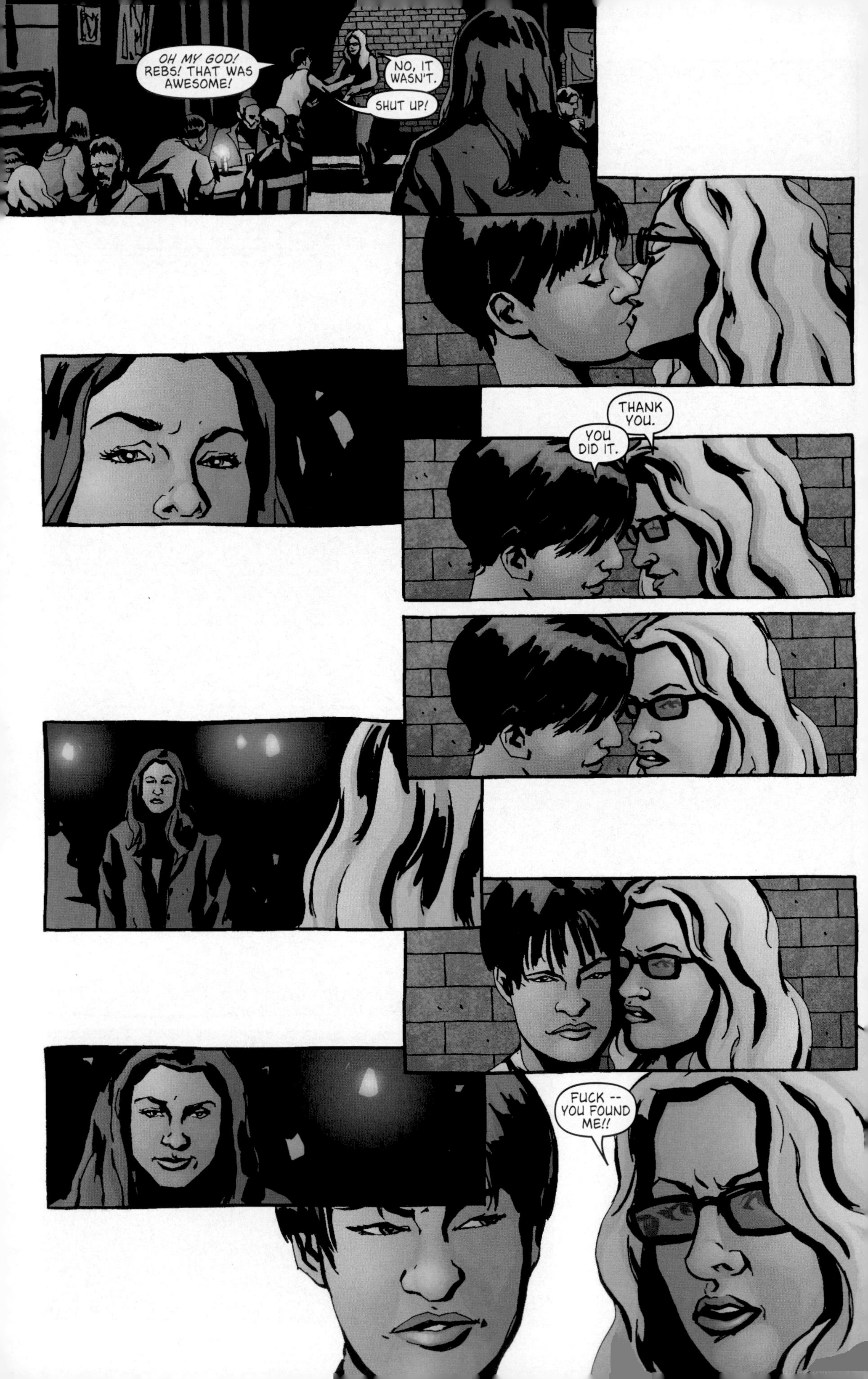
OH MY GOD! REBS! THAT WAS AWESOME!
NO, IT WASN'T.
SHUT UP!
YOU DID IT.
THANK YOU.
FUCK -- YOU FOUND ME!!

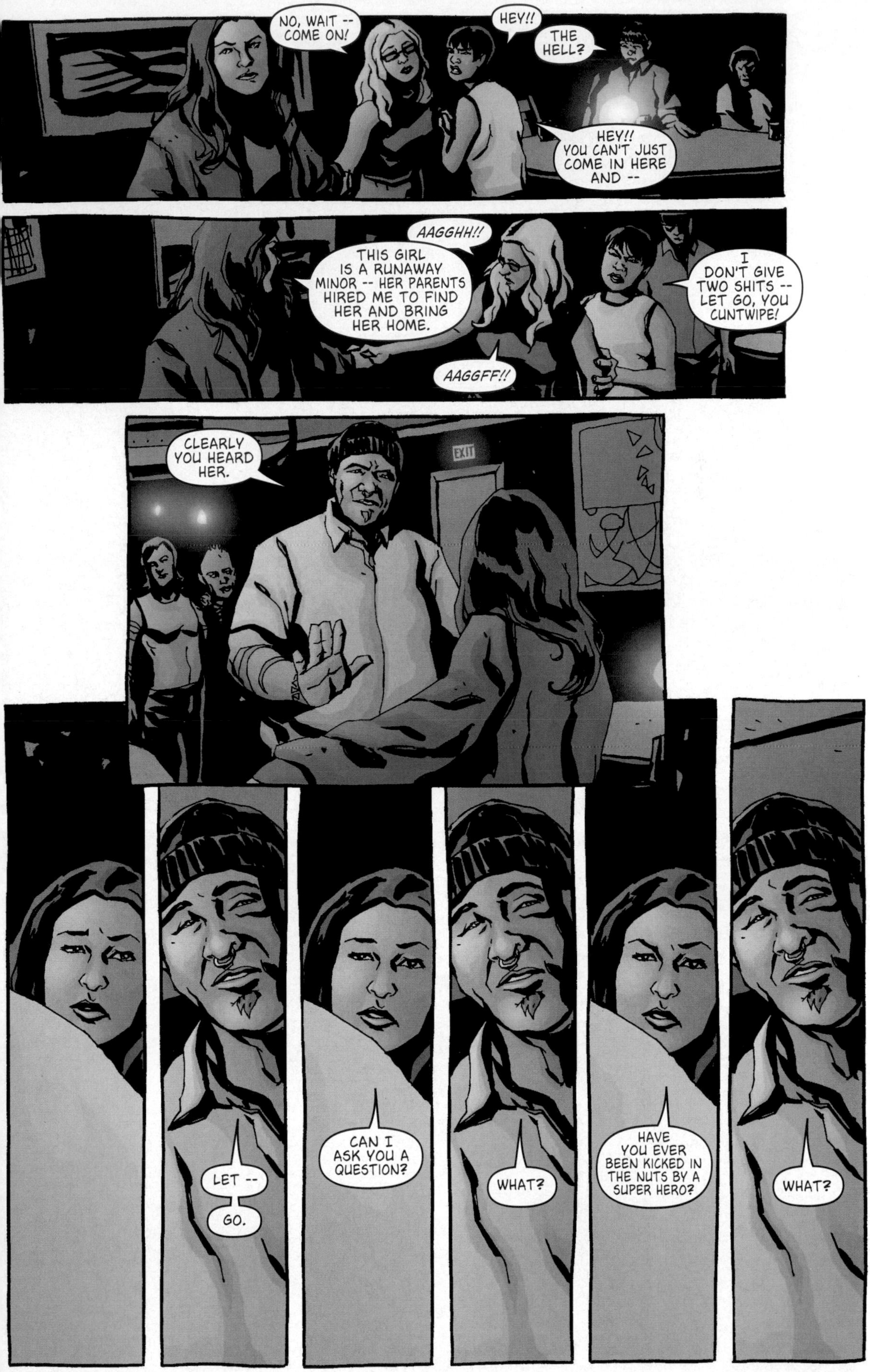
NO, WAIT -- COME ON!
HEY!!
THE HELL?
HEY!! YOU CAN'T JUST COME IN HERE AND --
AAGGHH!!
THIS GIRL IS A RUNAWAY MINOR -- HER PARENTS HIRED ME TO FIND HER AND BRING HER HOME.
I DON'T GIVE TWO SHITS -- LET GO, YOU CUNTWIPE!
AAGGFF!!
CLEARLY YOU HEARD HER.
EXIT
LET --
GO.
CAN I ASK YOU A QUESTION?
WHAT?
HAVE YOU EVER BEEN KICKED IN THE NUTS BY A SUPER HERO?
WHAT?

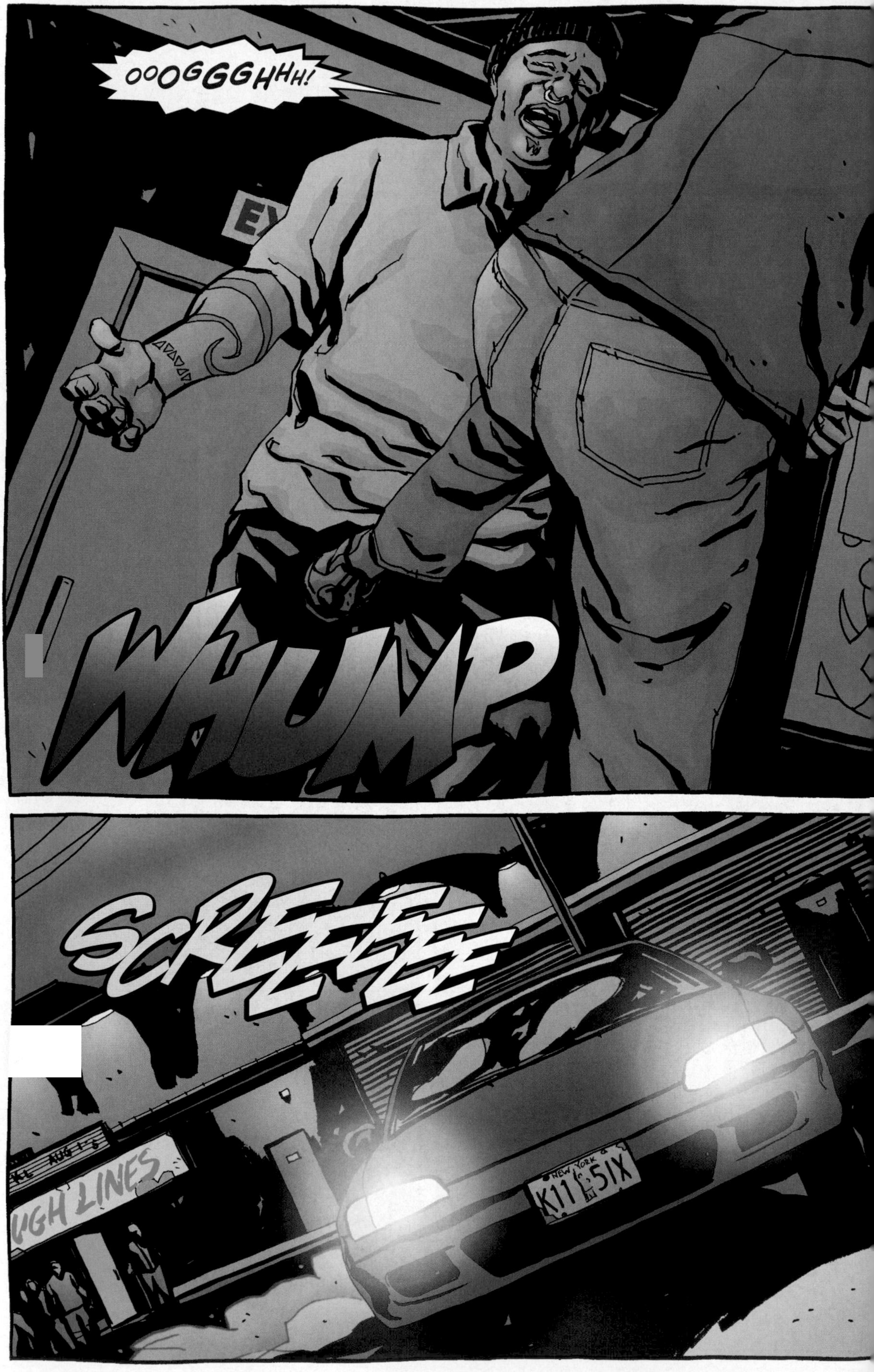
OOOGGGHHH!
WHUMP
SCREEEE
UGH LINES
NEW YORK
K11 5IX

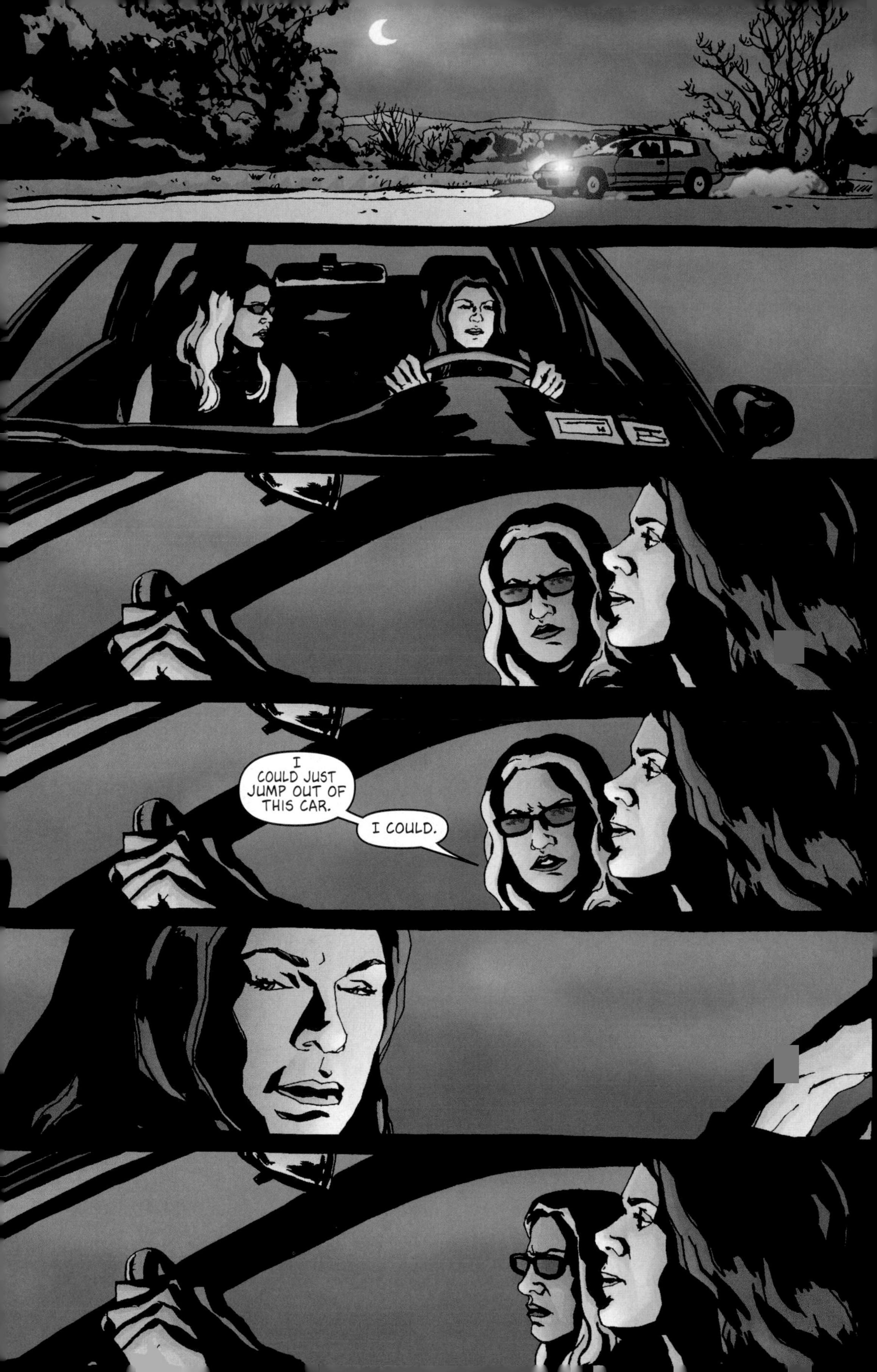
I COULD JUST JUMP OUT OF THIS CAR.
I COULD.

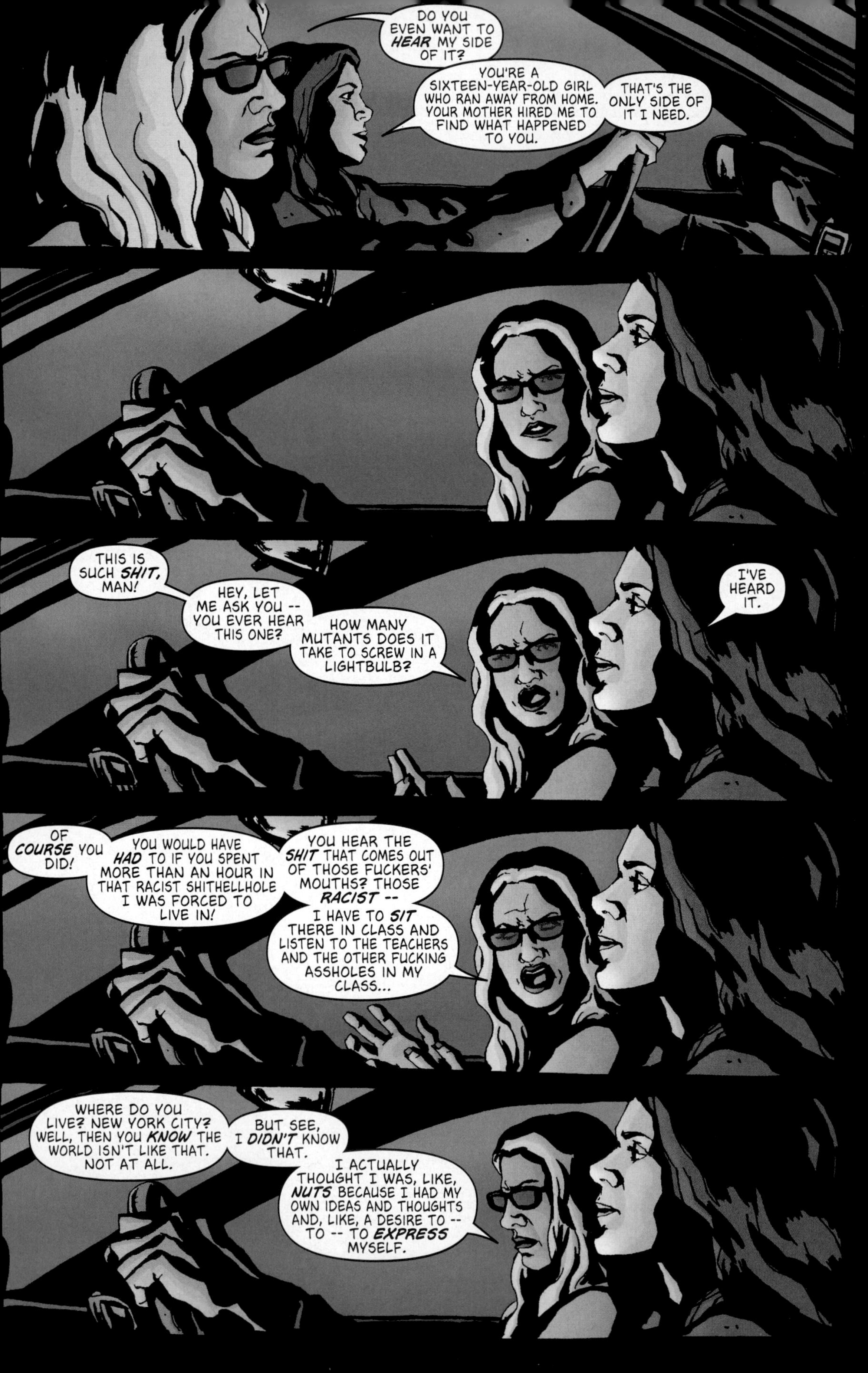

DO YOU EVEN WANT TO HEAR MY SIDE OF IT?
YOU'RE A SIXTEEN-YEAR-OLD GIRL WHO RAN AWAY FROM HOME. YOUR MOTHER HIRED ME TO FIND WHAT HAPPENED TO YOU.
THAT'S THE ONLY SIDE OF IT I NEED.
THIS IS SUCH SHIT, MAN!
HEY, LET ME ASK YOU -- YOU EVER HEAR THIS ONE?
HOW MANY MUTANTS DOES IT TAKE TO SCREW IN A LIGHTBULB?
I'VE HEARD IT.
OF COURSE YOU DID!
YOU WOULD HAVE HAD TO IF YOU SPENT MORE THAN AN HOUR IN THAT RACIST SHITHELLHOLE I WAS FORCED TO LIVE IN!
YOU HEAR THE SHIT THAT COMES OUT OF THOSE FUCKERS' MOUTHS? THOSE RACIST --
I HAVE TO SIT THERE IN CLASS AND LISTEN TO THE TEACHERS AND THE OTHER FUCKING ASSHOLES IN MY CLASS...
WHERE DO YOU LIVE? NEW YORK CITY? WELL, THEN YOU KNOW THE WORLD ISN'T LIKE THAT. NOT AT ALL.
BUT SEE, I DIDN'T KNOW THAT.
I ACTUALLY THOUGHT I WAS, LIKE, NUTS BECAUSE I HAD MY OWN IDEAS AND THOUGHTS AND, LIKE, A DESIRE TO -- TO -- TO EXPRESS MYSELF.

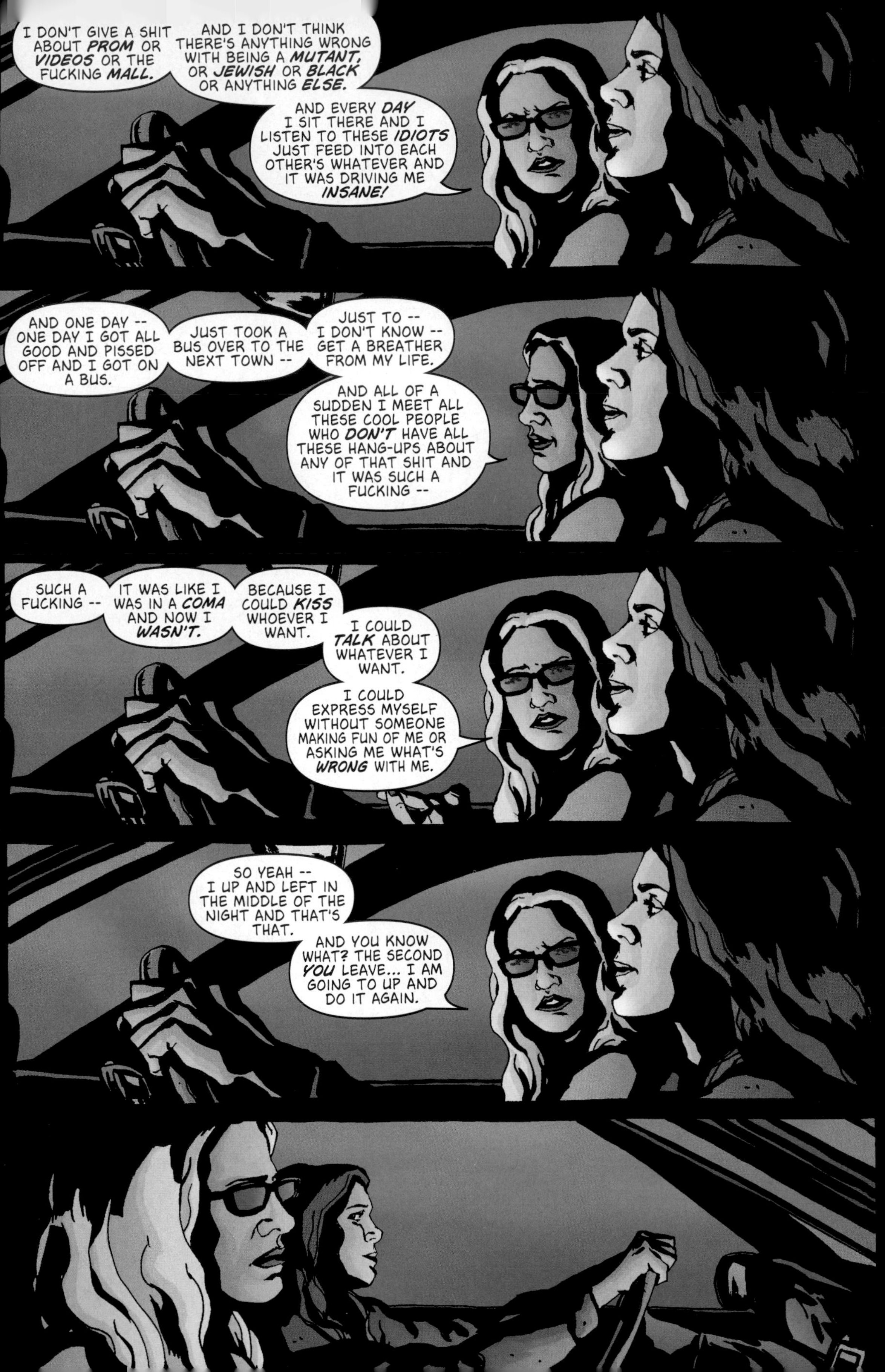
I DON'T GIVE A SHIT ABOUT PROM OR VIDEOS OR THE FUCKING MALL.
AND I DON'T THINK THERE'S ANYTHING WRONG WITH BEING A MUTANT, OR JEWISH OR BLACK OR ANYTHING ELSE.
AND EVERY DAY I SIT THERE AND I LISTEN TO THESE IDIOTS JUST FEED INTO EACH OTHER'S WHATEVER AND IT WAS DRIVING ME INSANE!
AND ONE DAY -- ONE DAY I GOT ALL GOOD AND PISSED OFF AND I GOT ON A BUS.
JUST TOOK A BUS OVER TO THE NEXT TOWN --
JUST TO -- I DON'T KNOW -- GET A BREATHER FROM MY LIFE.
AND ALL OF A SUDDEN I MEET ALL THESE COOL PEOPLE WHO DON'T HAVE ALL THESE HANG-UPS ABOUT ANY OF THAT SHIT AND IT WAS SUCH A FUCKING --
SUCH A FUCKING --
IT WAS LIKE I WAS IN A COMA AND NOW I WASN'T.
BECAUSE I COULD KISS WHOEVER I WANT.
I COULD TALK ABOUT WHATEVER I WANT.
I COULD EXPRESS MYSELF WITHOUT SOMEONE MAKING FUN OF ME OR ASKING ME WHAT'S WRONG WITH ME.
SO YEAH -- I UP AND LEFT IN THE MIDDLE OF THE NIGHT AND THAT'S THAT.
AND YOU KNOW WHAT? THE SECOND YOU LEAVE... I AM GOING TO UP AND DO IT AGAIN.

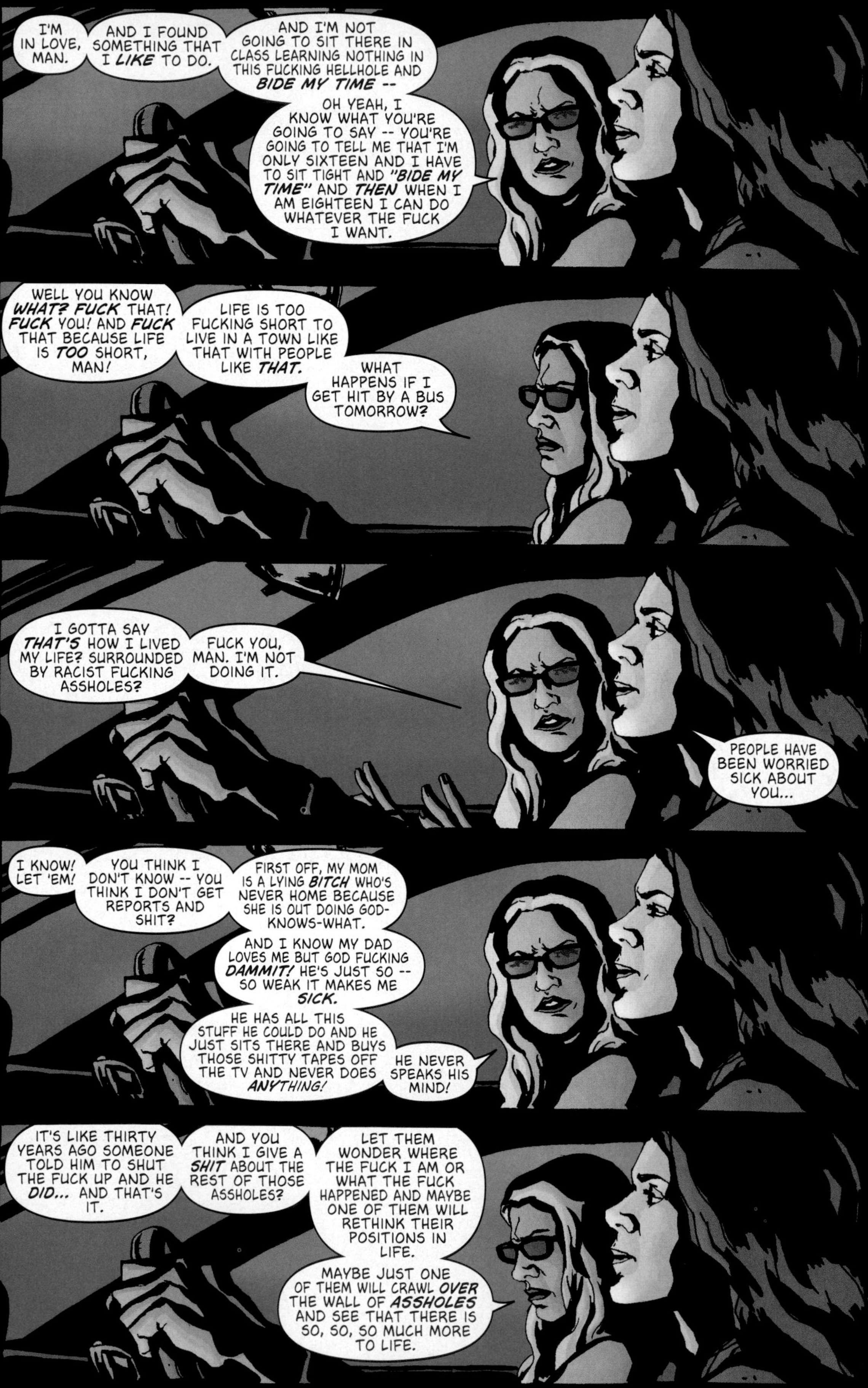
I'M IN LOVE, MAN.
AND I FOUND SOMETHING THAT I *LIKE* TO DO.
AND I'M NOT GOING TO SIT THERE IN CLASS LEARNING NOTHING IN THIS FUCKING HELLHOLE AND *BIDE MY TIME* --
OH YEAH, I KNOW WHAT YOU'RE GOING TO SAY -- YOU'RE GOING TO TELL ME THAT I'M ONLY SIXTEEN AND I HAVE TO SIT TIGHT AND *"BIDE MY TIME"* AND *THEN* WHEN I AM EIGHTEEN I CAN DO WHATEVER THE FUCK I WANT.
WELL YOU KNOW *WHAT? FUCK* THAT! *FUCK* YOU! AND *FUCK* THAT BECAUSE LIFE IS *TOO* SHORT, MAN!
LIFE IS TOO FUCKING SHORT TO LIVE IN A TOWN LIKE THAT WITH PEOPLE LIKE *THAT.*
WHAT HAPPENS IF I GET HIT BY A BUS TOMORROW?
I GOTTA SAY *THAT'S* HOW I LIVED MY LIFE? SURROUNDED BY RACIST FUCKING ASSHOLES?
FUCK YOU, MAN. I'M NOT DOING IT.
PEOPLE HAVE BEEN WORRIED SICK ABOUT YOU...
I KNOW! LET 'EM!
YOU THINK I DON'T KNOW -- YOU THINK I DON'T GET REPORTS AND SHIT?
FIRST OFF, MY MOM IS A LYING *BITCH* WHO'S NEVER HOME BECAUSE SHE IS OUT DOING GOD-KNOWS-WHAT.
AND I KNOW MY DAD LOVES ME BUT GOD FUCKING *DAMMIT!* HE'S JUST SO -- SO WEAK IT MAKES ME *SICK.*
HE HAS ALL THIS STUFF HE COULD DO AND HE JUST SITS THERE AND BUYS THOSE SHITTY TAPES OFF THE TV AND NEVER DOES *ANY*THING!
HE NEVER SPEAKS HIS MIND!
IT'S LIKE THIRTY YEARS AGO SOMEONE TOLD HIM TO SHUT THE FUCK UP AND HE *DID...* AND THAT'S IT.
AND YOU THINK I GIVE A *SHIT* ABOUT THE REST OF THOSE ASSHOLES?
LET THEM WONDER WHERE THE FUCK I AM OR WHAT THE FUCK HAPPENED AND MAYBE ONE OF THEM WILL RETHINK THEIR POSITIONS IN LIFE.
MAYBE JUST ONE OF THEM WILL CRAWL *OVER* THE WALL OF *ASSHOLES* AND SEE THAT THERE IS SO, SO, SO MUCH MORE TO LIFE.

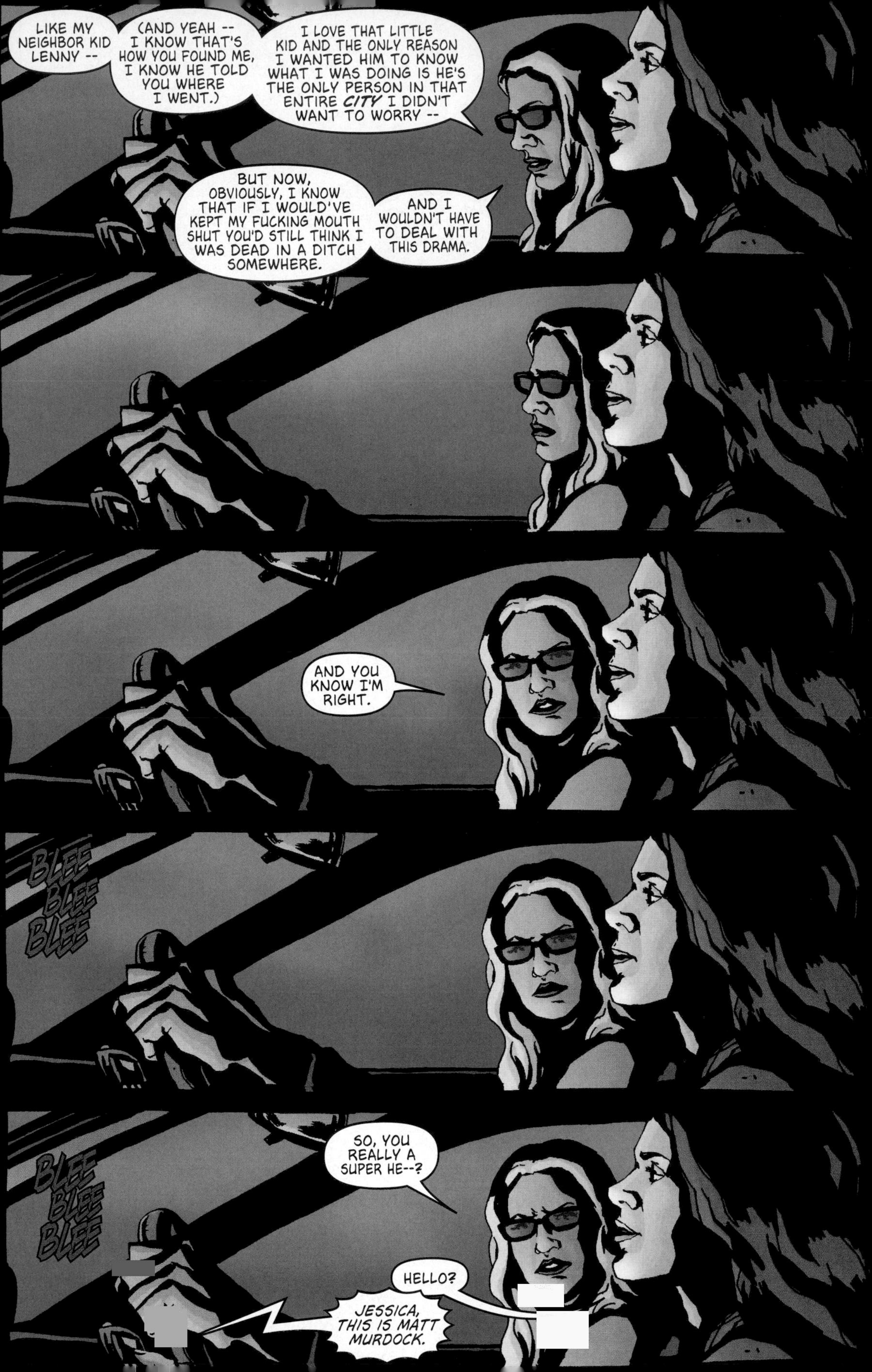
LIKE MY NEIGHBOR KID LENNY --
(AND YEAH -- I KNOW THAT'S HOW YOU FOUND ME, I KNOW HE TOLD YOU WHERE I WENT.)
I LOVE THAT LITTLE KID AND THE ONLY REASON I WANTED HIM TO KNOW WHAT I WAS DOING IS HE'S THE ONLY PERSON IN THAT ENTIRE *CITY* I DIDN'T WANT TO WORRY --
BUT NOW, OBVIOUSLY, I KNOW THAT IF I WOULD'VE KEPT MY FUCKING MOUTH SHUT YOU'D STILL THINK I WAS DEAD IN A DITCH SOMEWHERE.
AND I WOULDN'T HAVE TO DEAL WITH THIS DRAMA.
AND YOU KNOW I'M RIGHT.
BLEE BLEE BLEE
BLEE BLEE BLEE
SO, YOU REALLY A SUPER HE--?
HELLO?
JESSICA, THIS IS MATT MURDOCK.

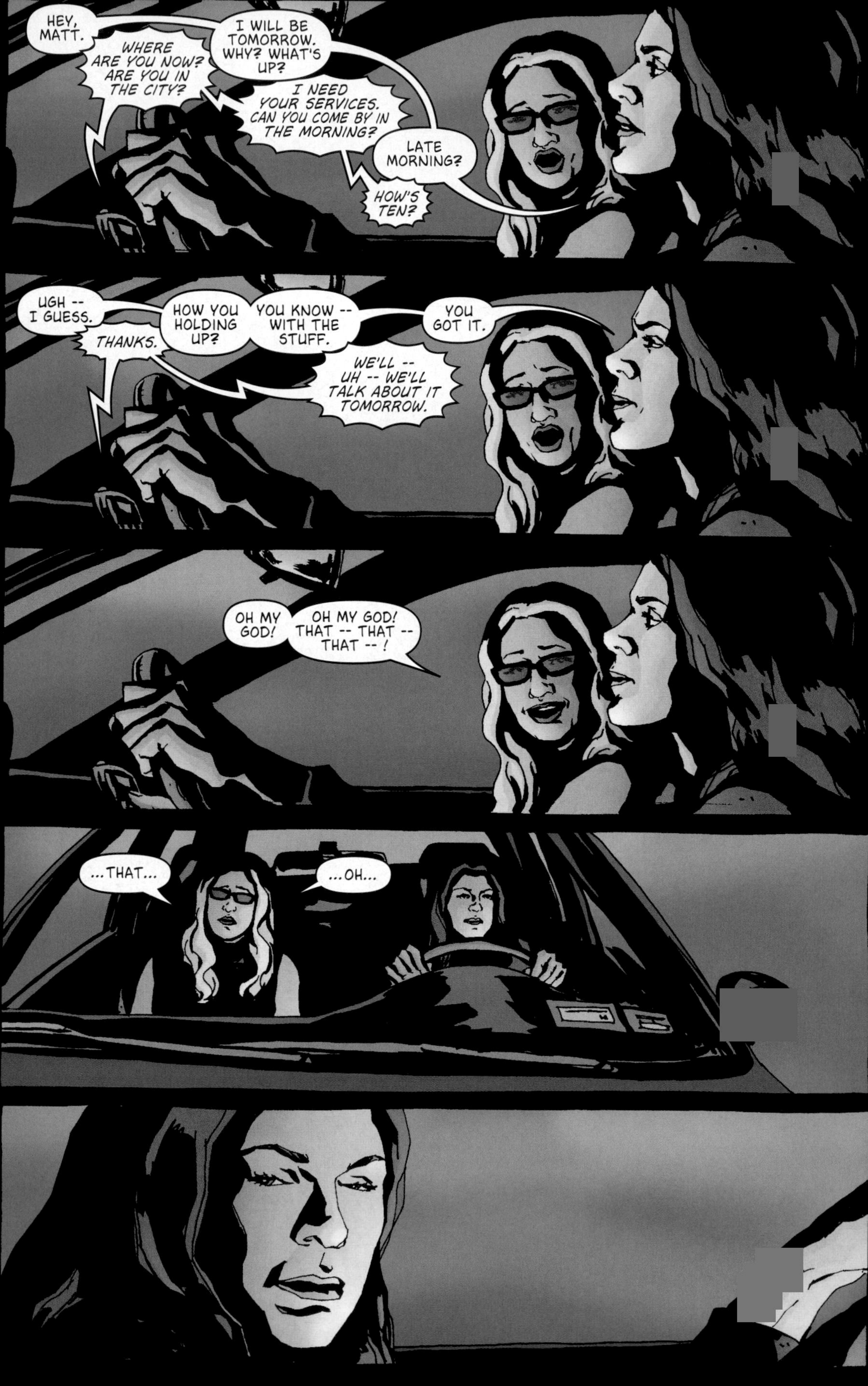
HEY, MATT.
WHERE ARE YOU NOW? ARE YOU IN THE CITY?
I WILL BE TOMORROW. WHY? WHAT'S UP?
I NEED YOUR SERVICES. CAN YOU COME BY IN THE MORNING?
LATE MORNING?
HOW'S TEN?
UGH -- I GUESS.
THANKS.
HOW YOU HOLDING UP?
YOU KNOW -- WITH THE STUFF.
WE'LL -- UH -- WE'LL TALK ABOUT IT TOMORROW.
YOU GOT IT.
OH MY GOD!
OH MY GOD! THAT -- THAT -- THAT -- !
...THAT...
...OH...

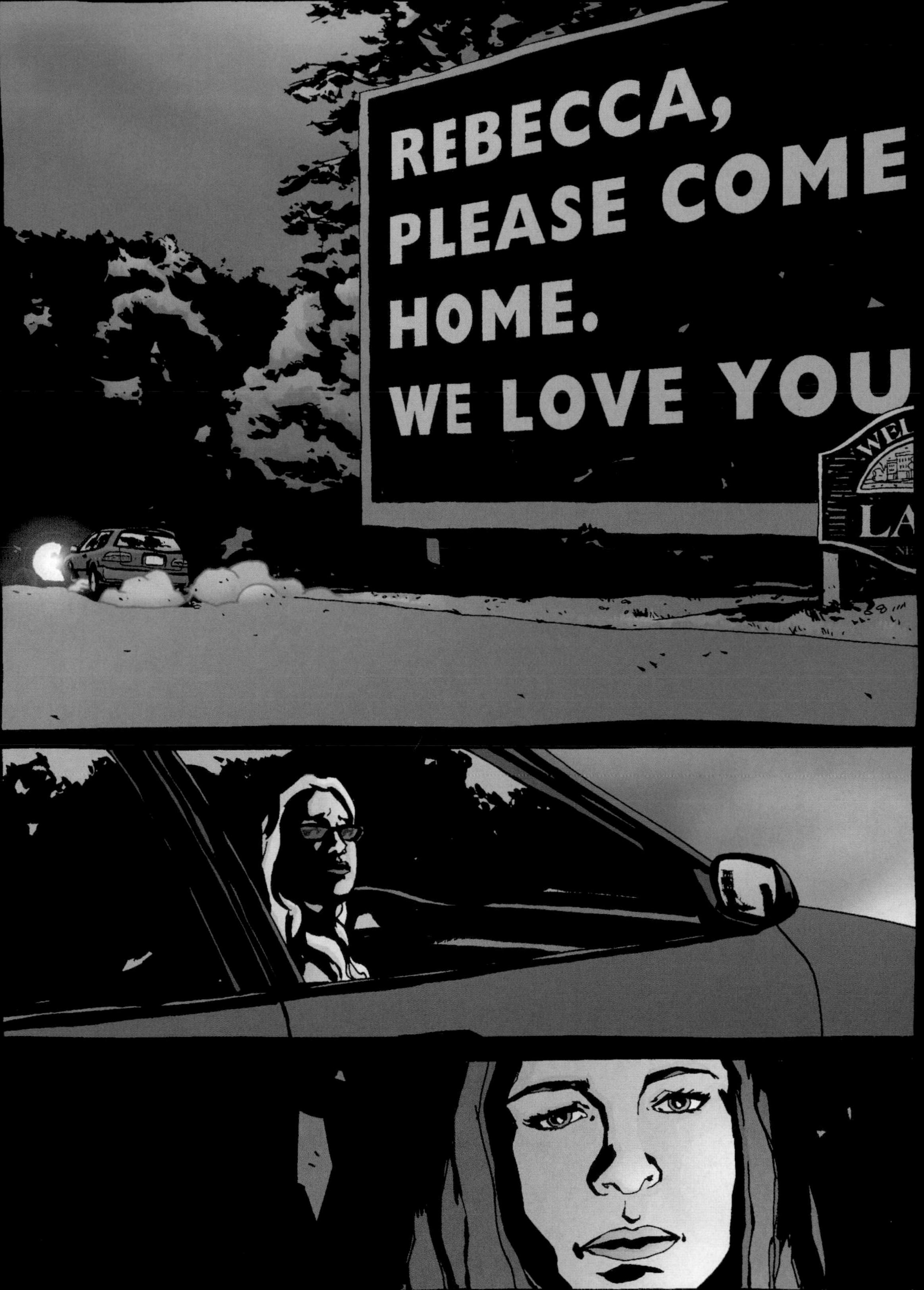
REBECCA,
PLEASE COME
HOME.
WE LOVE YOU

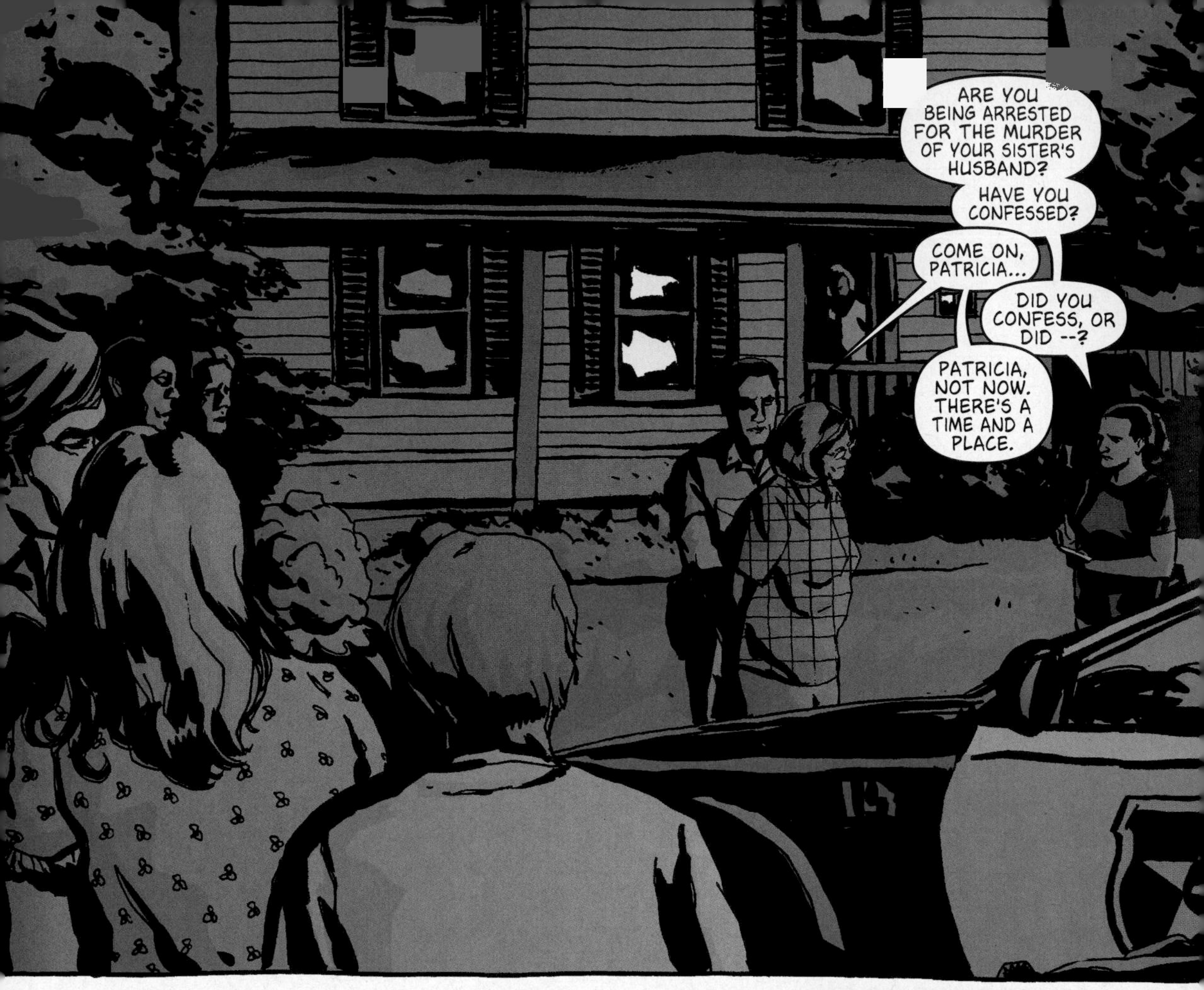
ARE YOU BEING ARRESTED FOR THE MURDER OF YOUR SISTER'S HUSBAND?
HAVE YOU CONFESSED?
COME ON, PATRICIA...
DID YOU CONFESS, OR DID --?
PATRICIA, NOT NOW. THERE'S A TIME AND A PLACE.

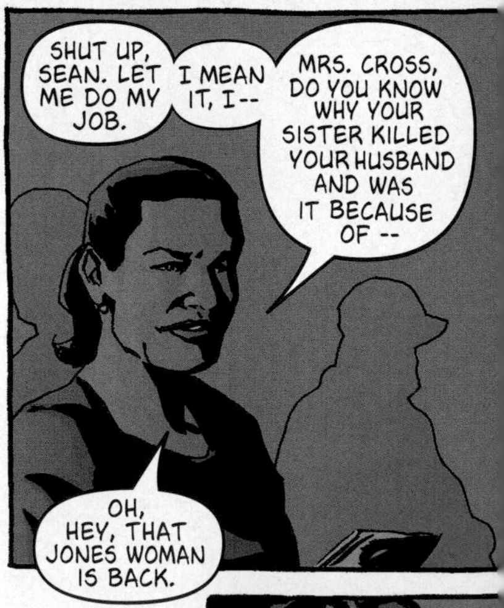
SHUT UP, SEAN. LET ME DO MY JOB.
I MEAN IT, I--
MRS. CROSS, DO YOU KNOW WHY YOUR SISTER KILLED YOUR HUSBAND AND WAS IT BECAUSE OF --
OH, HEY, THAT JONES WOMAN IS BACK.

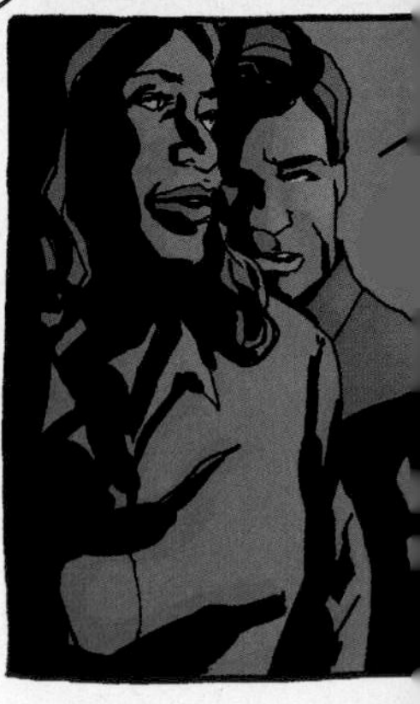

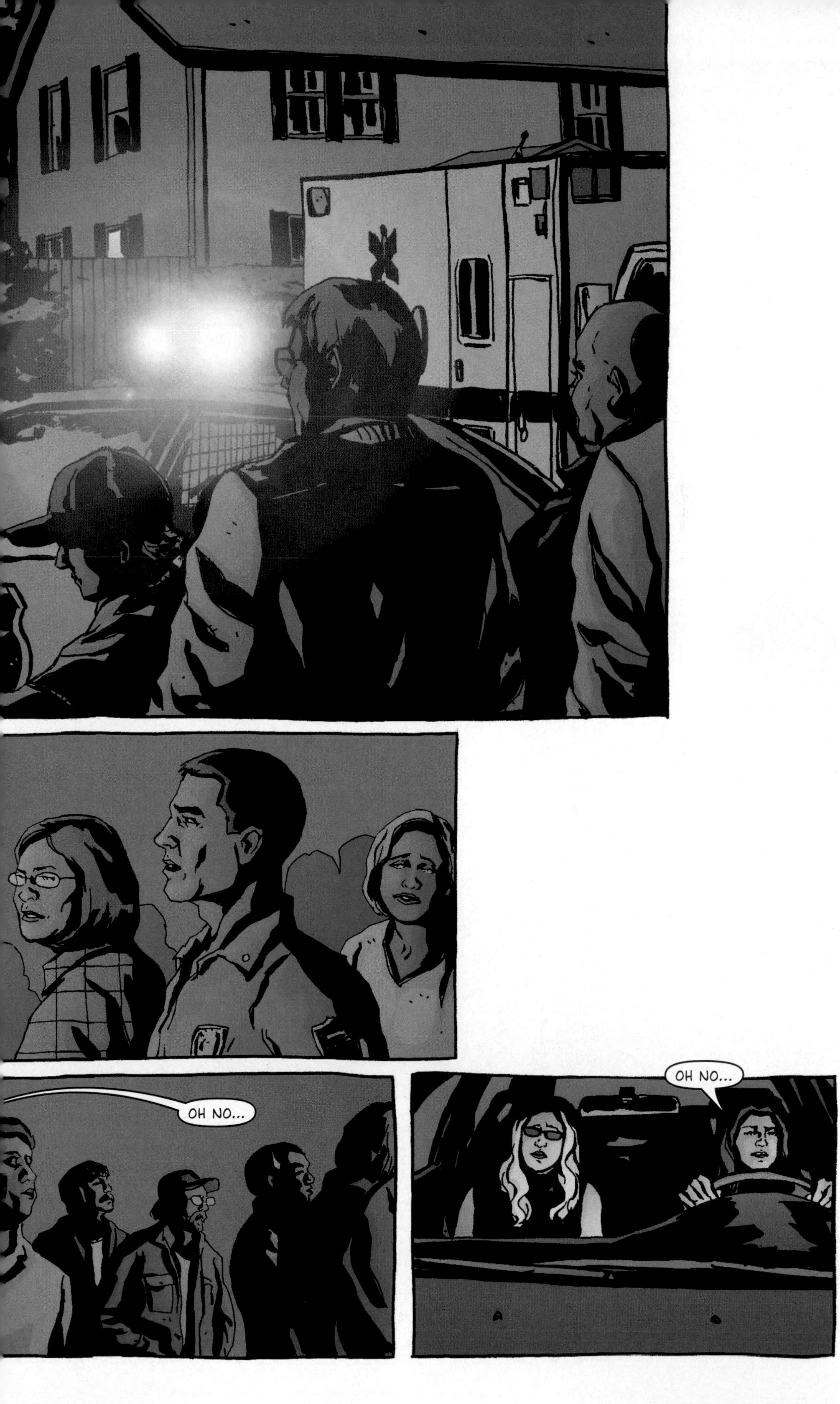
OH NO...
OH NO...

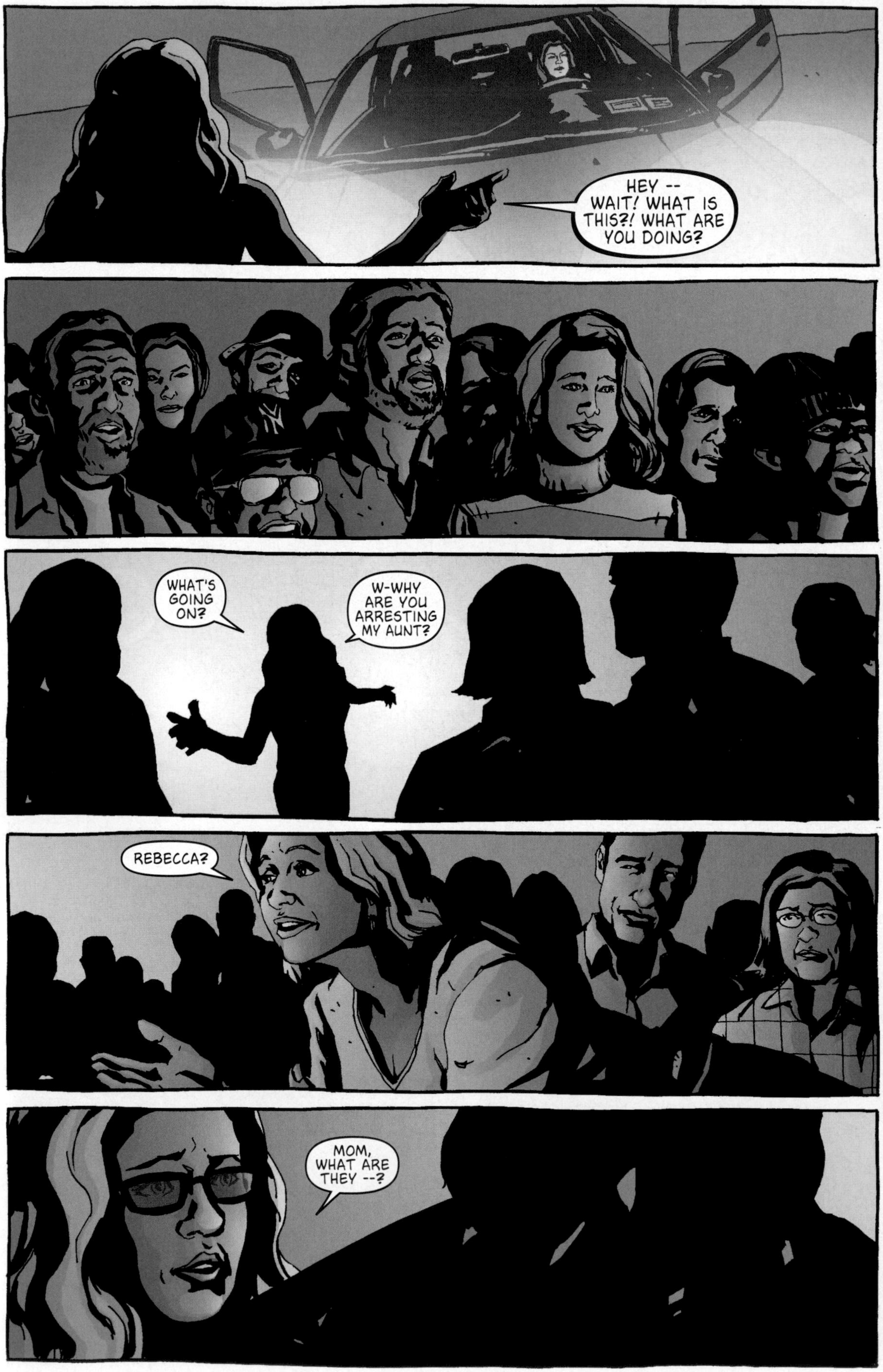
HEY -- WAIT! WHAT IS THIS?! WHAT ARE YOU DOING?
WHAT'S GOING ON?
W-WHY ARE YOU ARRESTING MY AUNT?
REBECCA?
MOM, WHAT ARE THEY --?

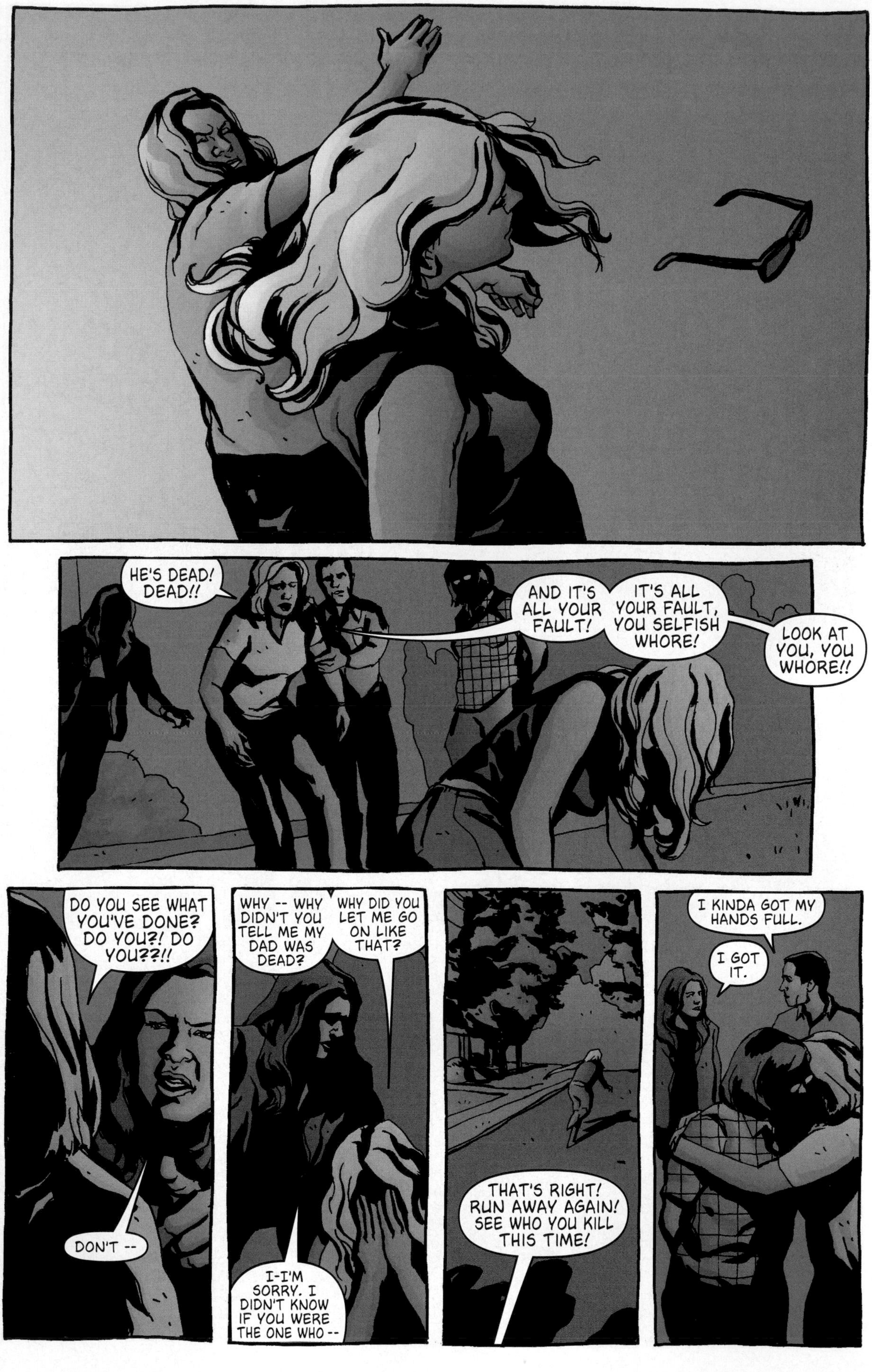
HE'S DEAD! DEAD!!
AND IT'S ALL YOUR FAULT!
IT'S ALL YOUR FAULT, YOU SELFISH WHORE!
LOOK AT YOU, YOU WHORE!!
DO YOU SEE WHAT YOU'VE DONE? DO YOU?! DO YOU??!!
DON'T --
WHY -- WHY DIDN'T YOU TELL ME MY DAD WAS DEAD?
WHY DID YOU LET ME GO ON LIKE THAT?
I-I'M SORRY. I DIDN'T KNOW IF YOU WERE THE ONE WHO --
THAT'S RIGHT! RUN AWAY AGAIN! SEE WHO YOU KILL THIS TIME!
I KINDA GOT MY HANDS FULL.
I GOT IT.

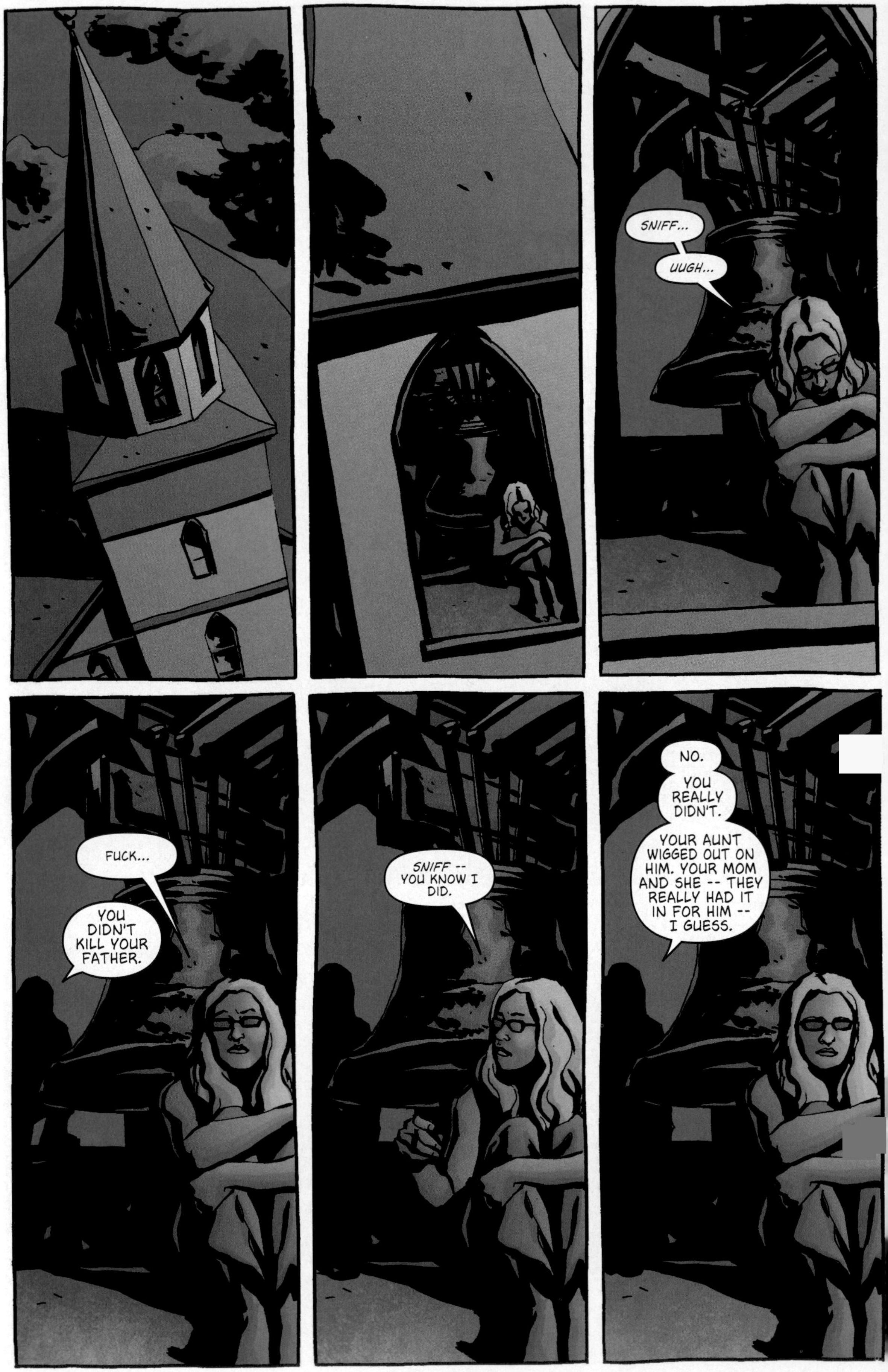
SNIFF...
UUGH...
FUCK...
YOU DIDN'T KILL YOUR FATHER.
SNIFF -- YOU KNOW I DID.
NO.
YOU REALLY DIDN'T.
YOUR AUNT WIGGED OUT ON HIM. YOUR MOM AND SHE -- THEY REALLY HAD IT IN FOR HIM -- I GUESS.

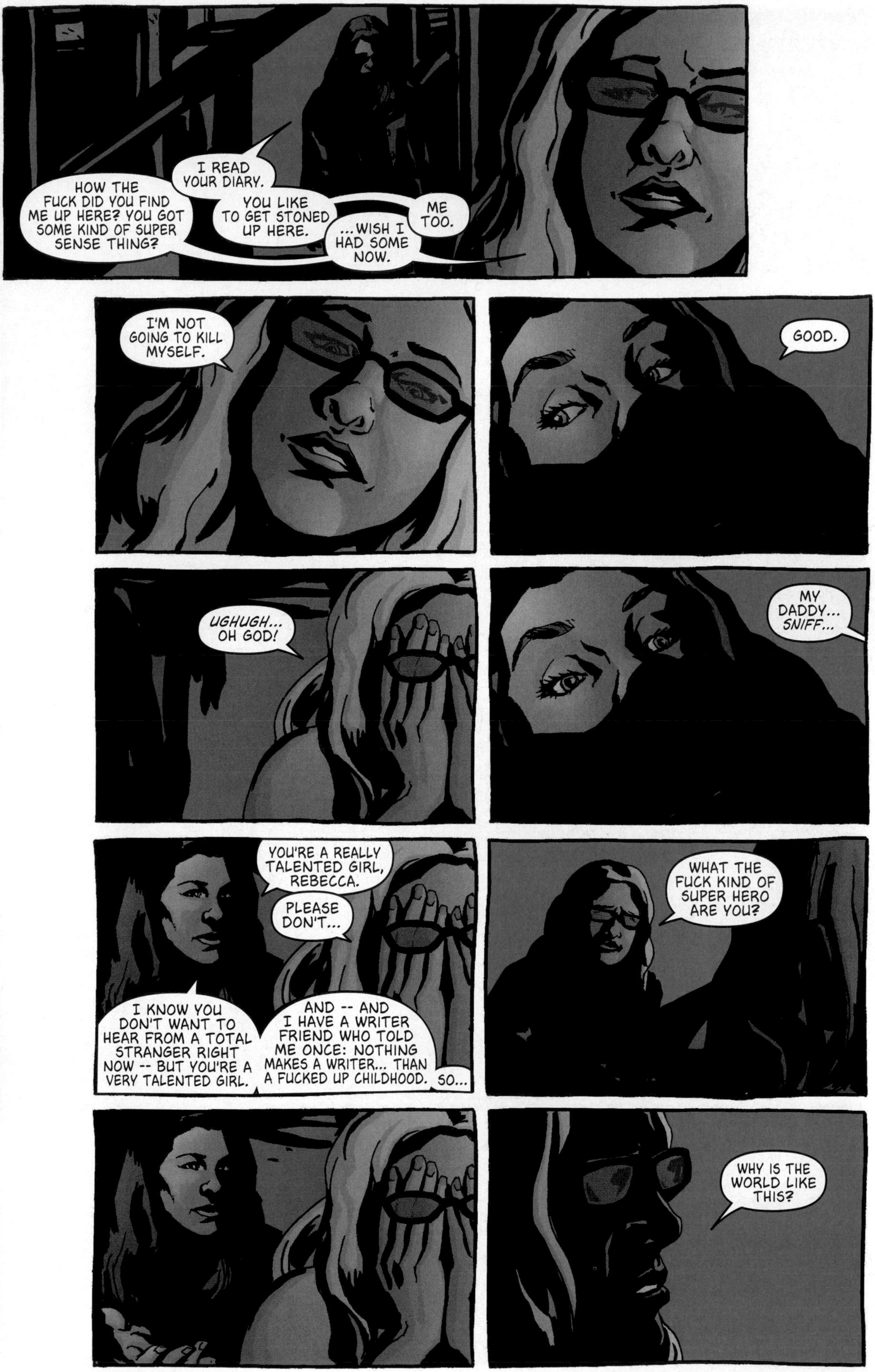
HOW THE FUCK DID YOU FIND ME UP HERE? YOU GOT SOME KIND OF SUPER SENSE THING?
I READ YOUR DIARY.
YOU LIKE TO GET STONED UP HERE.
...WISH I HAD SOME NOW.
ME TOO.
I'M NOT GOING TO KILL MYSELF.
GOOD.
UGHUGH... OH GOD!
MY DADDY... SNIFF...
YOU'RE A REALLY TALENTED GIRL, REBECCA.
PLEASE DON'T...
I KNOW YOU DON'T WANT TO HEAR FROM A TOTAL STRANGER RIGHT NOW -- BUT YOU'RE A VERY TALENTED GIRL.
AND -- AND I HAVE A WRITER FRIEND WHO TOLD ME ONCE: NOTHING MAKES A WRITER... THAN A FUCKED UP CHILDHOOD.
SO...
WHAT THE FUCK KIND OF SUPER HERO ARE YOU?
WHY IS THE WORLD LIKE THIS?

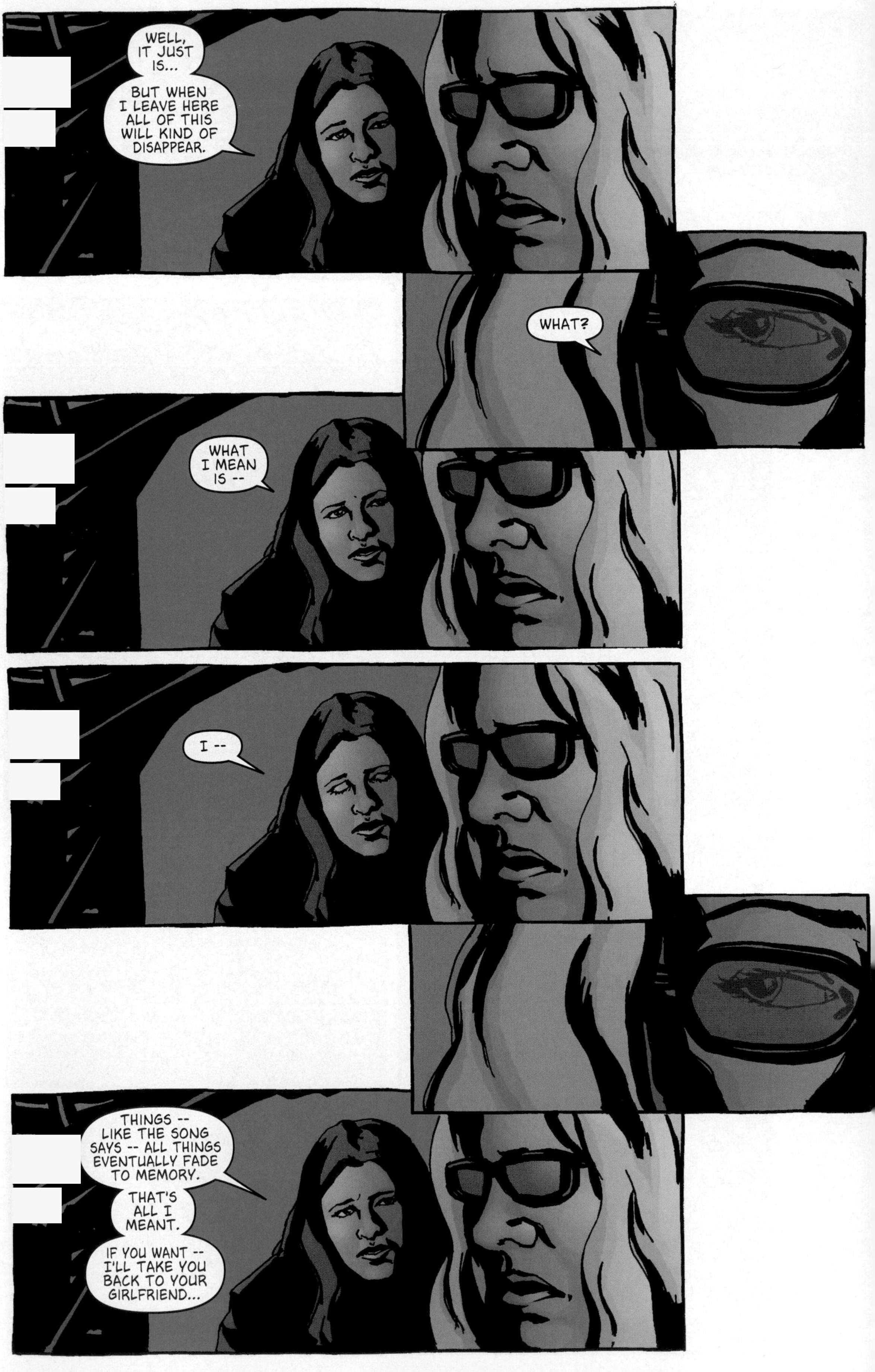
WELL, IT JUST IS...
BUT WHEN I LEAVE HERE ALL OF THIS WILL KIND OF DISAPPEAR.
WHAT?
WHAT I MEAN IS --
I --
THINGS -- LIKE THE SONG SAYS -- ALL THINGS EVENTUALLY FADE TO MEMORY.
THAT'S ALL I MEANT.
IF YOU WANT -- I'LL TAKE YOU BACK TO YOUR GIRLFRIEND...

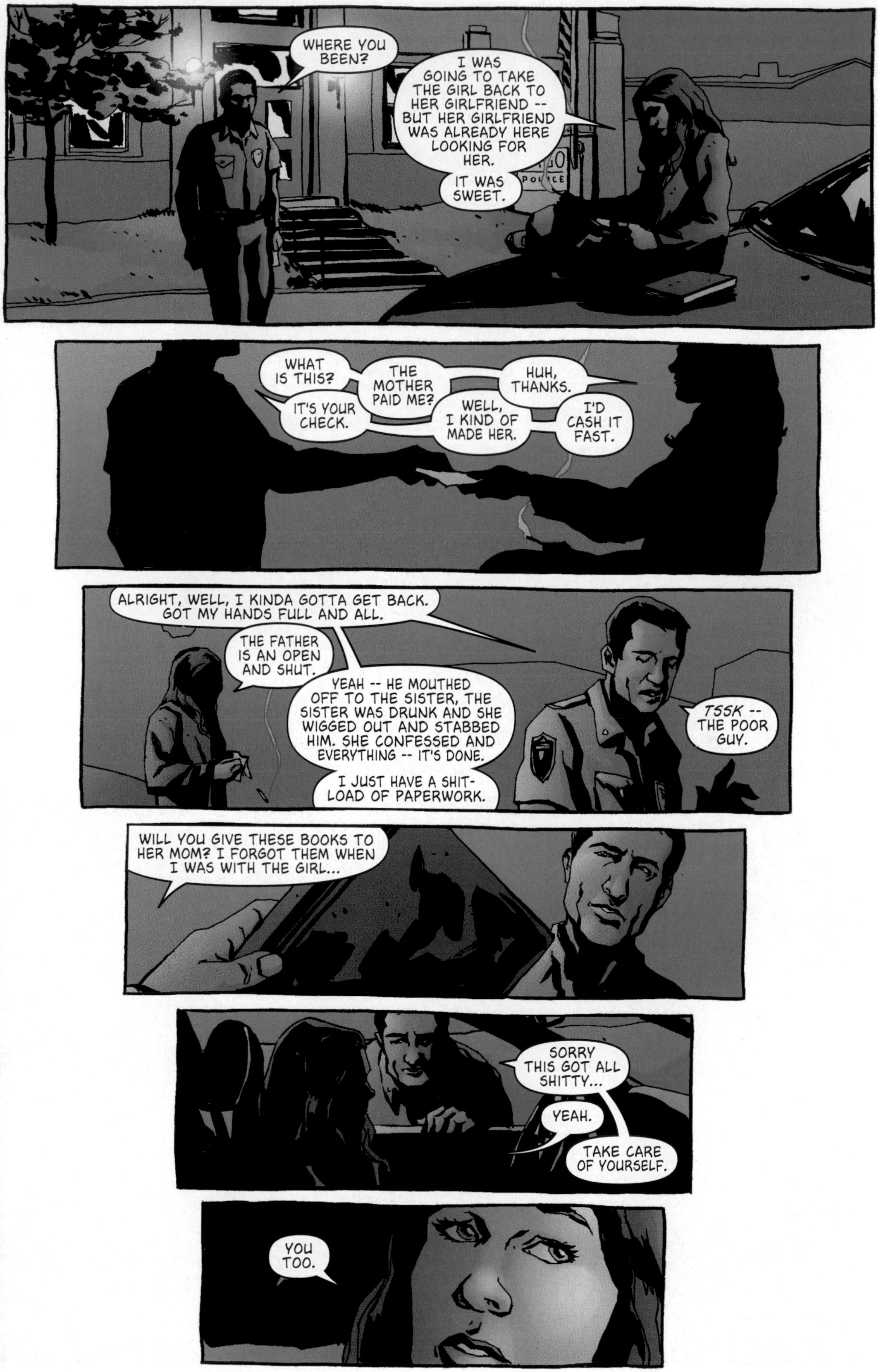
WHERE YOU BEEN?
I WAS GOING TO TAKE THE GIRL BACK TO HER GIRLFRIEND -- BUT HER GIRLFRIEND WAS ALREADY HERE LOOKING FOR HER.
IT WAS SWEET.
POLICE
WHAT IS THIS?
IT'S YOUR CHECK.
THE MOTHER PAID ME?
WELL, I KIND OF MADE HER.
HUH, THANKS.
I'D CASH IT FAST.
ALRIGHT, WELL, I KINDA GOTTA GET BACK. GOT MY HANDS FULL AND ALL.
THE FATHER IS AN OPEN AND SHUT.
YEAH -- HE MOUTHED OFF TO THE SISTER, THE SISTER WAS DRUNK AND SHE WIGGED OUT AND STABBED HIM. SHE CONFESSED AND EVERYTHING -- IT'S DONE.
I JUST HAVE A SHIT-LOAD OF PAPERWORK.
TSSK -- THE POOR GUY.
WILL YOU GIVE THESE BOOKS TO HER MOM? I FORGOT THEM WHEN I WAS WITH THE GIRL...
SORRY THIS GOT ALL SHITTY...
YEAH.
TAKE CARE OF YOURSELF.
YOU TOO.

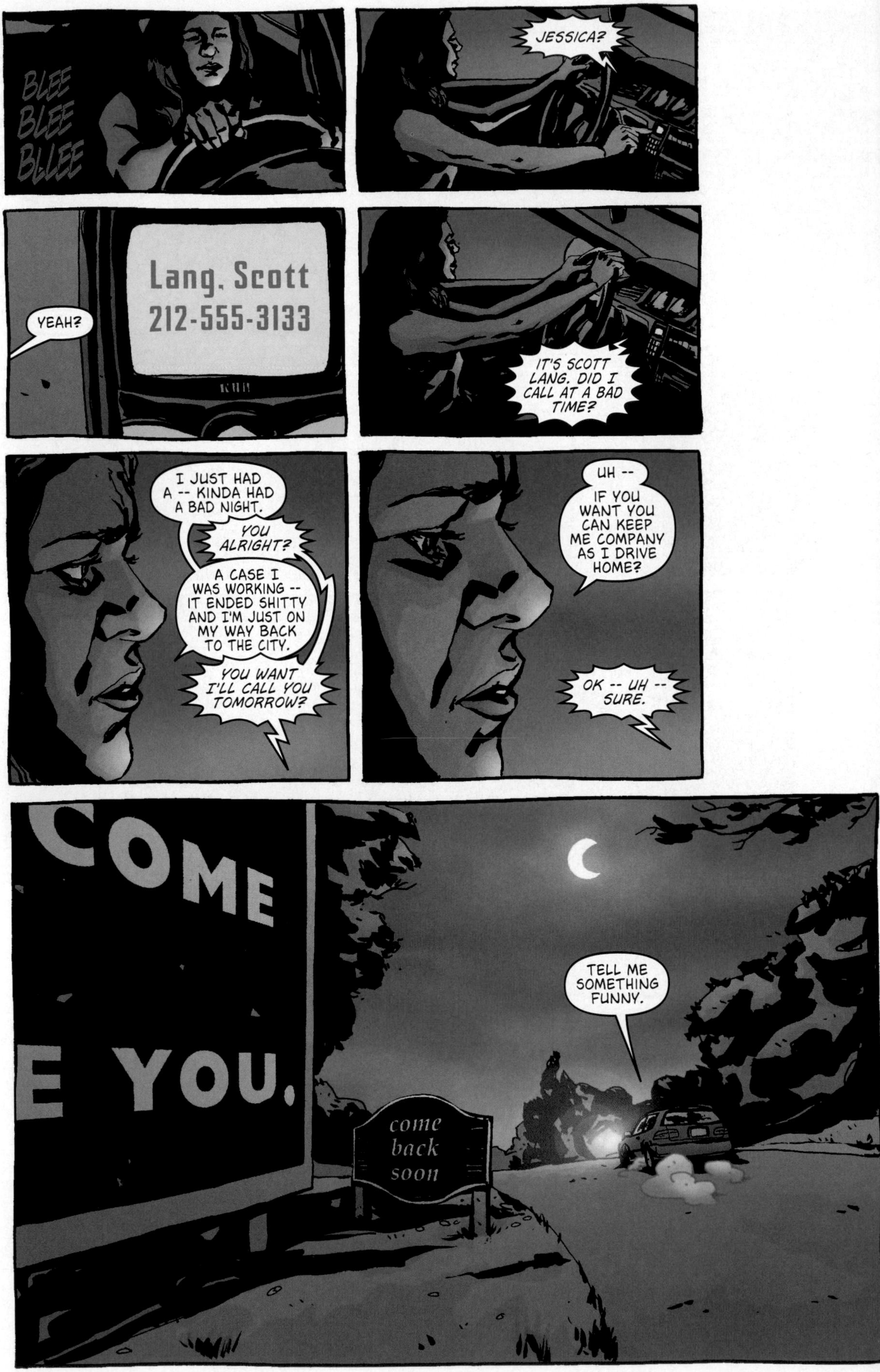
BLEE
BLEE
BLEE
JESSICA?
Lang, Scott
212-555-3133
YEAH?
IT'S SCOTT LANG. DID I CALL AT A BAD TIME?
I JUST HAD A -- KINDA HAD A BAD NIGHT.
YOU ALRIGHT?
A CASE I WAS WORKING -- IT ENDED SHITTY AND I'M JUST ON MY WAY BACK TO THE CITY.
YOU WANT I'LL CALL YOU TOMORROW?
UH --
IF YOU WANT YOU CAN KEEP ME COMPANY AS I DRIVE HOME?
OK -- UH -- SURE.
COME
E YOU.
come back soon
TELL ME SOMETHING FUNNY.

LAW OFFICES OF [redacted] & M[redacted]

ISSUE #15

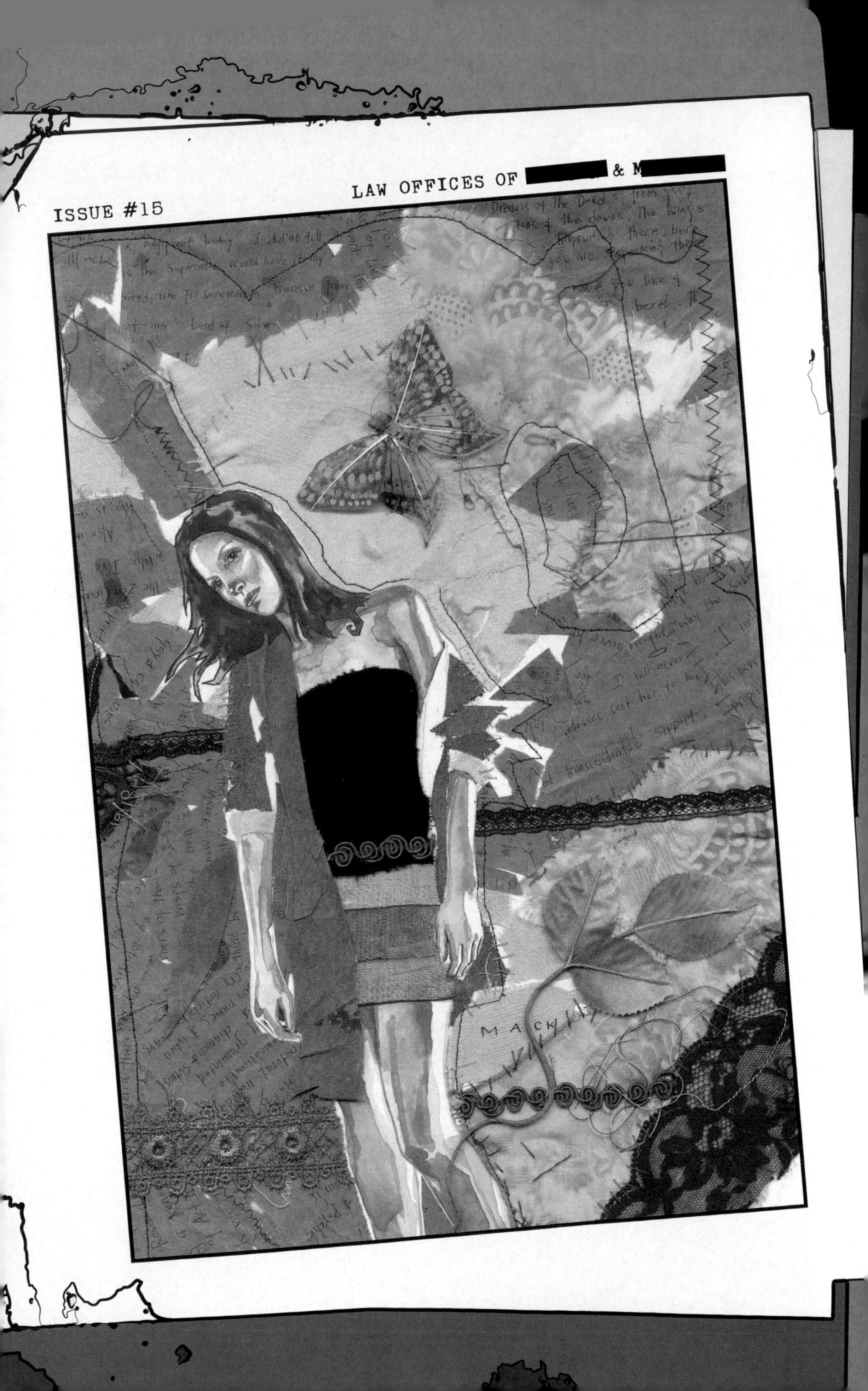
MACK

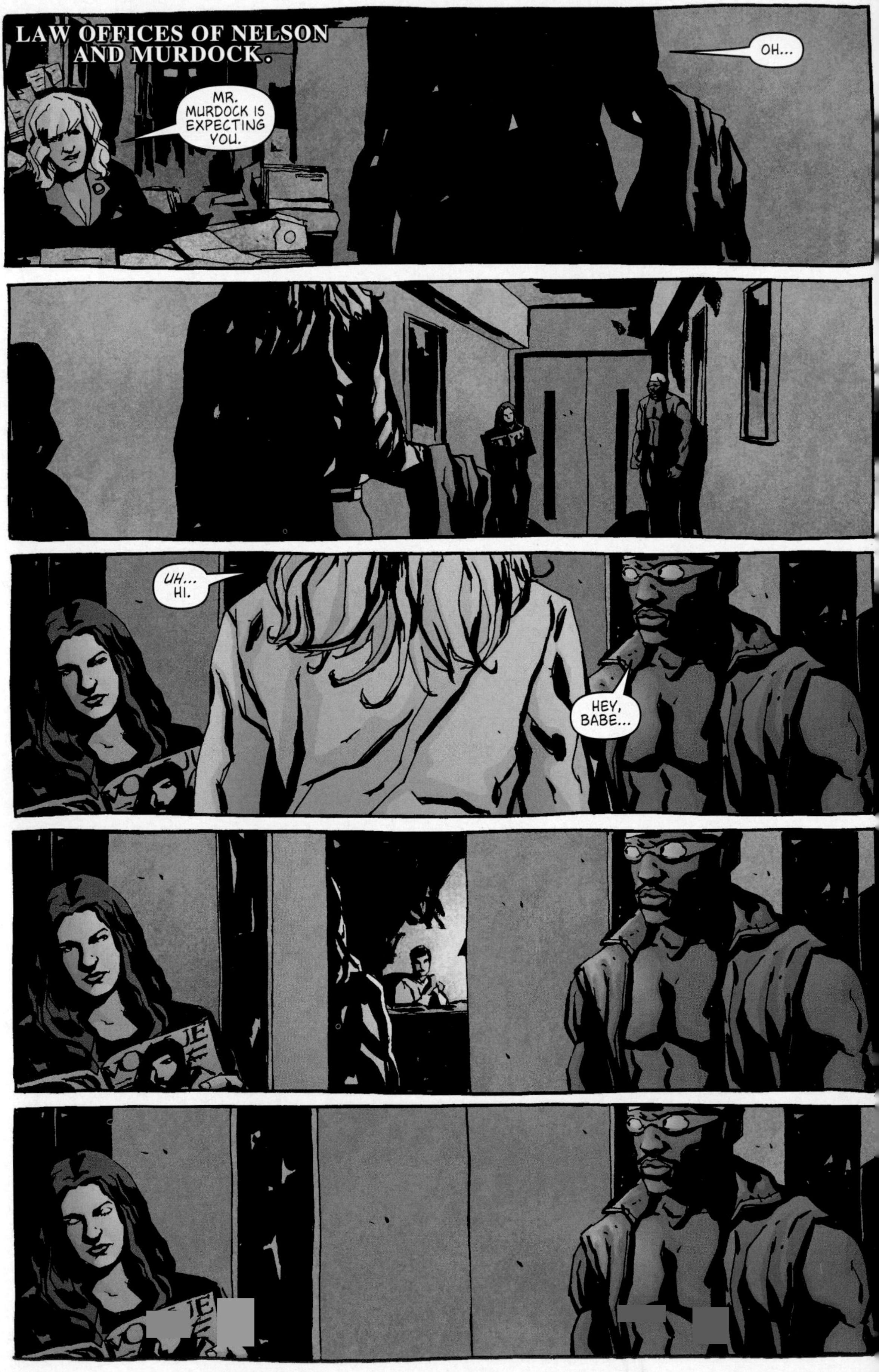
LAW OFFICES OF NELSON AND MURDOCK.
MR. MURDOCK IS EXPECTING YOU.
OH...
UH... HI.
HEY, BABE...

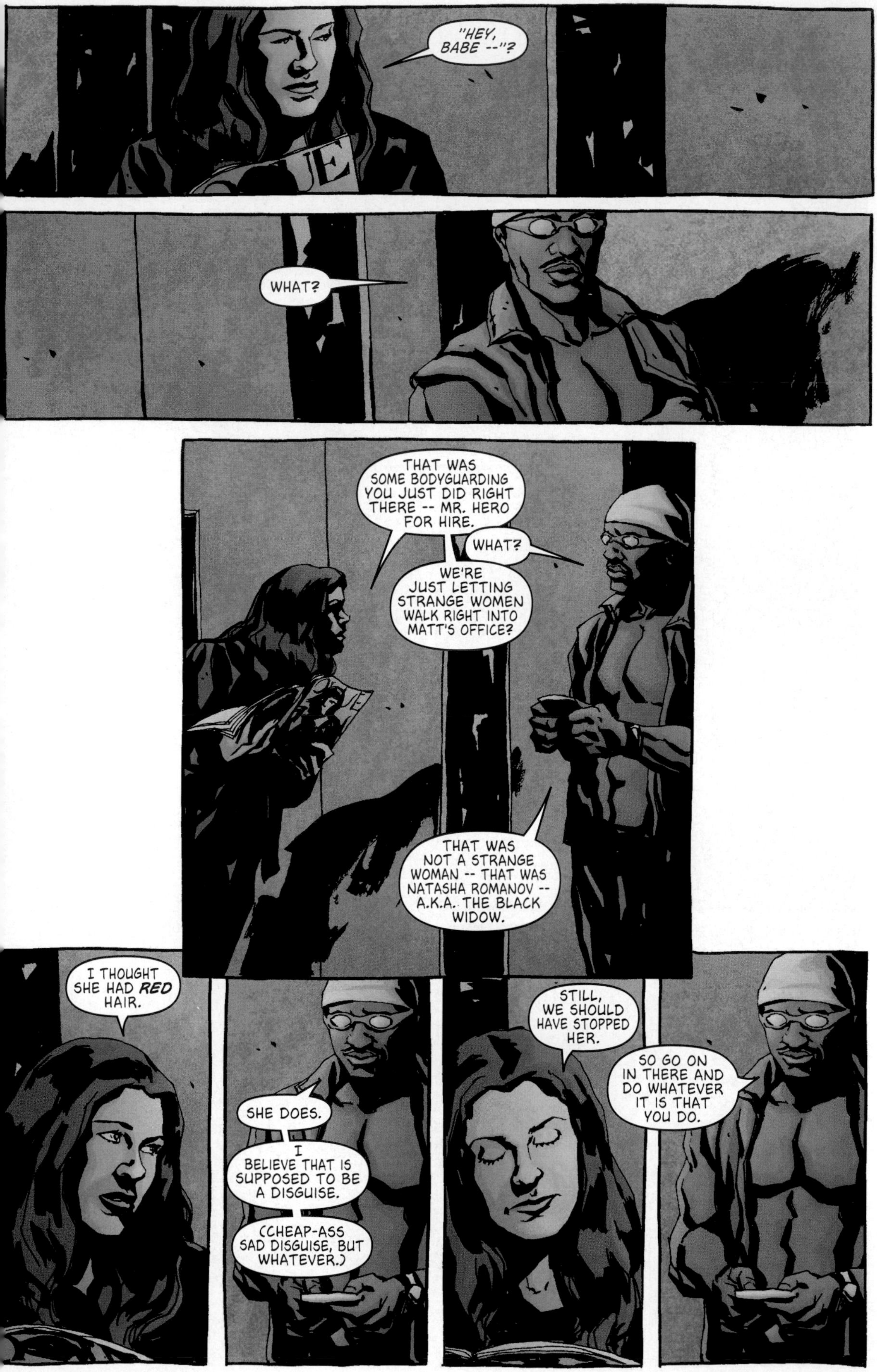
"HEY, BABE --"?
WHAT?
THAT WAS SOME BODYGUARDING YOU JUST DID RIGHT THERE -- MR. HERO FOR HIRE.
WHAT?
WE'RE JUST LETTING STRANGE WOMEN WALK RIGHT INTO MATT'S OFFICE?
THAT WAS NOT A STRANGE WOMAN -- THAT WAS NATASHA ROMANOV -- A.K.A. THE BLACK WIDOW.
I THOUGHT SHE HAD RED HAIR.
SHE DOES.
I BELIEVE THAT IS SUPPOSED TO BE A DISGUISE.
(CHEAP-ASS SAD DISGUISE, BUT WHATEVER.)
STILL, WE SHOULD HAVE STOPPED HER.
SO GO ON IN THERE AND DO WHATEVER IT IS THAT YOU DO.

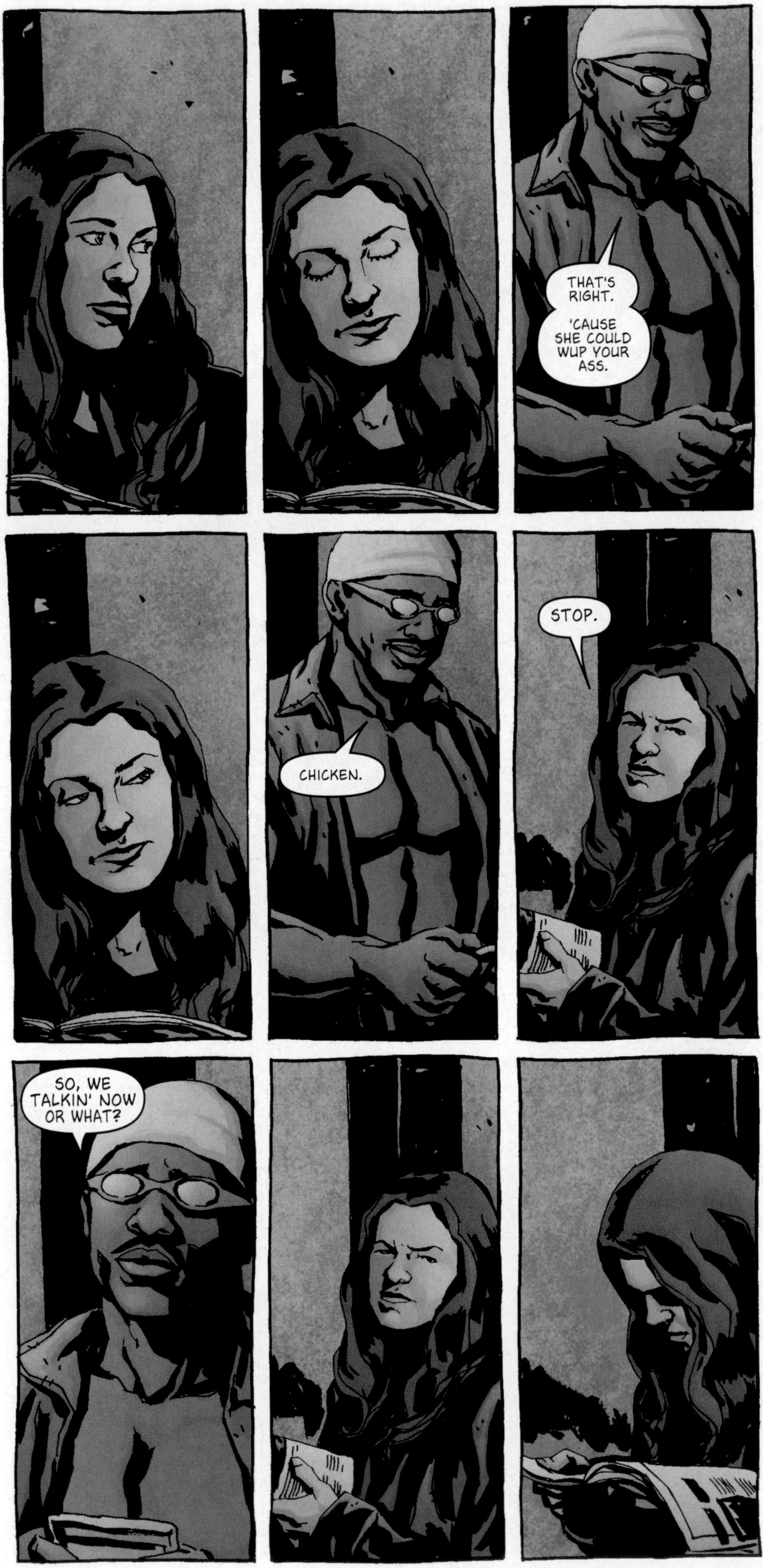
THAT'S RIGHT.
'CAUSE SHE COULD WUP YOUR ASS.
CHICKEN.
STOP.
SO, WE TALKIN' NOW OR WHAT?

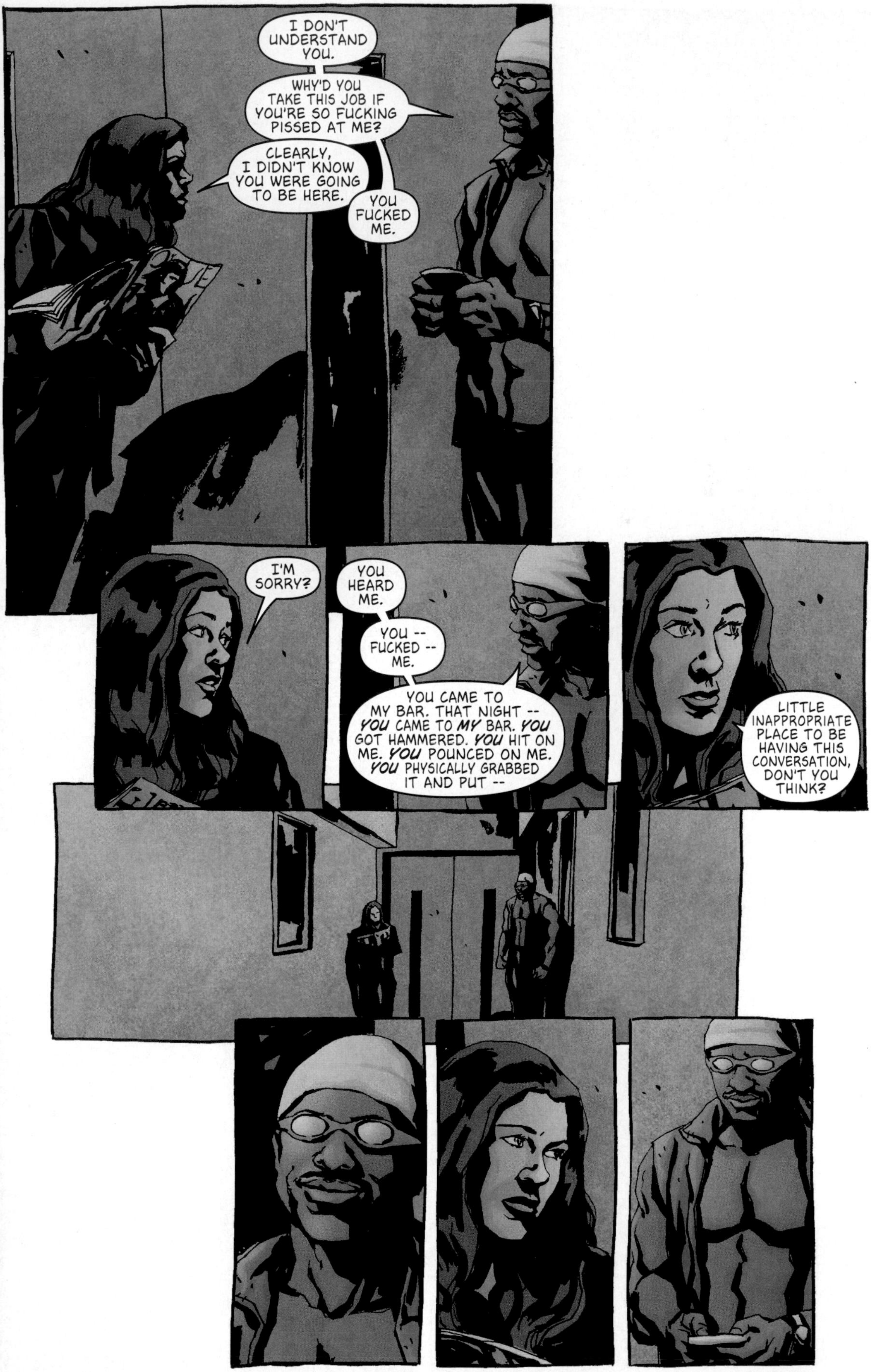
I DON'T UNDERSTAND YOU.
WHY'D YOU TAKE THIS JOB IF YOU'RE SO FUCKING PISSED AT ME?
CLEARLY, I DIDN'T KNOW YOU WERE GOING TO BE HERE.
YOU FUCKED ME.
I'M SORRY?
YOU HEARD ME.
YOU -- FUCKED -- ME.
YOU CAME TO MY BAR. THAT NIGHT -- YOU CAME TO MY BAR. YOU GOT HAMMERED. YOU HIT ON ME. YOU POUNCED ON ME. YOU PHYSICALLY GRABBED IT AND PUT --
LITTLE INAPPROPRIATE PLACE TO BE HAVING THIS CONVERSATION, DON'T YOU THINK?

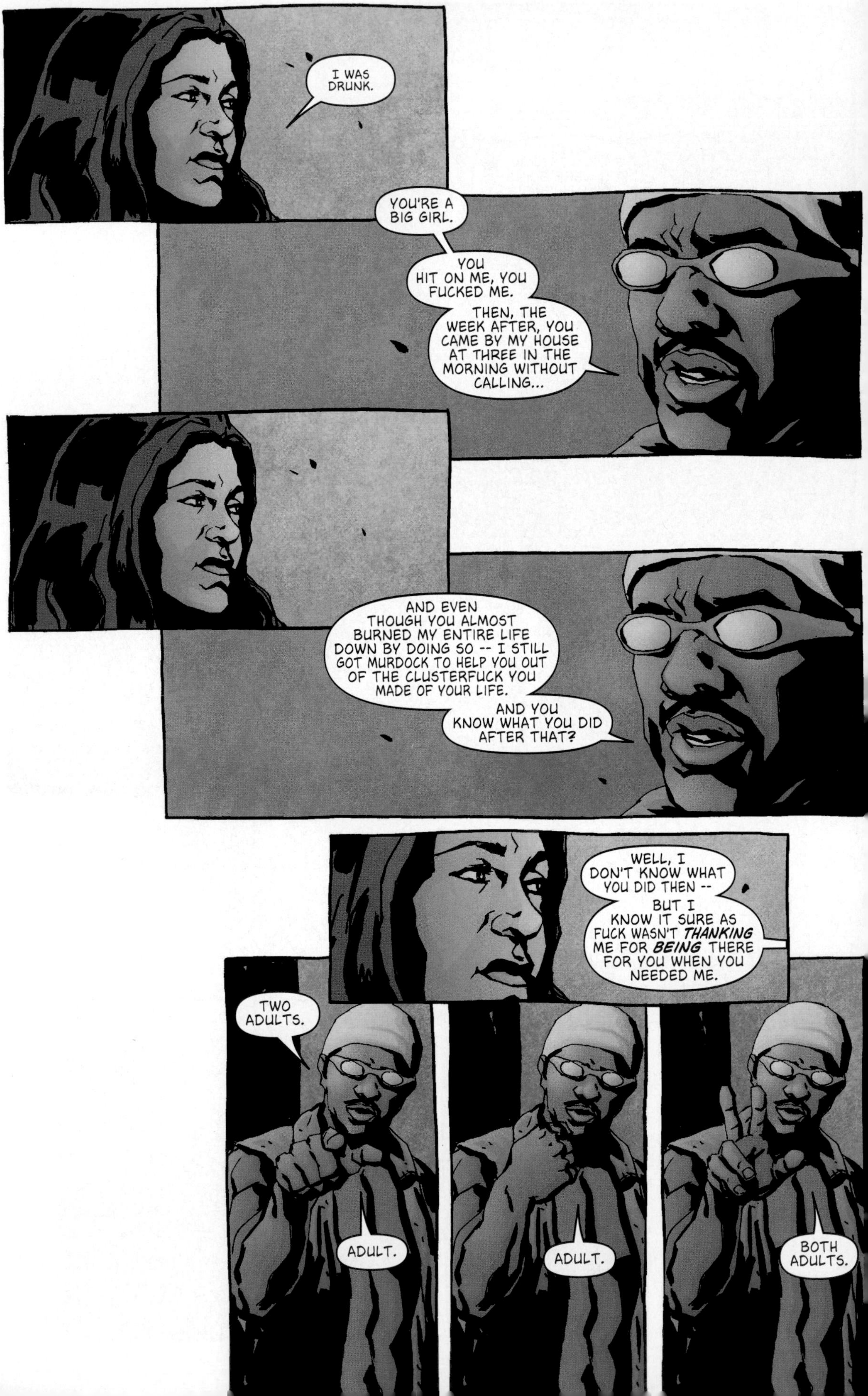
I WAS DRUNK.
YOU'RE A BIG GIRL.
YOU HIT ON ME, YOU FUCKED ME.
THEN, THE WEEK AFTER, YOU CAME BY MY HOUSE AT THREE IN THE MORNING WITHOUT CALLING...
AND EVEN THOUGH YOU ALMOST BURNED MY ENTIRE LIFE DOWN BY DOING SO -- I STILL GOT MURDOCK TO HELP YOU OUT OF THE CLUSTERFUCK YOU MADE OF YOUR LIFE.
AND YOU KNOW WHAT YOU DID AFTER THAT?
WELL, I DON'T KNOW WHAT YOU DID THEN --
BUT I KNOW IT SURE AS FUCK WASN'T *THANKING* ME FOR *BEING* THERE FOR YOU WHEN YOU NEEDED ME.
TWO ADULTS.
ADULT.
ADULT.
BOTH ADULTS.

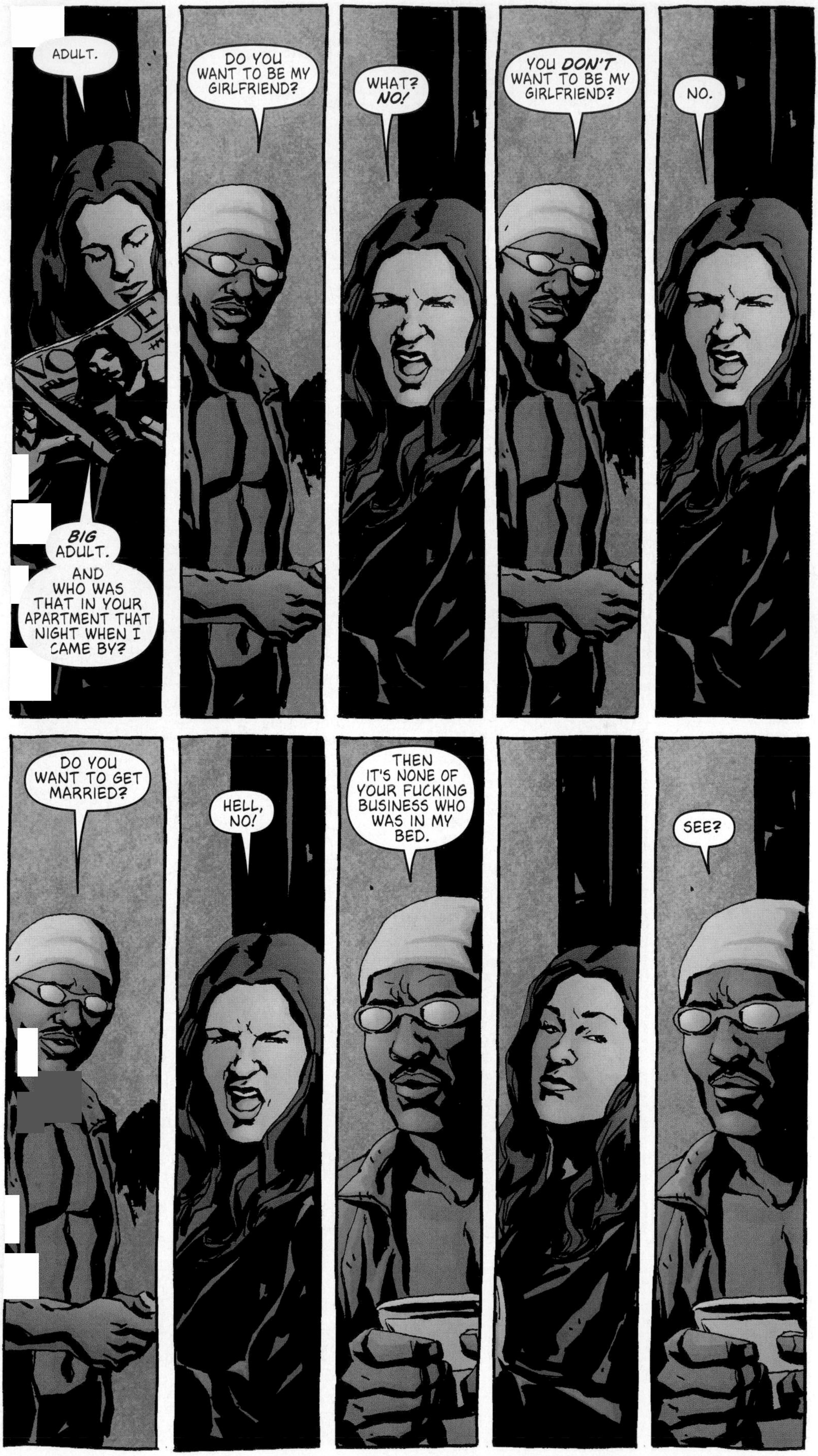
ADULT.
BIG ADULT.
AND WHO WAS THAT IN YOUR APARTMENT THAT NIGHT WHEN I CAME BY?
DO YOU WANT TO BE MY GIRLFRIEND?
WHAT? NO!
YOU DON'T WANT TO BE MY GIRLFRIEND?
NO.
DO YOU WANT TO GET MARRIED?
HELL, NO!
THEN IT'S NONE OF YOUR FUCKING BUSINESS WHO WAS IN MY BED.
SEE?

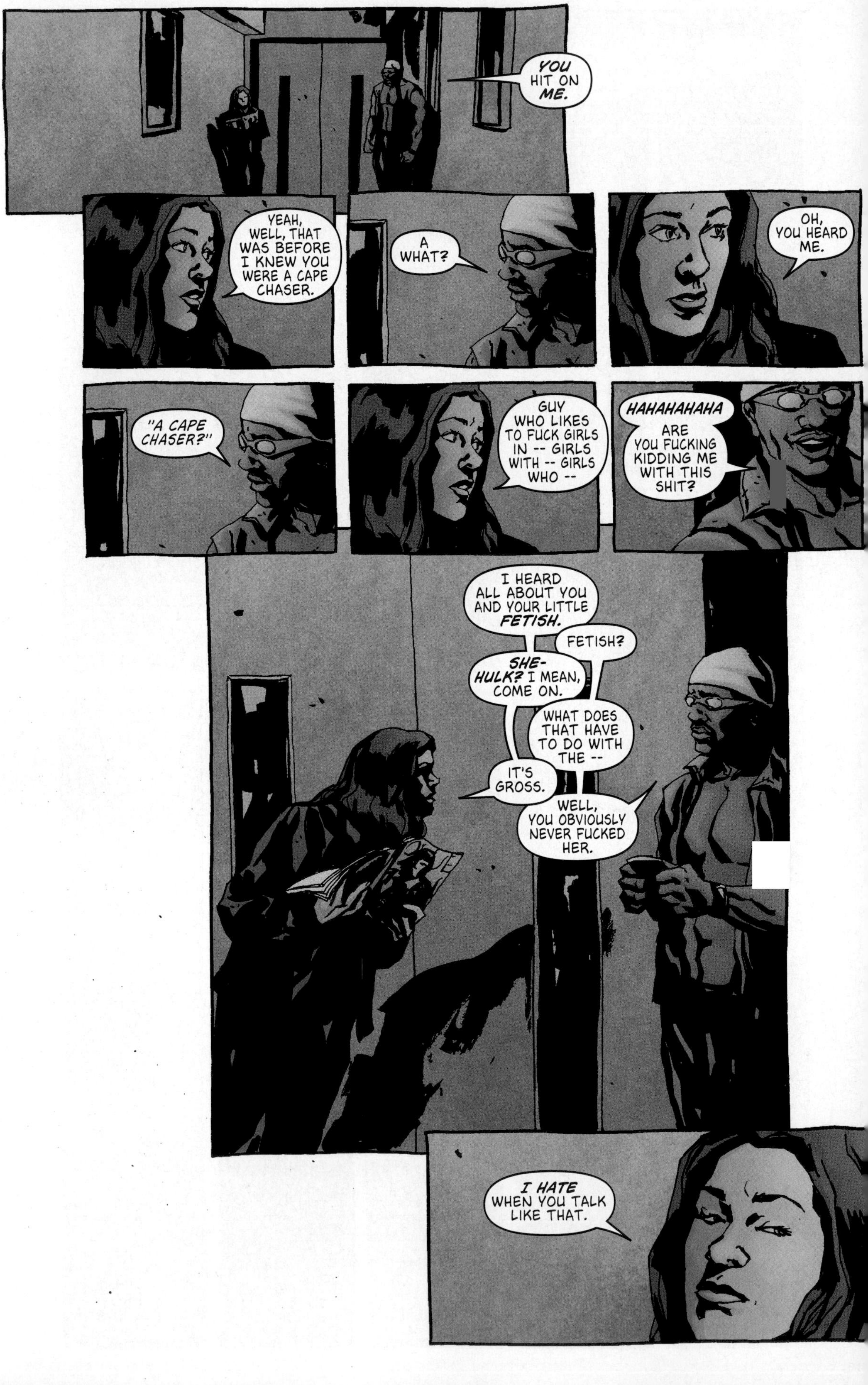
YOU HIT ON ME.
YEAH, WELL, THAT WAS BEFORE I KNEW YOU WERE A CAPE CHASER.
A WHAT?
OH, YOU HEARD ME.
"A CAPE CHASER?"
GUY WHO LIKES TO FUCK GIRLS IN -- GIRLS WITH -- GIRLS WHO --
HAHAHAHAHA
ARE YOU FUCKING KIDDING ME WITH THIS SHIT?
I HEARD ALL ABOUT YOU AND YOUR LITTLE FETISH.
FETISH?
SHE-HULK? I MEAN, COME ON.
WHAT DOES THAT HAVE TO DO WITH THE --
IT'S GROSS.
WELL, YOU OBVIOUSLY NEVER FUCKED HER.
I HATE WHEN YOU TALK LIKE THAT.

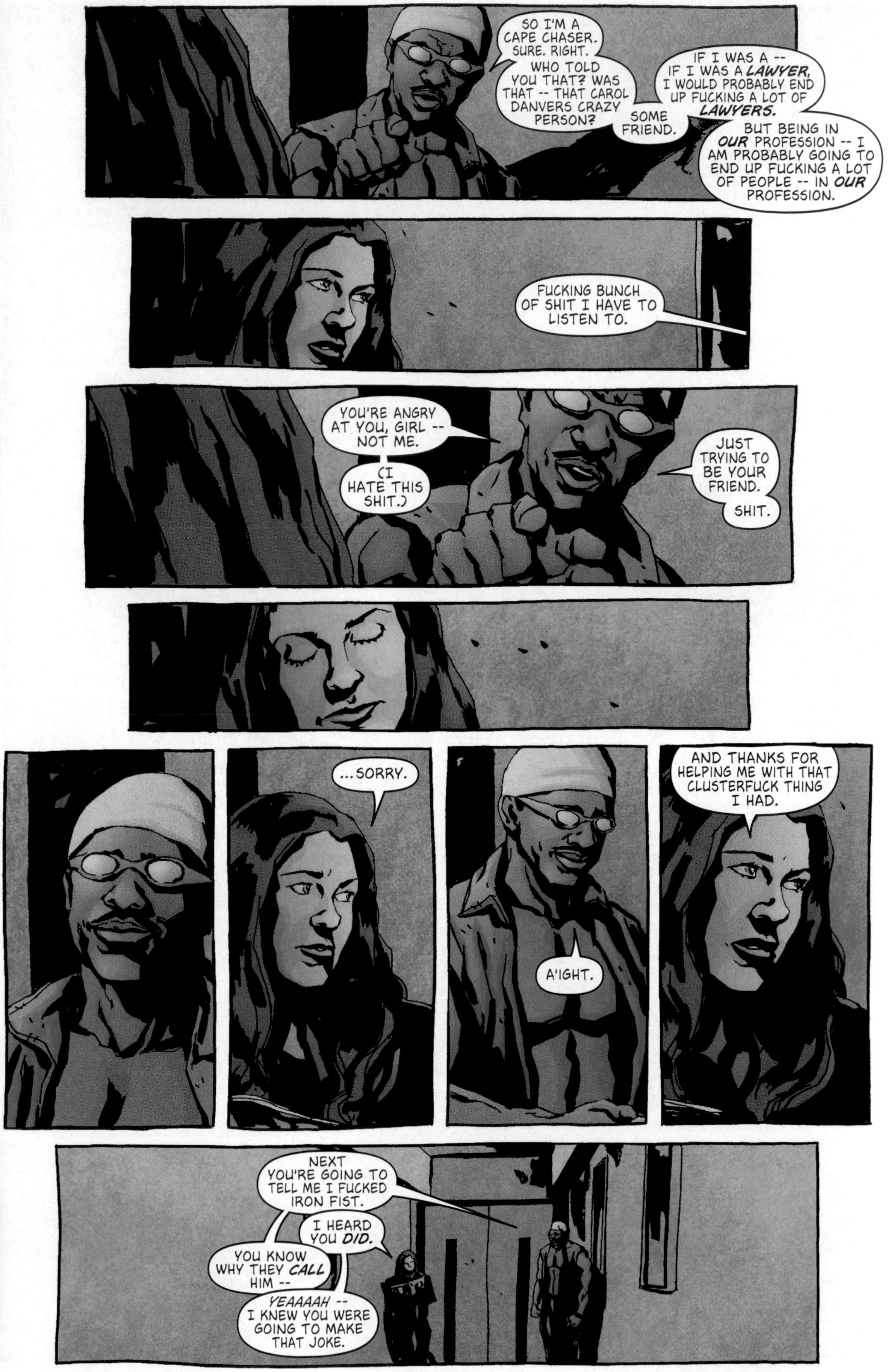

SO I'M A CAPE CHASER. SURE. RIGHT.
WHO TOLD YOU THAT? WAS THAT -- THAT CAROL DANVERS CRAZY PERSON?
SOME FRIEND.
IF I WAS A -- IF I WAS A LAWYER, I WOULD PROBABLY END UP FUCKING A LOT OF LAWYERS.
BUT BEING IN OUR PROFESSION -- I AM PROBABLY GOING TO END UP FUCKING A LOT OF PEOPLE -- IN OUR PROFESSION.
FUCKING BUNCH OF SHIT I HAVE TO LISTEN TO.
YOU'RE ANGRY AT YOU, GIRL -- NOT ME.
(I HATE THIS SHIT.)
JUST TRYING TO BE YOUR FRIEND.
SHIT.
...SORRY.
A'IGHT.
AND THANKS FOR HELPING ME WITH THAT CLUSTERFUCK THING I HAD.
NEXT YOU'RE GOING TO TELL ME I FUCKED IRON FIST.
I HEARD YOU DID.
YOU KNOW WHY THEY CALL HIM --
YEAAAAH -- I KNEW YOU WERE GOING TO MAKE THAT JOKE.

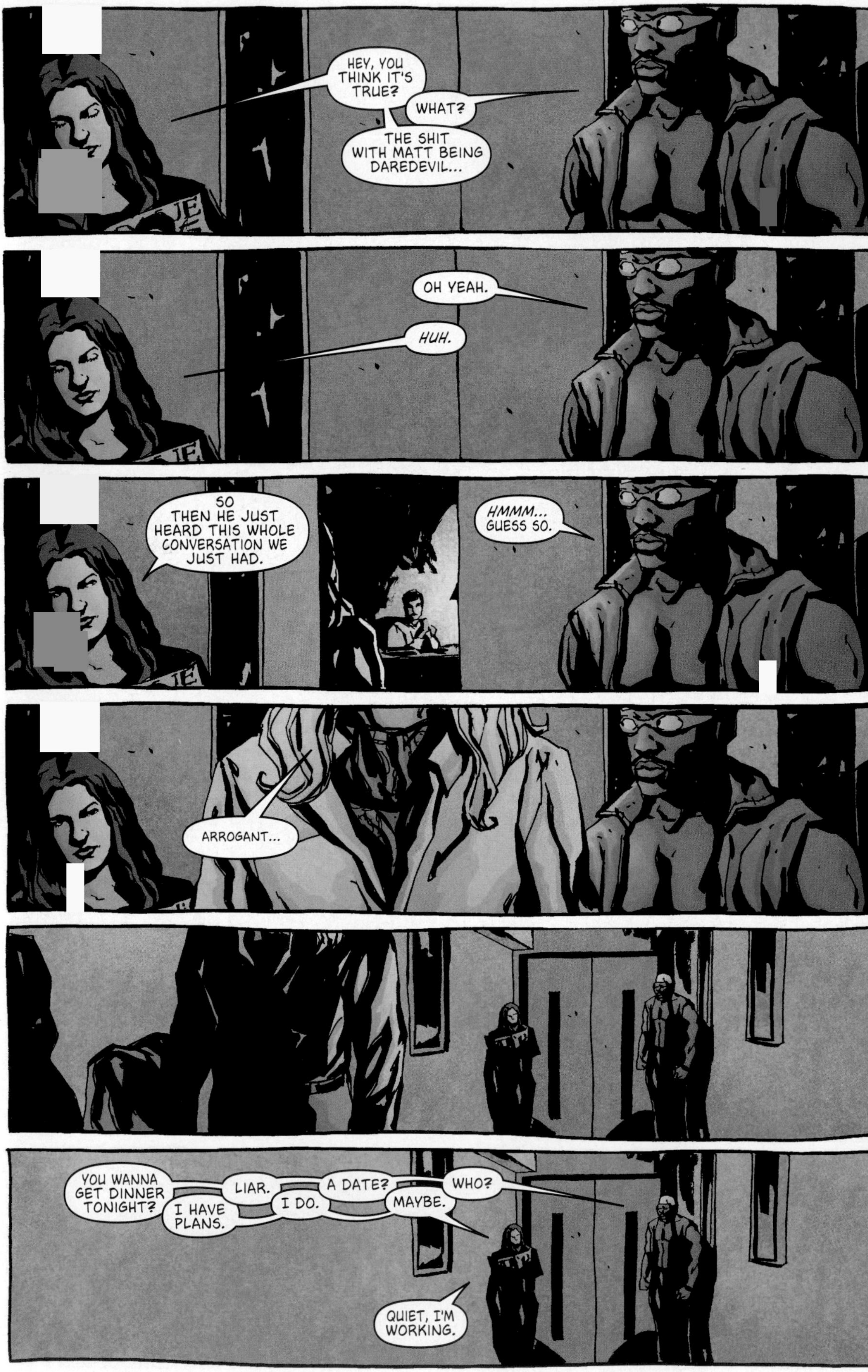
HEY, YOU THINK IT'S TRUE?
WHAT?
THE SHIT WITH MATT BEING DAREDEVIL...
OH YEAH.
HUH.
SO THEN HE JUST HEARD THIS WHOLE CONVERSATION WE JUST HAD.
HMMM... GUESS SO.
ARROGANT...
YOU WANNA GET DINNER TONIGHT?
I HAVE PLANS.
LIAR.
I DO.
A DATE?
MAYBE.
WHO?
QUIET, I'M WORKING.

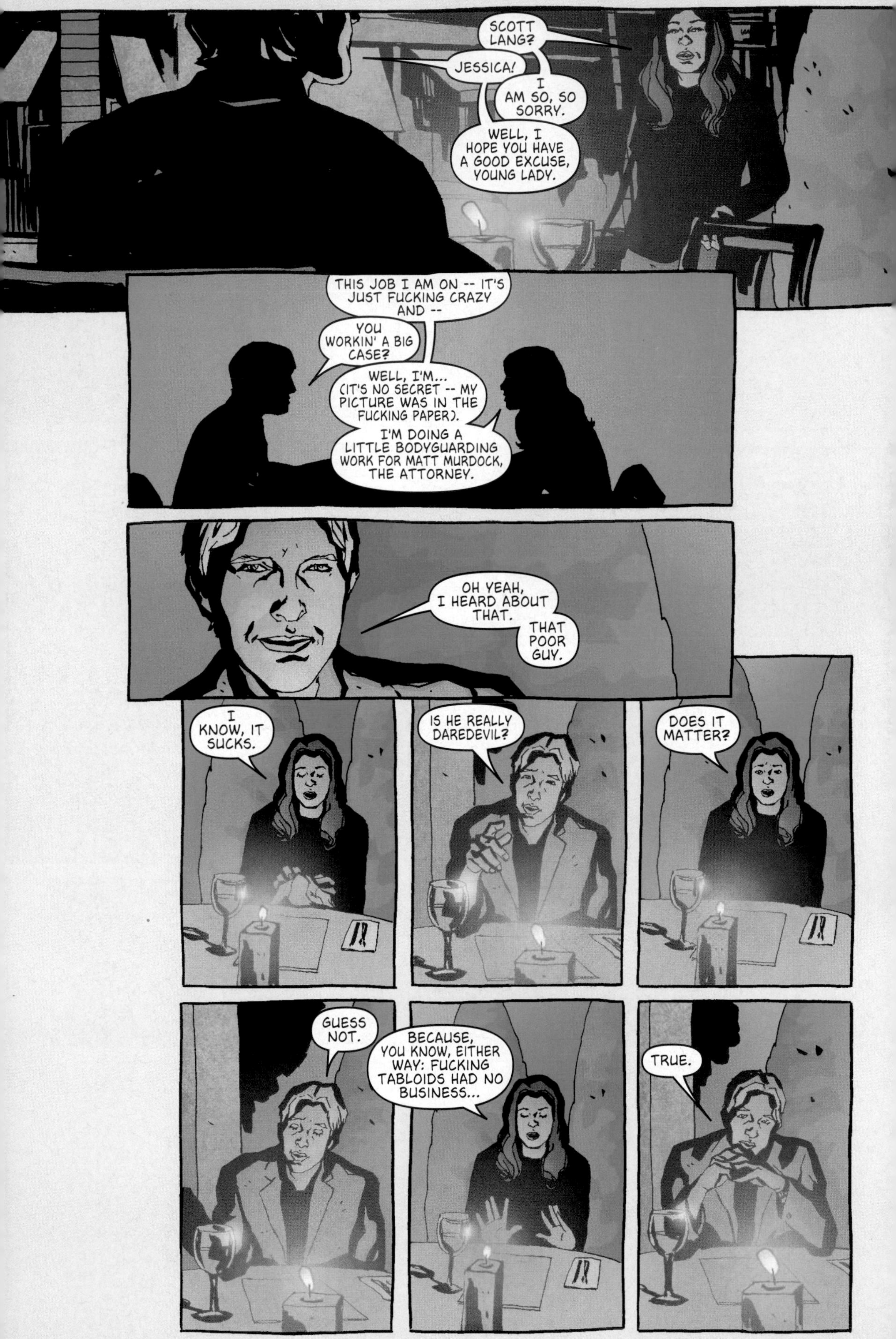
SCOTT LANG?
JESSICA!
I AM SO, SO SORRY.
WELL, I HOPE YOU HAVE A GOOD EXCUSE, YOUNG LADY.
THIS JOB I AM ON -- IT'S JUST FUCKING CRAZY AND --
YOU WORKIN' A BIG CASE?
WELL, I'M... (IT'S NO SECRET -- MY PICTURE WAS IN THE FUCKING PAPER).
I'M DOING A LITTLE BODYGUARDING WORK FOR MATT MURDOCK, THE ATTORNEY.
OH YEAH, I HEARD ABOUT THAT.
THAT POOR GUY.
I KNOW, IT SUCKS.
IS HE REALLY DAREDEVIL?
DOES IT MATTER?
GUESS NOT.
BECAUSE, YOU KNOW, EITHER WAY: FUCKING TABLOIDS HAD NO BUSINESS...
TRUE.

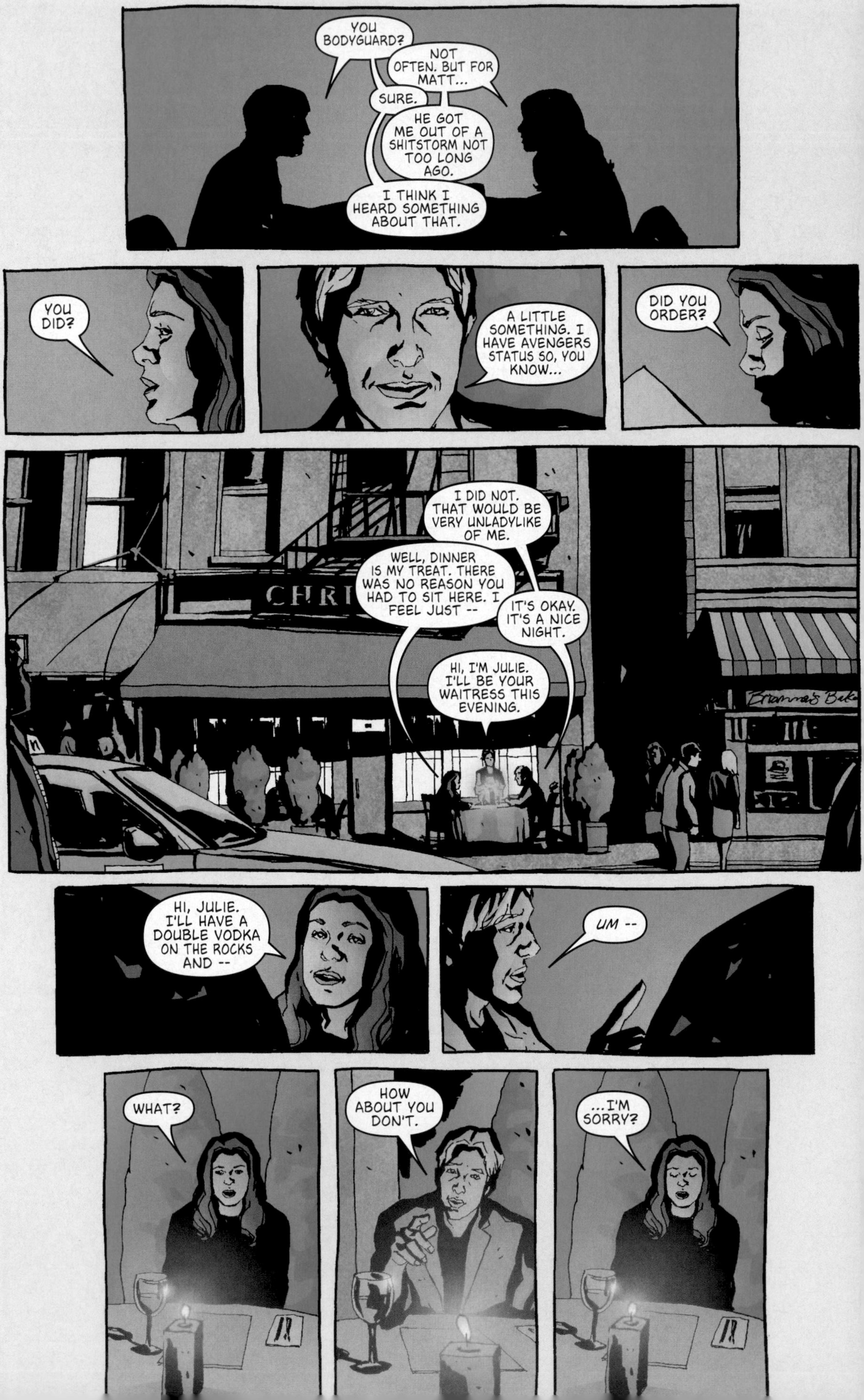
YOU BODYGUARD?
NOT OFTEN. BUT FOR MATT...
SURE.
HE GOT ME OUT OF A SHITSTORM NOT TOO LONG AGO.
I THINK I HEARD SOMETHING ABOUT THAT.
YOU DID?
A LITTLE SOMETHING. I HAVE AVENGERS STATUS SO, YOU KNOW...
DID YOU ORDER?
CHRI
I DID NOT. THAT WOULD BE VERY UNLADYLIKE OF ME.
WELL, DINNER IS MY TREAT. THERE WAS NO REASON YOU HAD TO SIT HERE. I FEEL JUST --
IT'S OKAY. IT'S A NICE NIGHT.
HI, I'M JULIE. I'LL BE YOUR WAITRESS THIS EVENING.
HI, JULIE. I'LL HAVE A DOUBLE VODKA ON THE ROCKS AND --
UM --
WHAT?
HOW ABOUT YOU DON'T.
...I'M SORRY?

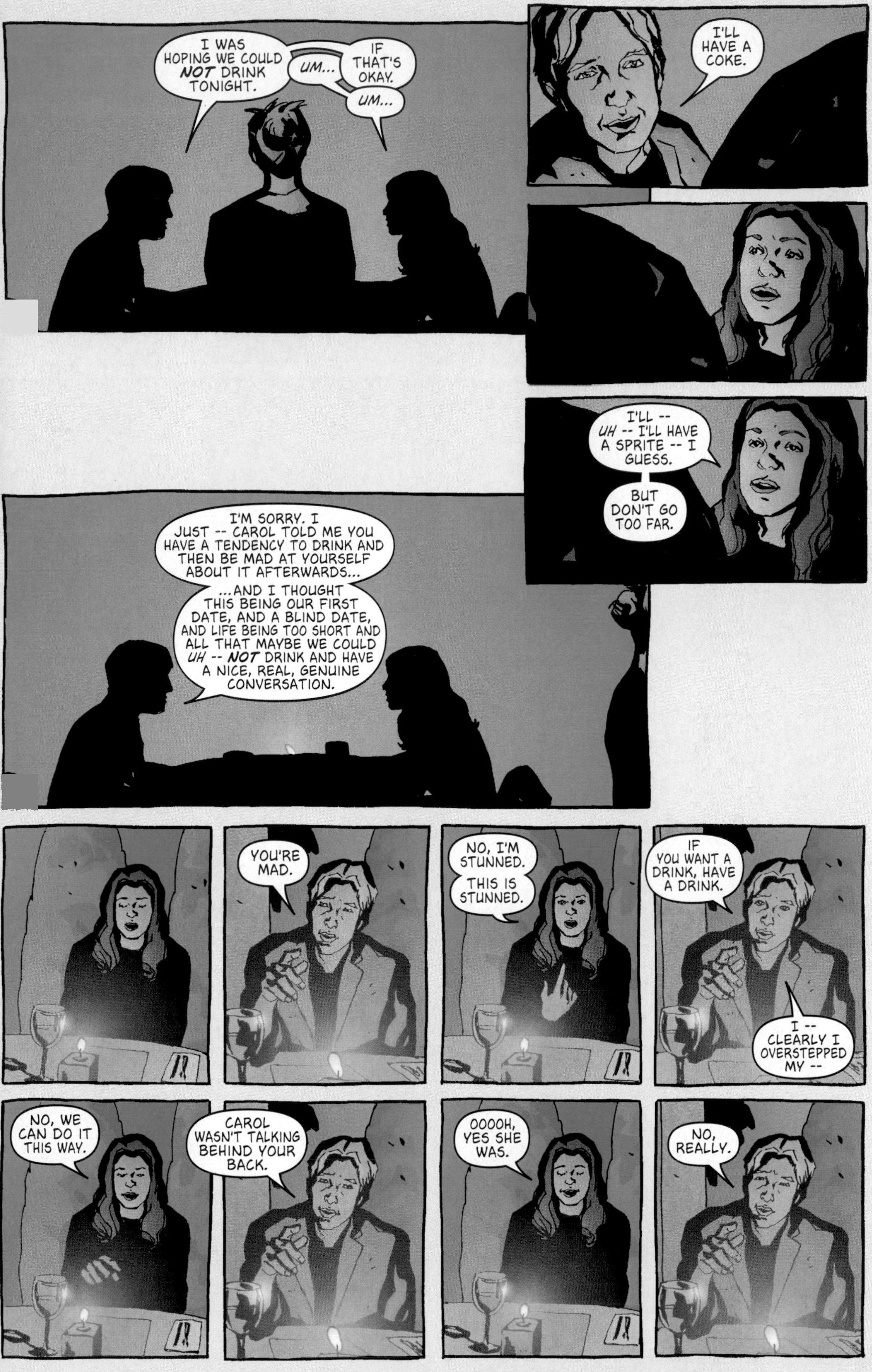

I WAS HOPING WE COULD NOT DRINK TONIGHT.
UM...
IF THAT'S OKAY.
UM...
I'LL HAVE A COKE.
I'LL -- UH -- I'LL HAVE A SPRITE -- I GUESS.
BUT DON'T GO TOO FAR.
I'M SORRY. I JUST -- CAROL TOLD ME YOU HAVE A TENDENCY TO DRINK AND THEN BE MAD AT YOURSELF ABOUT IT AFTERWARDS...
...AND I THOUGHT THIS BEING OUR FIRST DATE, AND A BLIND DATE, AND LIFE BEING TOO SHORT AND ALL THAT MAYBE WE COULD UH -- NOT DRINK AND HAVE A NICE, REAL, GENUINE CONVERSATION.
YOU'RE MAD.
NO, I'M STUNNED.
THIS IS STUNNED.
IF YOU WANT A DRINK, HAVE A DRINK.
I -- CLEARLY I OVERSTEPPED MY --
NO, WE CAN DO IT THIS WAY.
CAROL WASN'T TALKING BEHIND YOUR BACK.
OOOOH, YES SHE WAS.
NO, REALLY.

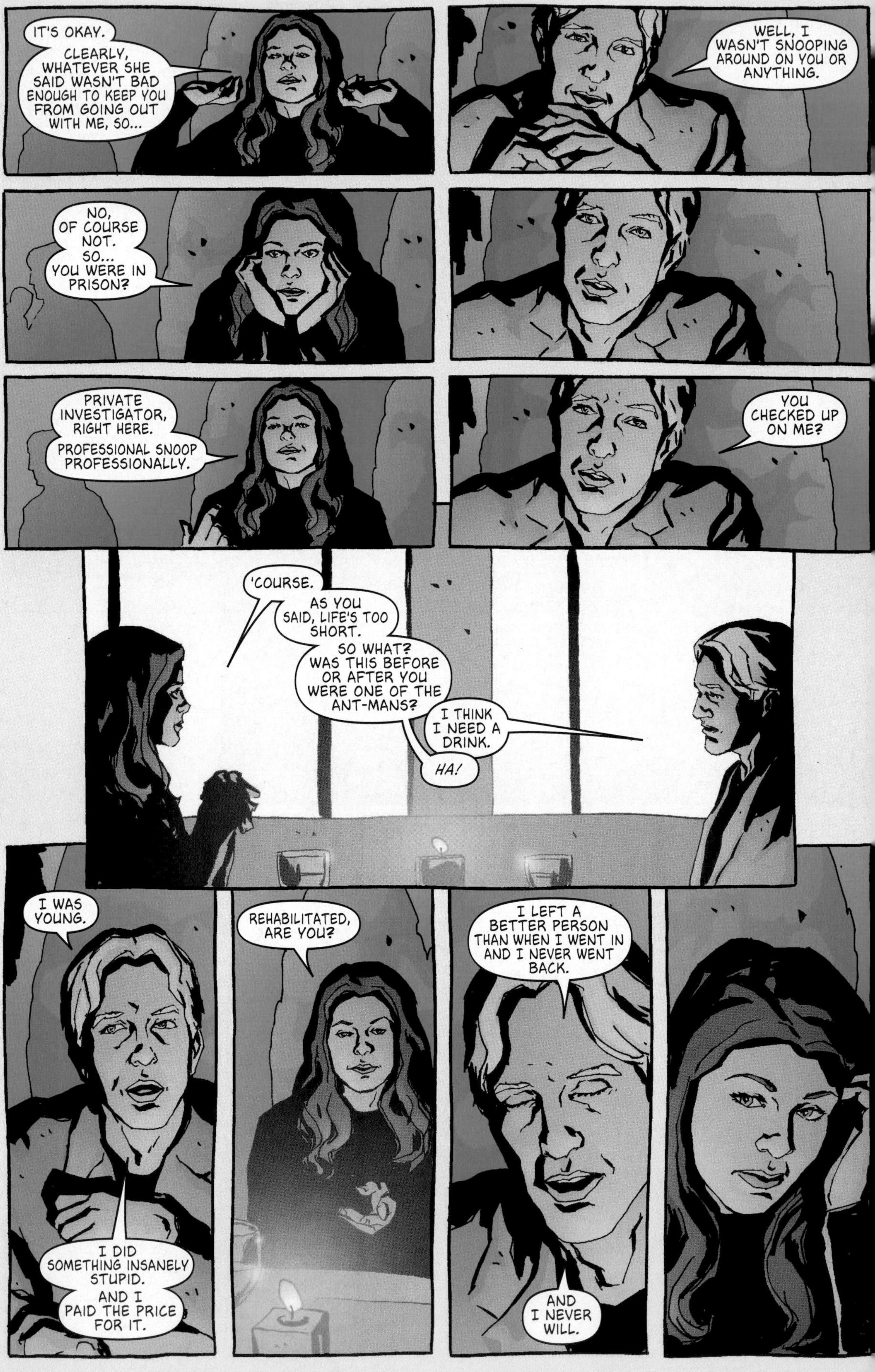
IT'S OKAY.
CLEARLY, WHATEVER SHE SAID WASN'T BAD ENOUGH TO KEEP YOU FROM GOING OUT WITH ME, SO...
WELL, I WASN'T SNOOPING AROUND ON YOU OR ANYTHING.
NO, OF COURSE NOT.
SO... YOU WERE IN PRISON?
PRIVATE INVESTIGATOR, RIGHT HERE.
PROFESSIONAL SNOOP PROFESSIONALLY.
YOU CHECKED UP ON ME?
'COURSE.
AS YOU SAID, LIFE'S TOO SHORT.
SO WHAT? WAS THIS BEFORE OR AFTER YOU WERE ONE OF THE ANT-MANS?
I THINK I NEED A DRINK.
HA!
I WAS YOUNG.
I DID SOMETHING INSANELY STUPID.
AND I PAID THE PRICE FOR IT.
REHABILITATED, ARE YOU?
I LEFT A BETTER PERSON THAN WHEN I WENT IN AND I NEVER WENT BACK.
AND I NEVER WILL.

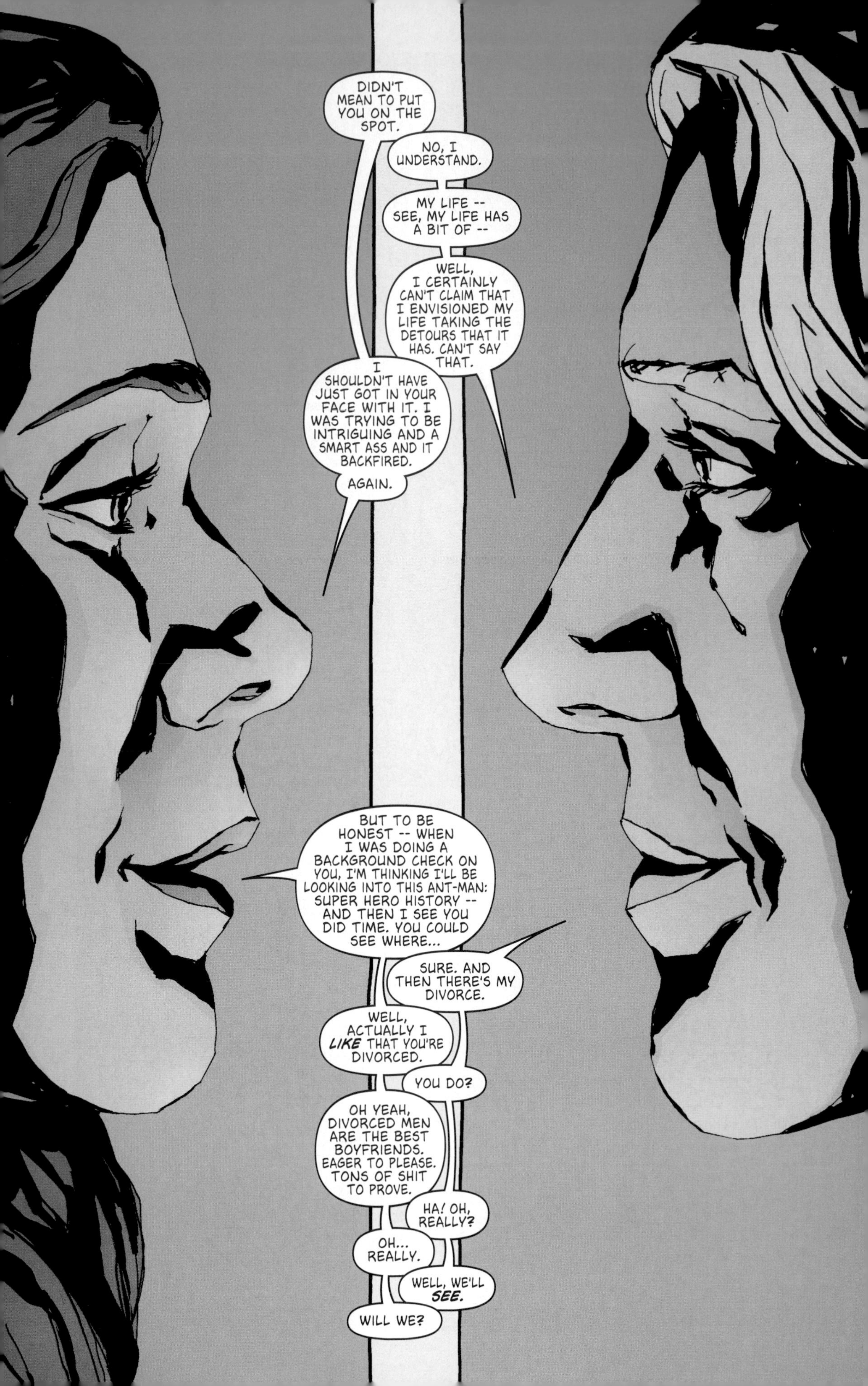
DIDN'T MEAN TO PUT YOU ON THE SPOT.
NO, I UNDERSTAND.
MY LIFE -- SEE, MY LIFE HAS A BIT OF --
WELL, I CERTAINLY CAN'T CLAIM THAT I ENVISIONED MY LIFE TAKING THE DETOURS THAT IT HAS. CAN'T SAY THAT.
I SHOULDN'T HAVE JUST GOT IN YOUR FACE WITH IT. I WAS TRYING TO BE INTRIGUING AND A SMART ASS AND IT BACKFIRED.
AGAIN.
BUT TO BE HONEST -- WHEN I WAS DOING A BACKGROUND CHECK ON YOU, I'M THINKING I'LL BE LOOKING INTO THIS ANT-MAN: SUPER HERO HISTORY -- AND THEN I SEE YOU DID TIME. YOU COULD SEE WHERE...
SURE. AND THEN THERE'S MY DIVORCE.
WELL, ACTUALLY I *LIKE* THAT YOU'RE DIVORCED.
YOU DO?
OH YEAH, DIVORCED MEN ARE THE BEST BOYFRIENDS. EAGER TO PLEASE. TONS OF SHIT TO PROVE.
HA! OH, REALLY?
OH... REALLY.
WELL, WE'LL **SEE.**
WILL WE?

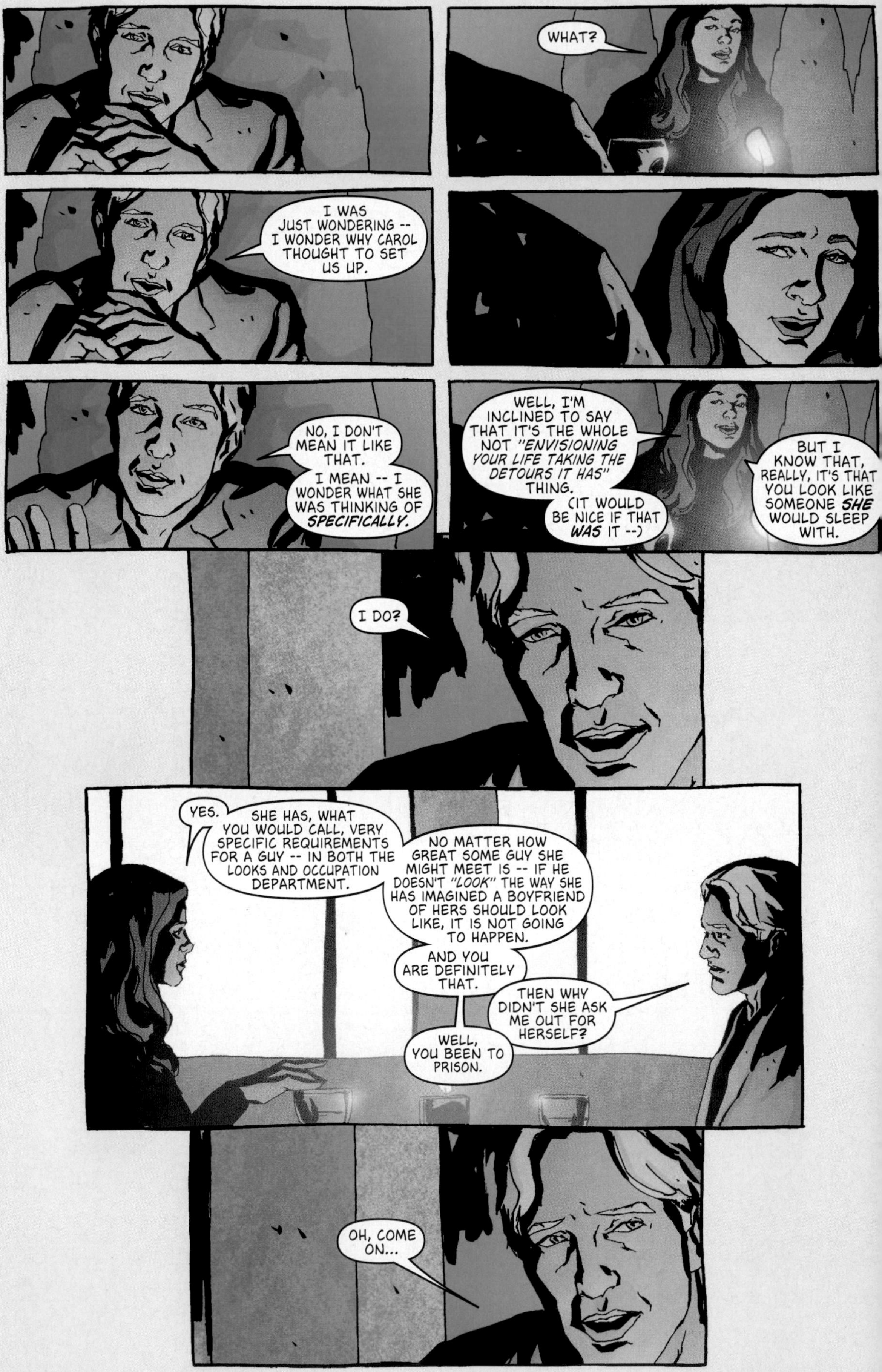

WHAT?
I WAS JUST WONDERING -- I WONDER WHY CAROL THOUGHT TO SET US UP.
NO, I DON'T MEAN IT LIKE THAT.
I MEAN -- I WONDER WHAT SHE WAS THINKING OF *SPECIFICALLY*.
WELL, I'M INCLINED TO SAY THAT IT'S THE WHOLE NOT *"ENVISIONING YOUR LIFE TAKING THE DETOURS IT HAS"* THING.
(IT WOULD BE NICE IF THAT ***WAS*** IT --)
BUT I KNOW THAT, REALLY, IT'S THAT YOU LOOK LIKE SOMEONE ***SHE*** WOULD SLEEP WITH.
I DO?
YES.
SHE HAS, WHAT YOU WOULD CALL, VERY SPECIFIC REQUIREMENTS FOR A GUY -- IN BOTH THE LOOKS AND OCCUPATION DEPARTMENT.
NO MATTER HOW GREAT SOME GUY SHE MIGHT MEET IS -- IF HE DOESN'T *"LOOK"* THE WAY SHE HAS IMAGINED A BOYFRIEND OF HERS SHOULD LOOK LIKE, IT IS NOT GOING TO HAPPEN.
AND YOU ARE DEFINITELY THAT.
THEN WHY DIDN'T SHE ASK ME OUT FOR HERSELF?
WELL, YOU BEEN TO PRISON.
OH, COME ON...

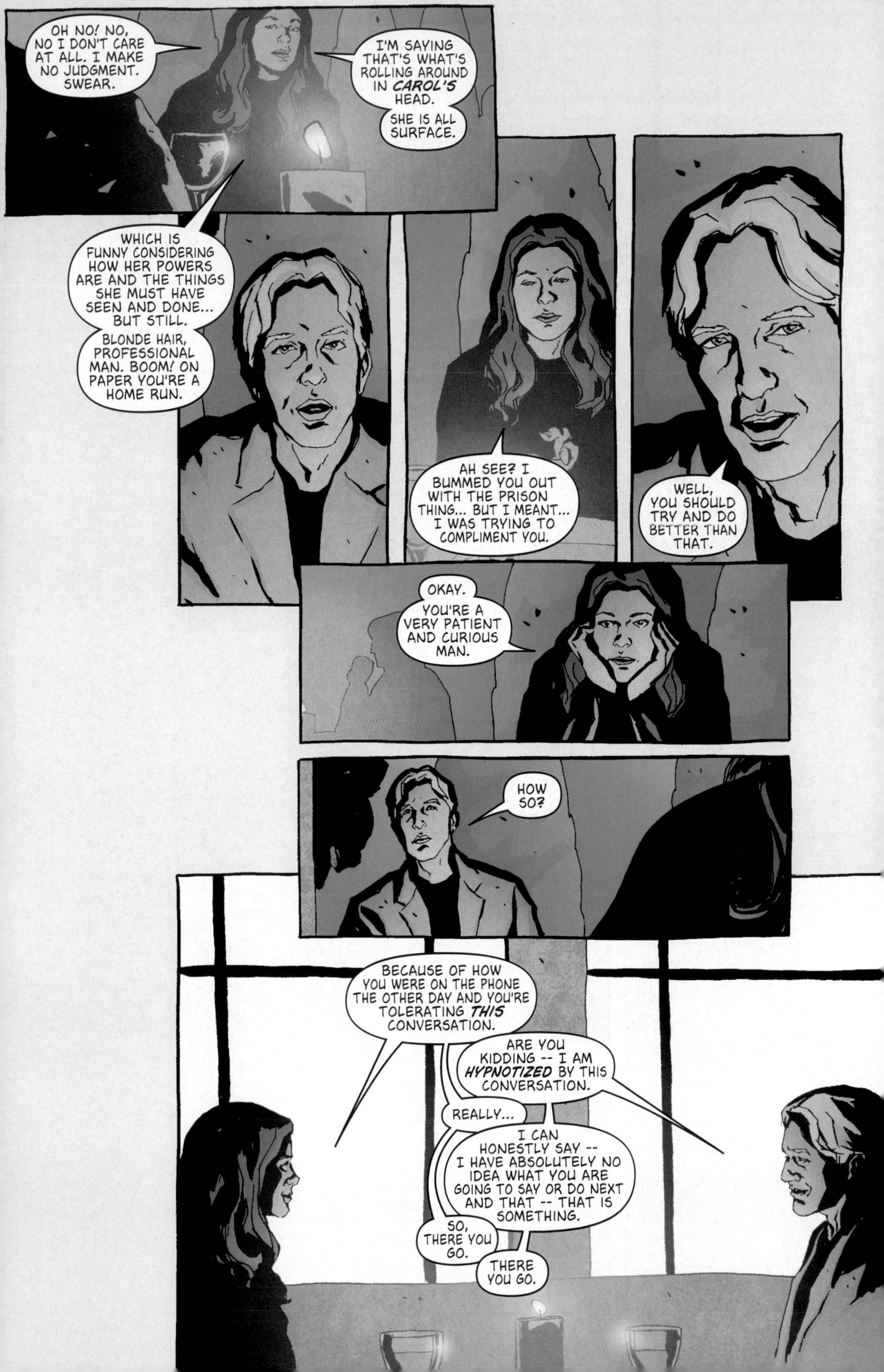
OH NO! NO, NO I DON'T CARE AT ALL. I MAKE NO JUDGMENT. SWEAR.
I'M SAYING THAT'S WHAT'S ROLLING AROUND IN *CAROL'S* HEAD.
SHE IS ALL SURFACE.
WHICH IS FUNNY CONSIDERING HOW HER POWERS ARE AND THE THINGS SHE MUST HAVE SEEN AND DONE... BUT STILL.
BLONDE HAIR, PROFESSIONAL MAN. BOOM! ON PAPER YOU'RE A HOME RUN.
AH SEE? I BUMMED YOU OUT WITH THE PRISON THING... BUT I MEANT... I WAS TRYING TO COMPLIMENT YOU.
WELL, YOU SHOULD TRY AND DO BETTER THAN THAT.
OKAY.
YOU'RE A VERY PATIENT AND CURIOUS MAN.
HOW SO?
BECAUSE OF HOW YOU WERE ON THE PHONE THE OTHER DAY AND YOU'RE TOLERATING *THIS* CONVERSATION.
ARE YOU KIDDING -- I AM *HYPNOTIZED* BY THIS CONVERSATION.
REALLY...
I CAN HONESTLY SAY -- I HAVE ABSOLUTELY NO IDEA WHAT YOU ARE GOING TO SAY OR DO NEXT AND THAT -- THAT IS SOMETHING.
SO, THERE YOU GO.
THERE YOU GO.

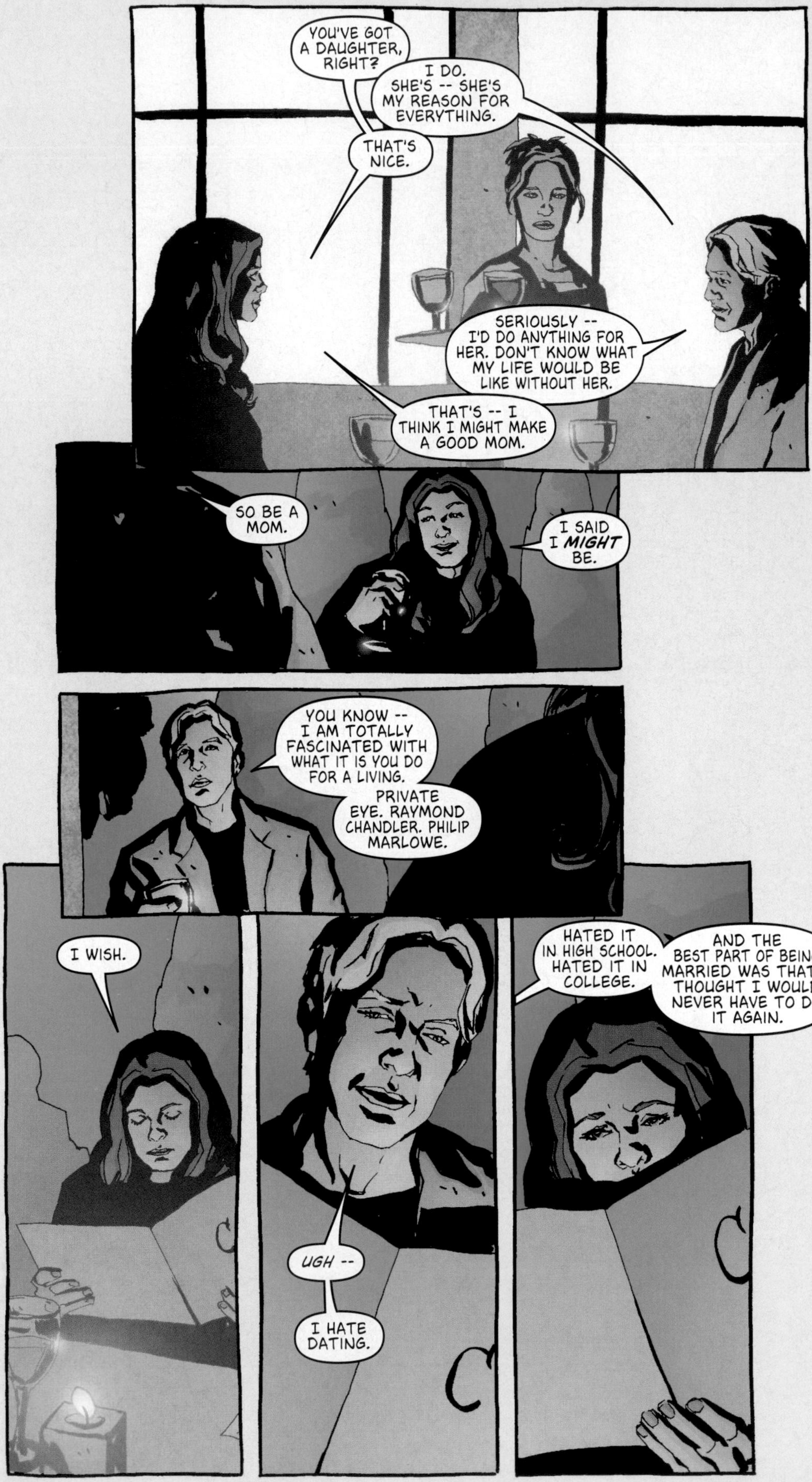
YOU'VE GOT A DAUGHTER, RIGHT?
I DO. SHE'S -- SHE'S MY REASON FOR EVERYTHING.
THAT'S NICE.
SERIOUSLY -- I'D DO ANYTHING FOR HER. DON'T KNOW WHAT MY LIFE WOULD BE LIKE WITHOUT HER.
THAT'S -- I THINK I MIGHT MAKE A GOOD MOM.
SO BE A MOM.
I SAID I *MIGHT* BE.
YOU KNOW -- I AM TOTALLY FASCINATED WITH WHAT IT IS YOU DO FOR A LIVING.
PRIVATE EYE. RAYMOND CHANDLER. PHILIP MARLOWE.
I WISH.
UGH --
I HATE DATING.
HATED IT IN HIGH SCHOOL. HATED IT IN COLLEGE.
AND THE BEST PART OF BEING MARRIED WAS THAT I THOUGHT I WOULD NEVER HAVE TO DO IT AGAIN.

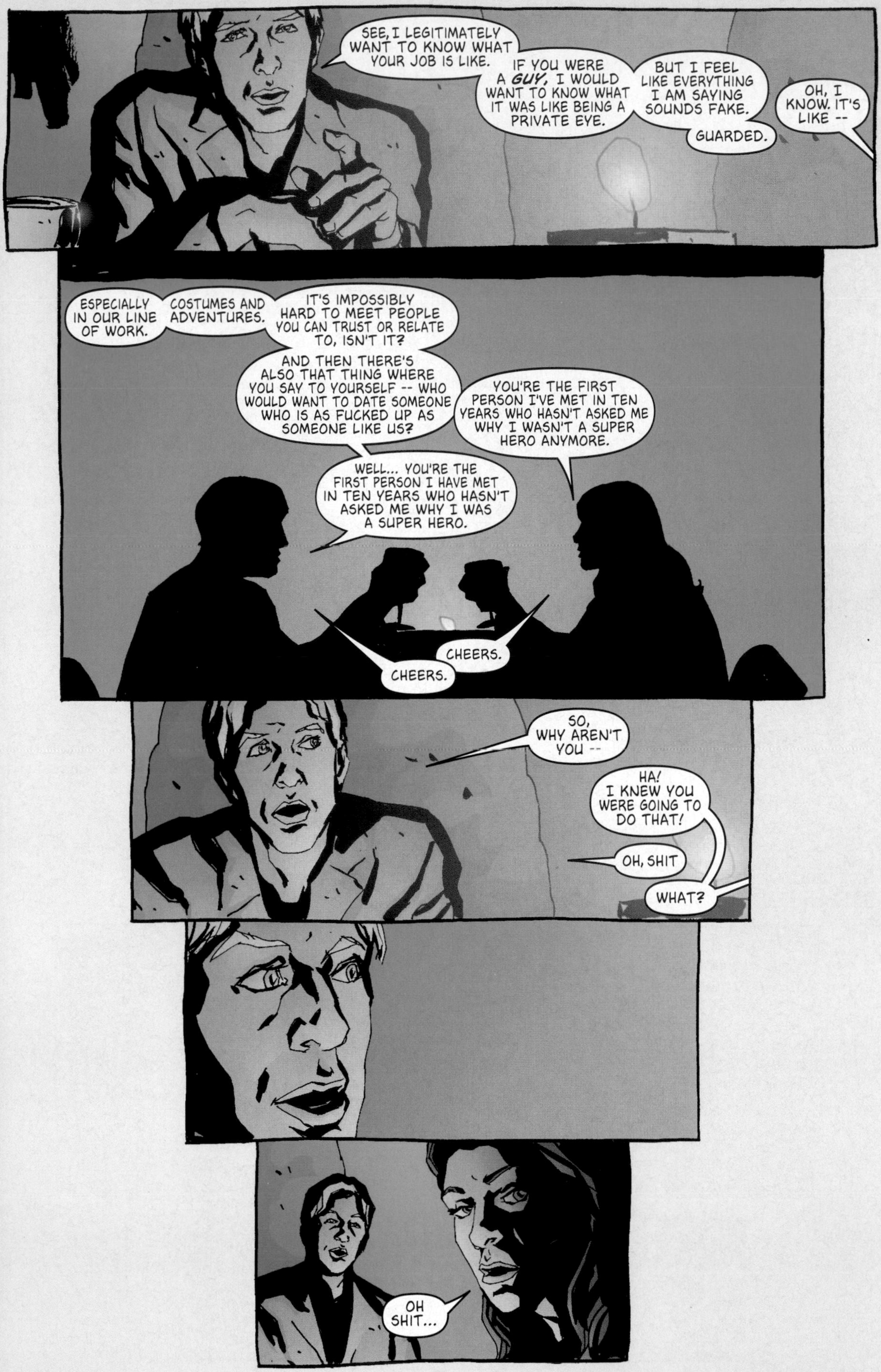
SEE, I LEGITIMATELY WANT TO KNOW WHAT YOUR JOB IS LIKE.
IF YOU WERE A GUY, I WOULD WANT TO KNOW WHAT IT WAS LIKE BEING A PRIVATE EYE.
BUT I FEEL LIKE EVERYTHING I AM SAYING SOUNDS FAKE.
GUARDED.
OH, I KNOW. IT'S LIKE --
ESPECIALLY IN OUR LINE OF WORK.
COSTUMES AND ADVENTURES.
IT'S IMPOSSIBLY HARD TO MEET PEOPLE YOU CAN TRUST OR RELATE TO, ISN'T IT?
AND THEN THERE'S ALSO THAT THING WHERE YOU SAY TO YOURSELF -- WHO WOULD WANT TO DATE SOMEONE WHO IS AS FUCKED UP AS SOMEONE LIKE US?
YOU'RE THE FIRST PERSON I'VE MET IN TEN YEARS WHO HASN'T ASKED ME WHY I WASN'T A SUPER HERO ANYMORE.
WELL... YOU'RE THE FIRST PERSON I HAVE MET IN TEN YEARS WHO HASN'T ASKED ME WHY I WAS A SUPER HERO.
CHEERS.
CHEERS.
SO, WHY AREN'T YOU --
HA! I KNEW YOU WERE GOING TO DO THAT!
OH, SHIT
WHAT?
OH SHIT...

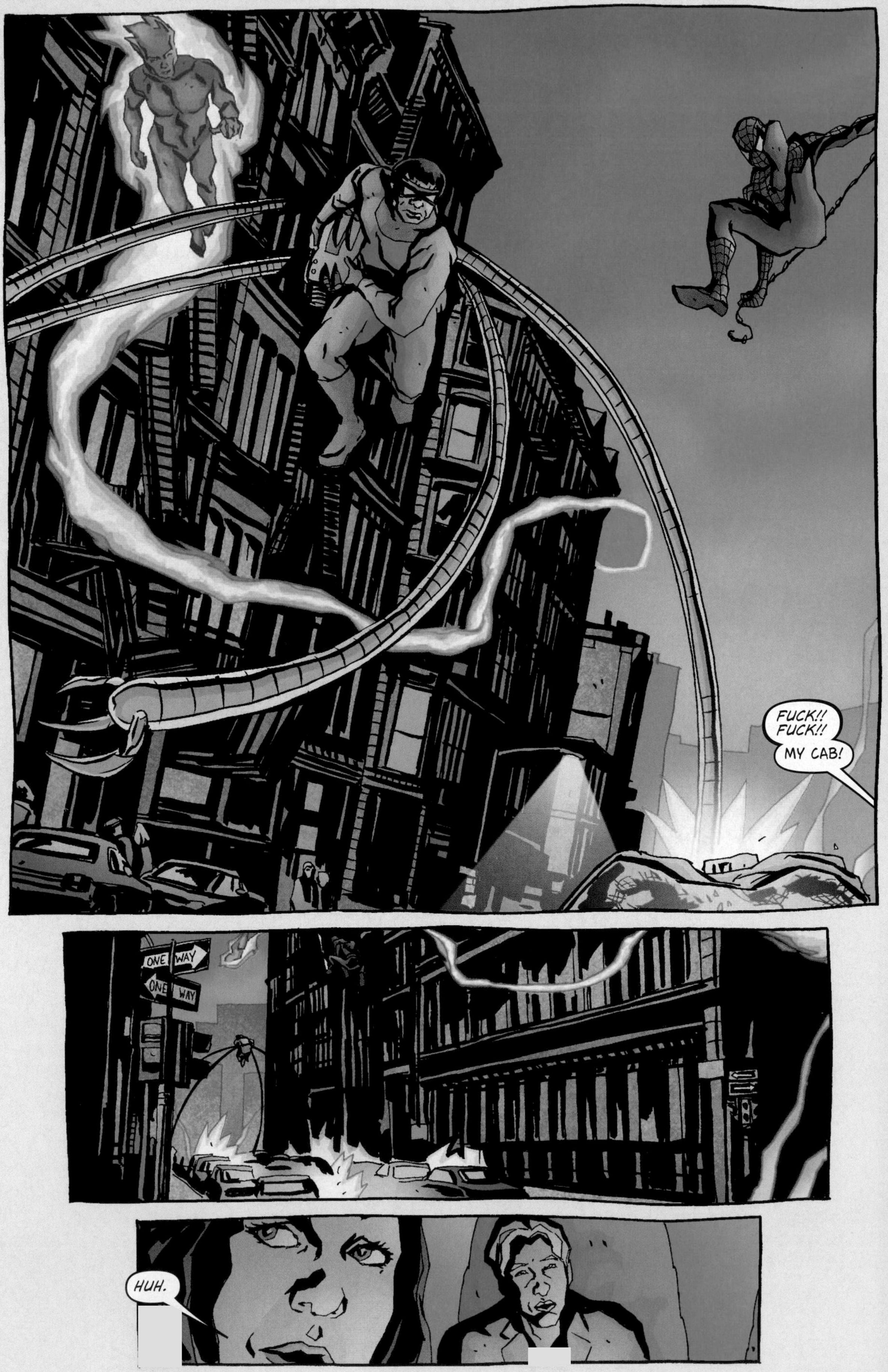
FUCK!! FUCK!!
MY CAB!
ONE WAY
ONE WAY
HUH.

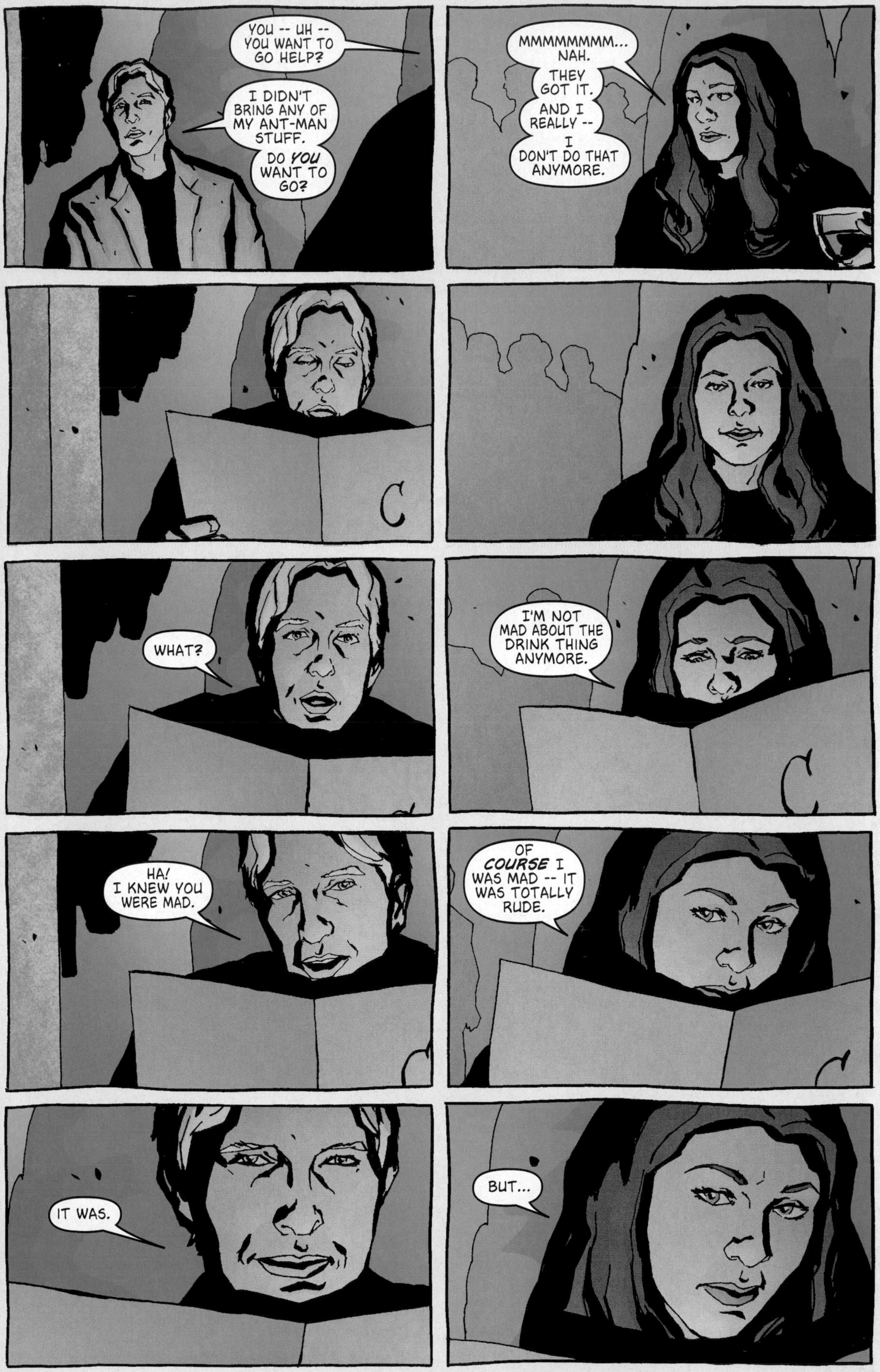
YOU -- UH -- YOU WANT TO GO HELP?
I DIDN'T BRING ANY OF MY ANT-MAN STUFF.
DO *YOU* WANT TO GO?
MMMMMMMM... NAH.
THEY GOT IT.
AND I REALLY --
I DON'T DO THAT ANYMORE.
WHAT?
I'M NOT MAD ABOUT THE DRINK THING ANYMORE.
HA! I KNEW YOU WERE MAD.
OF ***COURSE*** I WAS MAD -- IT WAS TOTALLY RUDE.
IT WAS.
BUT...

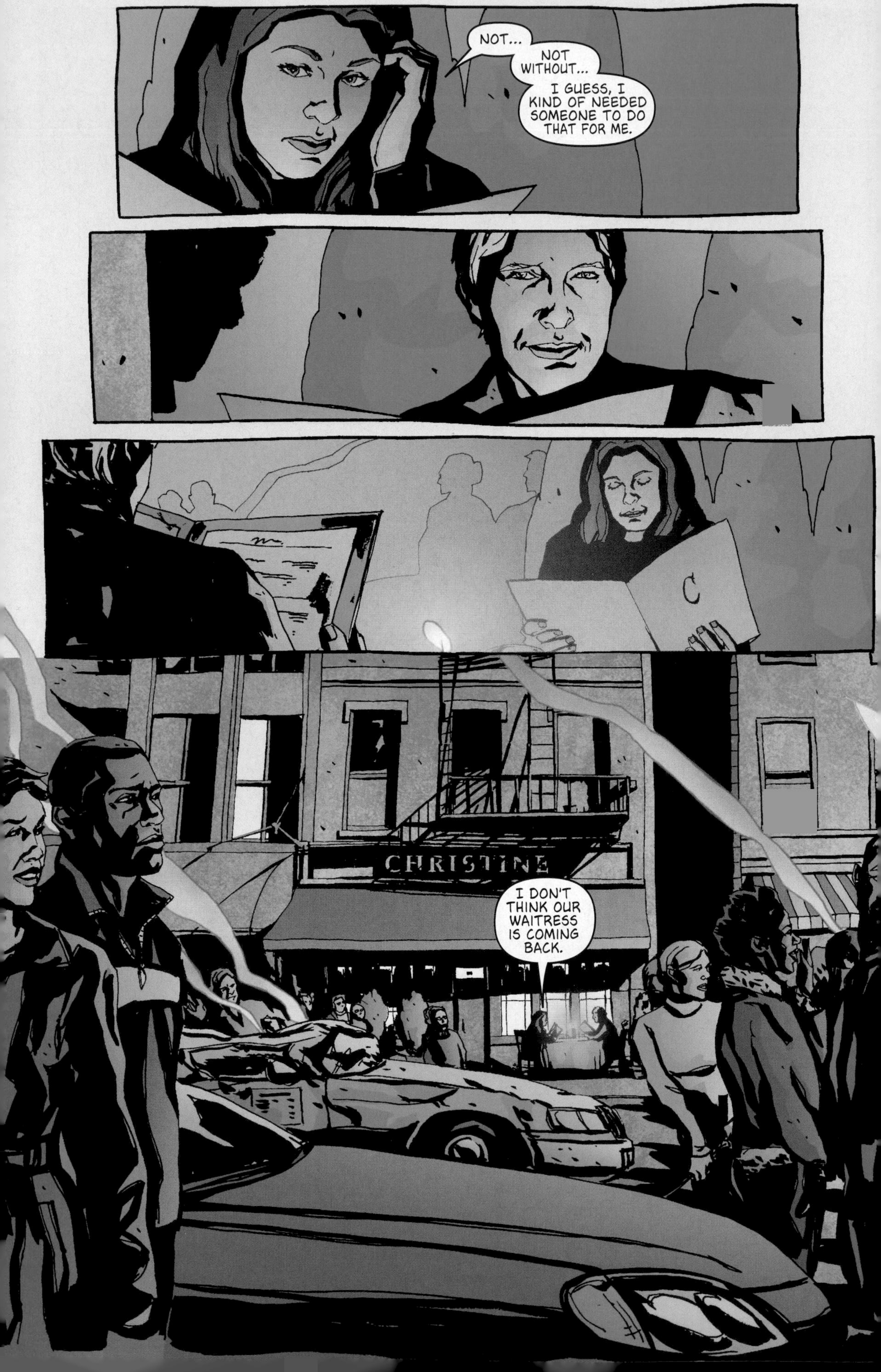
NOT...
NOT WITHOUT...
I GUESS, I KIND OF NEEDED SOMEONE TO DO THAT FOR ME.
CHRISTINE
I DON'T THINK OUR WAITRESS IS COMING BACK.

DAVID MACK SKETCHBOOK
INTRODUCTION

Hi,

OK. So this entire arc of *Alias* was written in my head about four seconds after I crapped out the initial idea for the series. It's hard to pinpoint exactly why this arc was so vivid and important to me, other than the sad truth that elements of it are actually based on a couple of true stories.

It also has one of those artistic conceits that I often come up with that end up just torturing everyone at Marvel. See, early on, I knew that David Mack's feminine-noir cover work would eventually bleed into a few sections of the interiors of Alias but didn't know where exactly. Not like I knew how I wanted Mark Bagley, my *Ultimate Spider-Man* collaborator, to render all *Alias* dream sequences and super-hero flashbacks.

Now I know this doesn't seem like that big a deal, but it's a logistical nightmare for my editors on a book that ships monthly.

Also, this is no slight to the powerful subtlety of the immensely talented Michael Gaydos, my hand-picked first choice for *Alias* artist. Not at all. All it is is another way to find new ways to express what I think is unique about the series and the character.

I called David Mack to discuss the cover motif for this arc. I explained that the missing girl would have a painterly and poetic sketchbook/diary that would mystify Jessica. This was based on a series of collage sketchbooks one of my ex-girlfriends kept at that age. I explained to him how almost every thought this girl had would be painted or clipped into the sketchbooks, and that there was no end to them.

It was mid-conversation that we both realized that it would be very cool to see the pages of her sketchbook in the story itself. Ooh! I was a little tingly. I was excited. David and I discussed this girl's alienation to her surroundings; her obsession with the darker side, the Marvel Knights' side, of the Marvel icons; and basically what other ideas would float around her young and feisty mind.

And then David went and created an entire sketchbook for her, from scratch. An entire sketchbook! He actually created an entire multimedia sketchbook in the voice of this mystery girl.

So here in this bonus section you will find a smattering of what David did following this conversation. And it was from this sketchbook we pulled the cover images and zoomed in on what elements should be featured in the story.

But what I really wanted to do was show all of it. I just love that the sketchbook exists. I love how David accomplished it, and I wanted to bump all the video-game ads in the comic and just run it, but Joe said something about not getting paid for the issue if there weren't any ads. So, you know...

One little side note to all of this is that David Mack's incredibly kind and talented girlfriend, Anh Trahn, had a large hand in these pages, as well. She drew all over them. We both wanted them to look as femme and arty as possible, and Ahn is both those things, so we all thank her for chipping in.

BENDIS!
December, 2002

HELLO
my name is

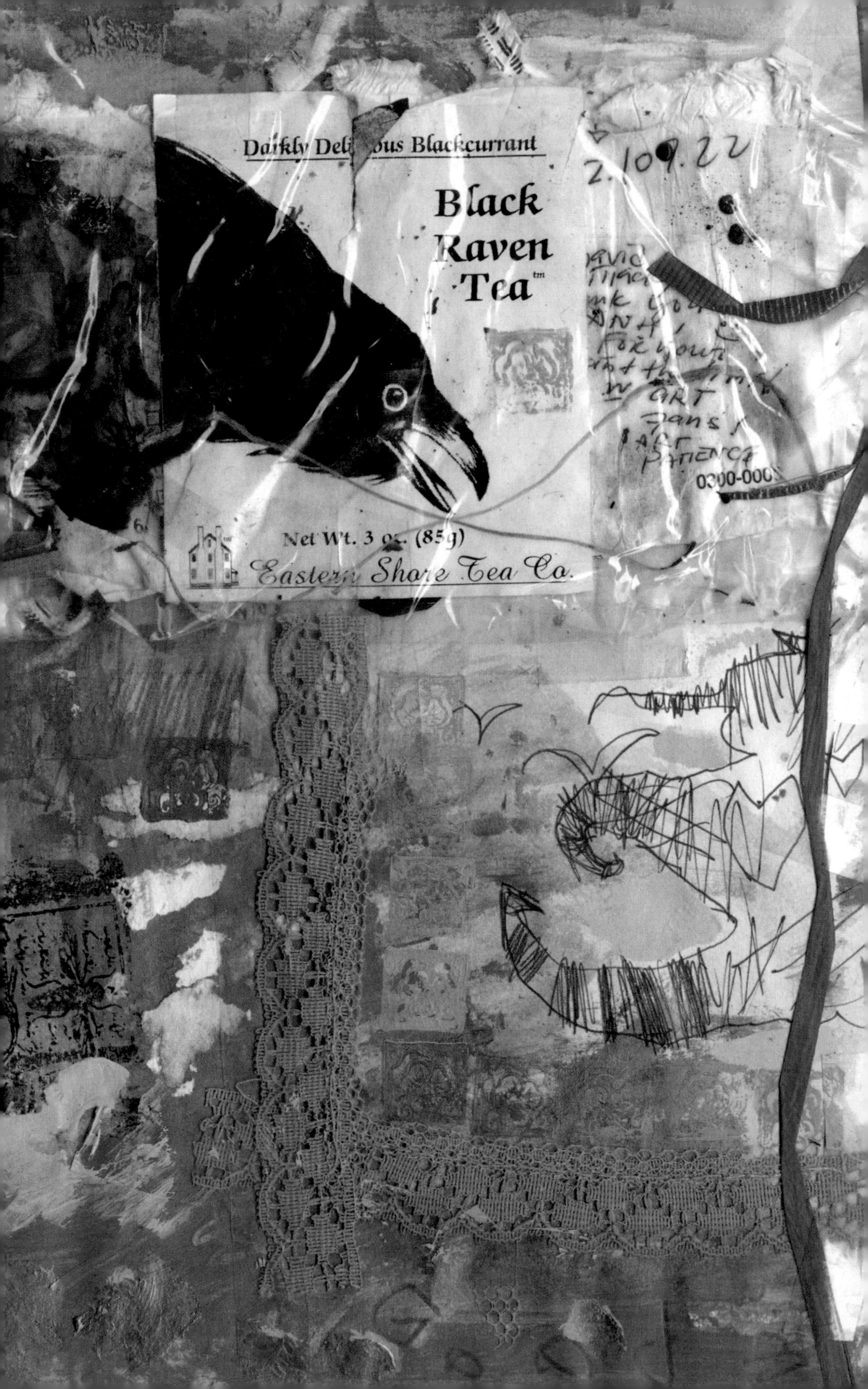

Blackcurrant
Black
Raven
Tea™
Net Wt. 3 oz. (85g)
Shore Tea Co.

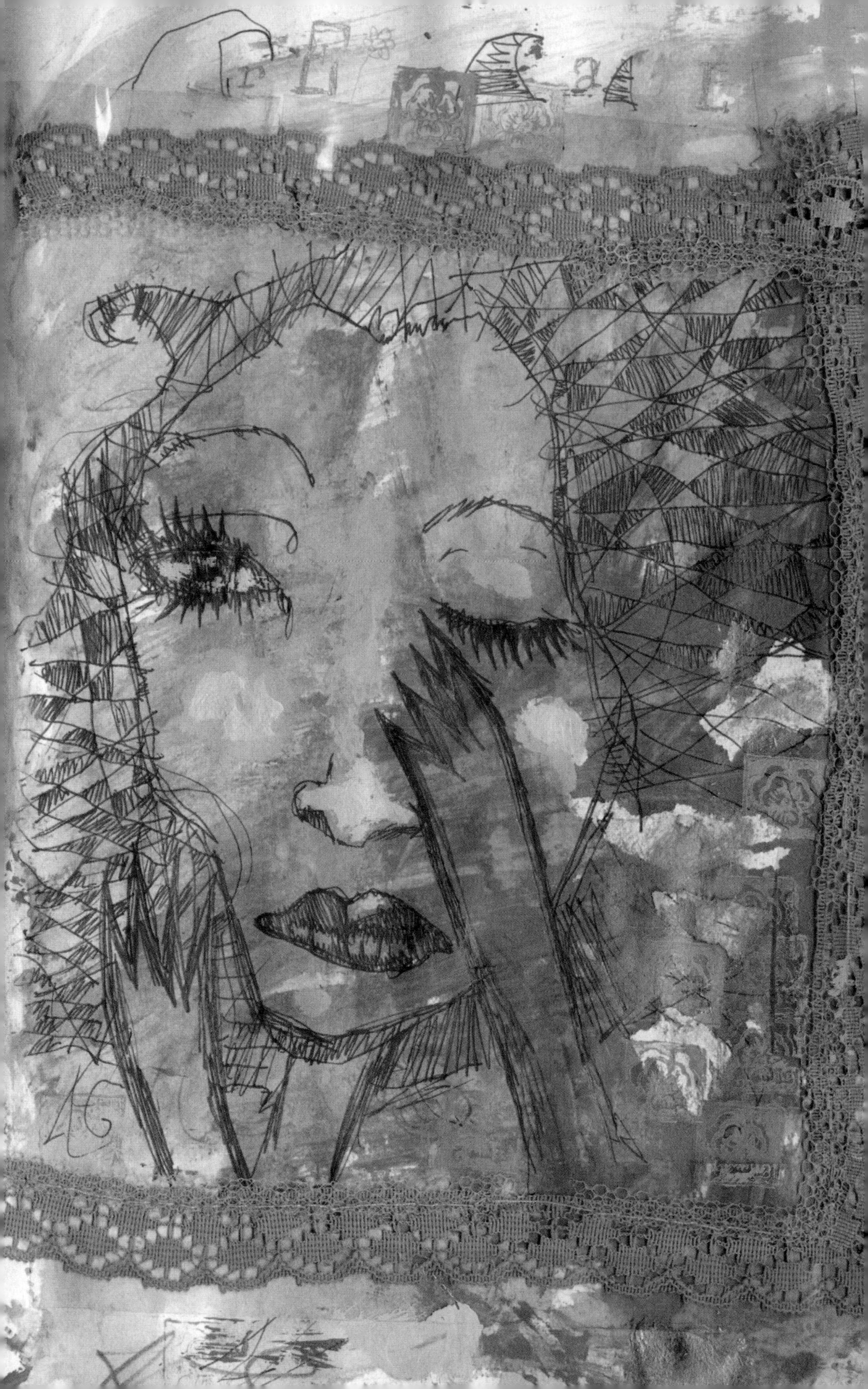

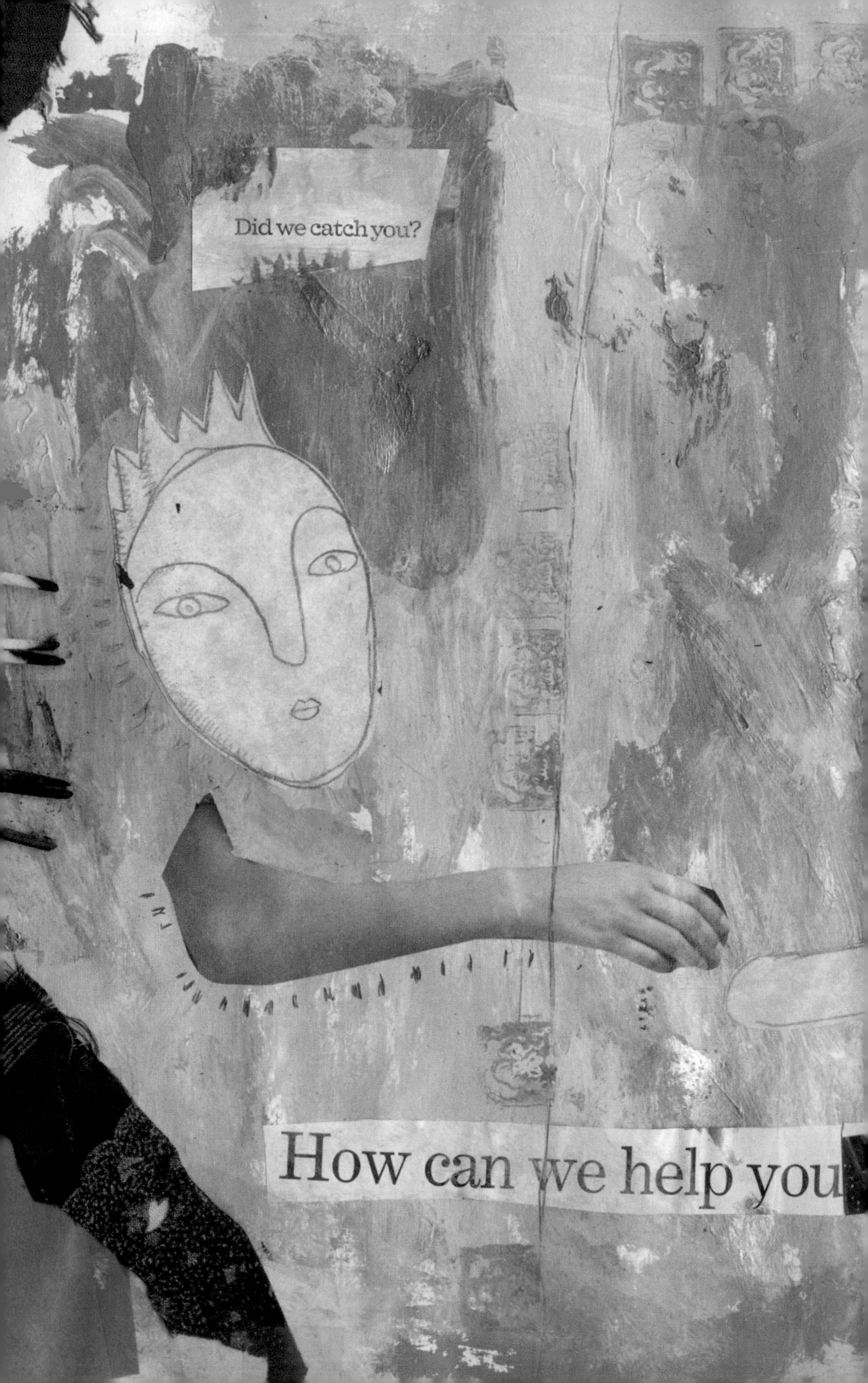
Did we catch you?
How can we help you

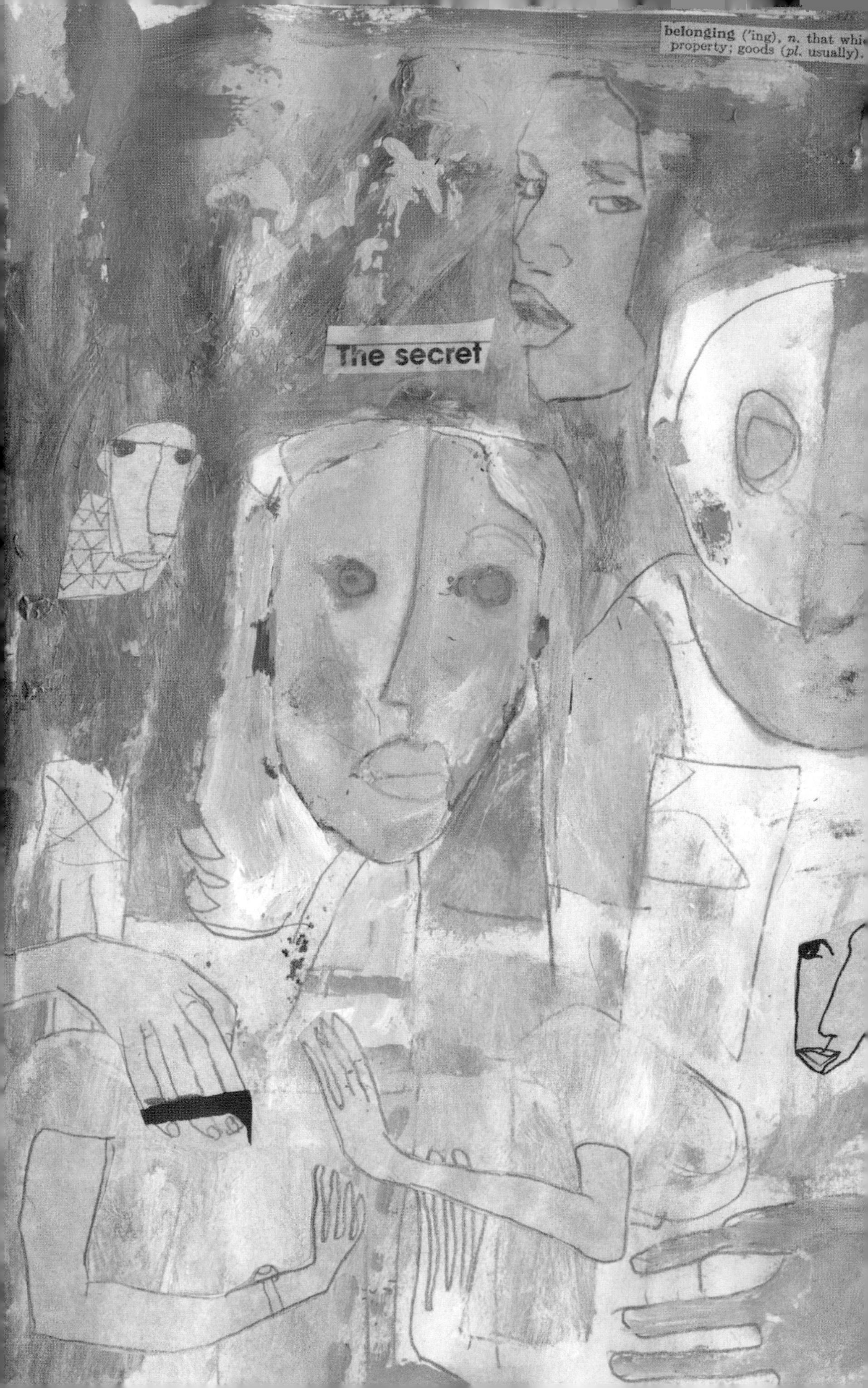

belonging ('ing), n. that whi
property; goods (pl. usually).
The secret

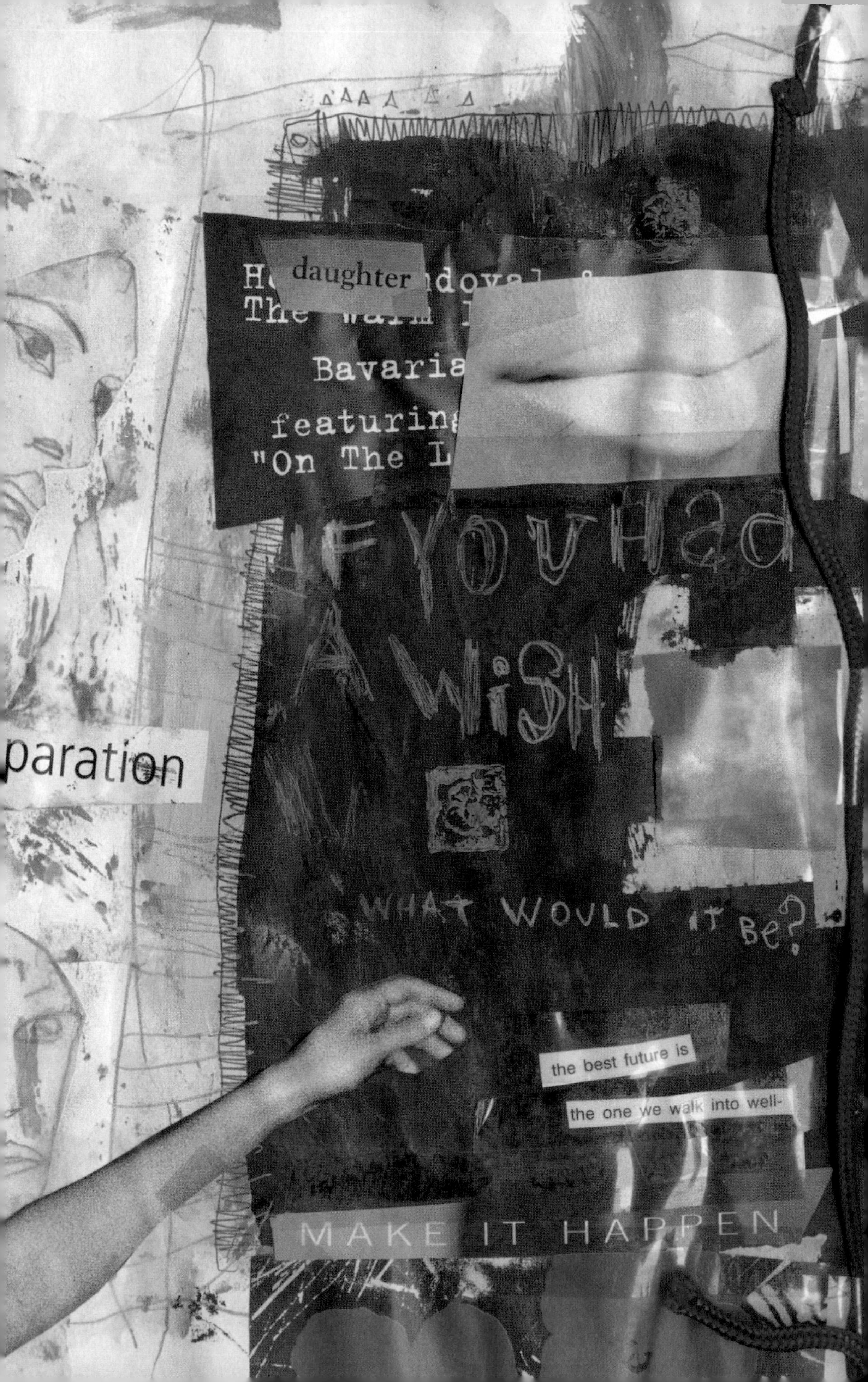
daughter
Bavaria
featurin
"On The L
IF YOU HAD A WISH
WHAT WOULD IT BE?
paration
the best future is
the one we walk into well-
MAKE IT HAPPEN

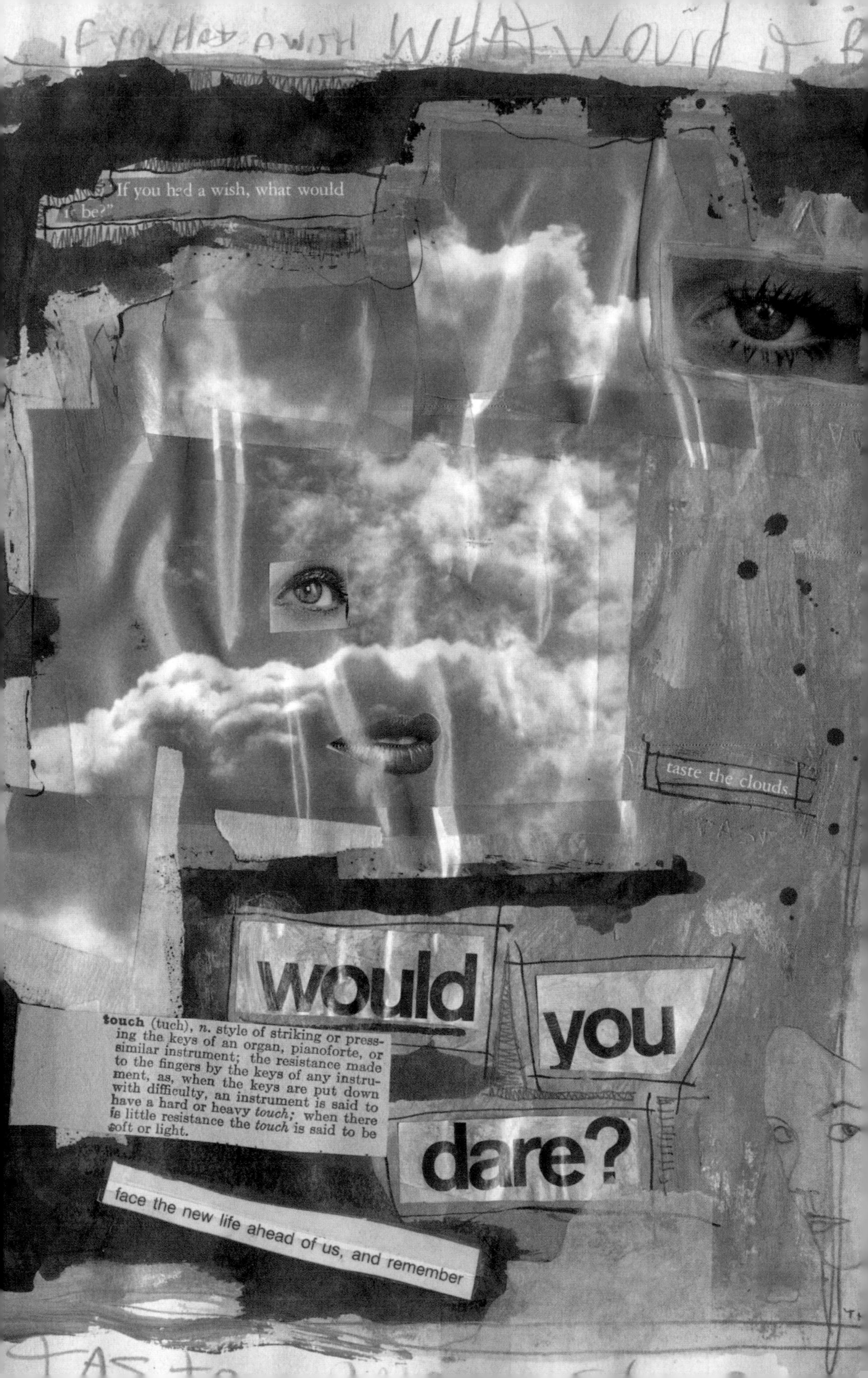
"If you had a wish, what would it be?"
taste the clouds.
would you dare?
touch (tuch), n. style of striking or pressing the keys of an organ, pianoforte, or similar instrument; the resistance made to the fingers by the keys of any instrument, as, when the keys are put down with difficulty, an instrument is said to have a hard or heavy touch; when there is little resistance the touch is said to be soft or light.
face the new life ahead of us, and remember

small mosquito

Blood
Suckers
INCorporated

your

some

disturbing

violin (vi-o-un'), n. a su
having four strings, an
bow; it is the most perfe
ment known, of brillian
ble of every variety of e

not to com
slave but to
most essential self; the
anything), and happy. Oh, right then.
"Emotions are stored in the body, often as physical pain."

the wounded child inside, and then all the
subsequent steps fitted in after that. [My charac-
ter]   is desperate to be
loved, who is desperate to love, desperate to be
needed, to have a role, to be seen and admired.
And I think that the wounded child inside   has
turned into a screaming psychopath because
those wounds have never been addressed.

truths

PUN

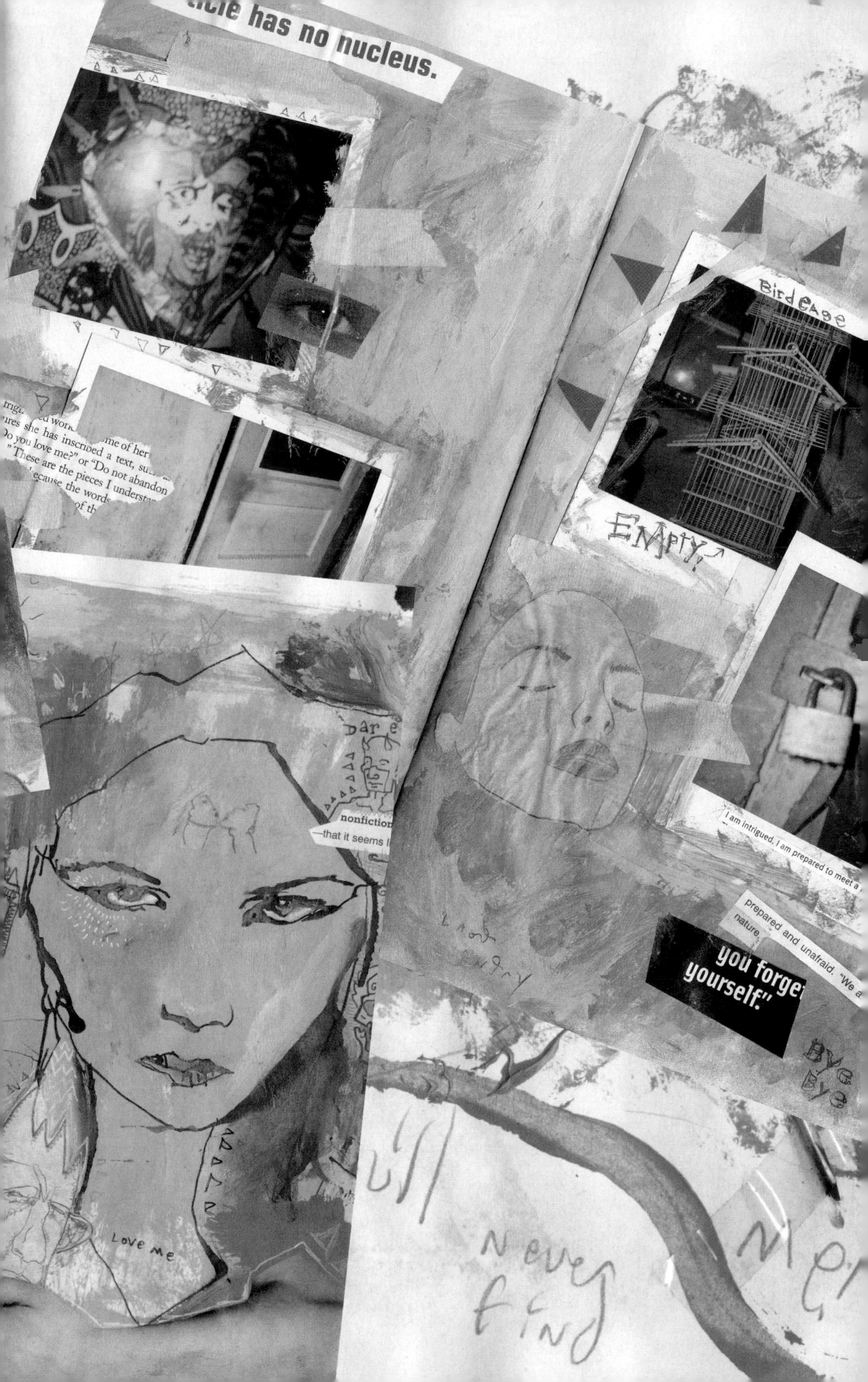

has no nucleus.
Bird cage
Empty
dare
nonfiction
—that it seems
I am intrigued. I am prepared to meet a
prepared and unafraid. "We a
nature.
you forget
yourself."
Bye Bye
Love me
never find

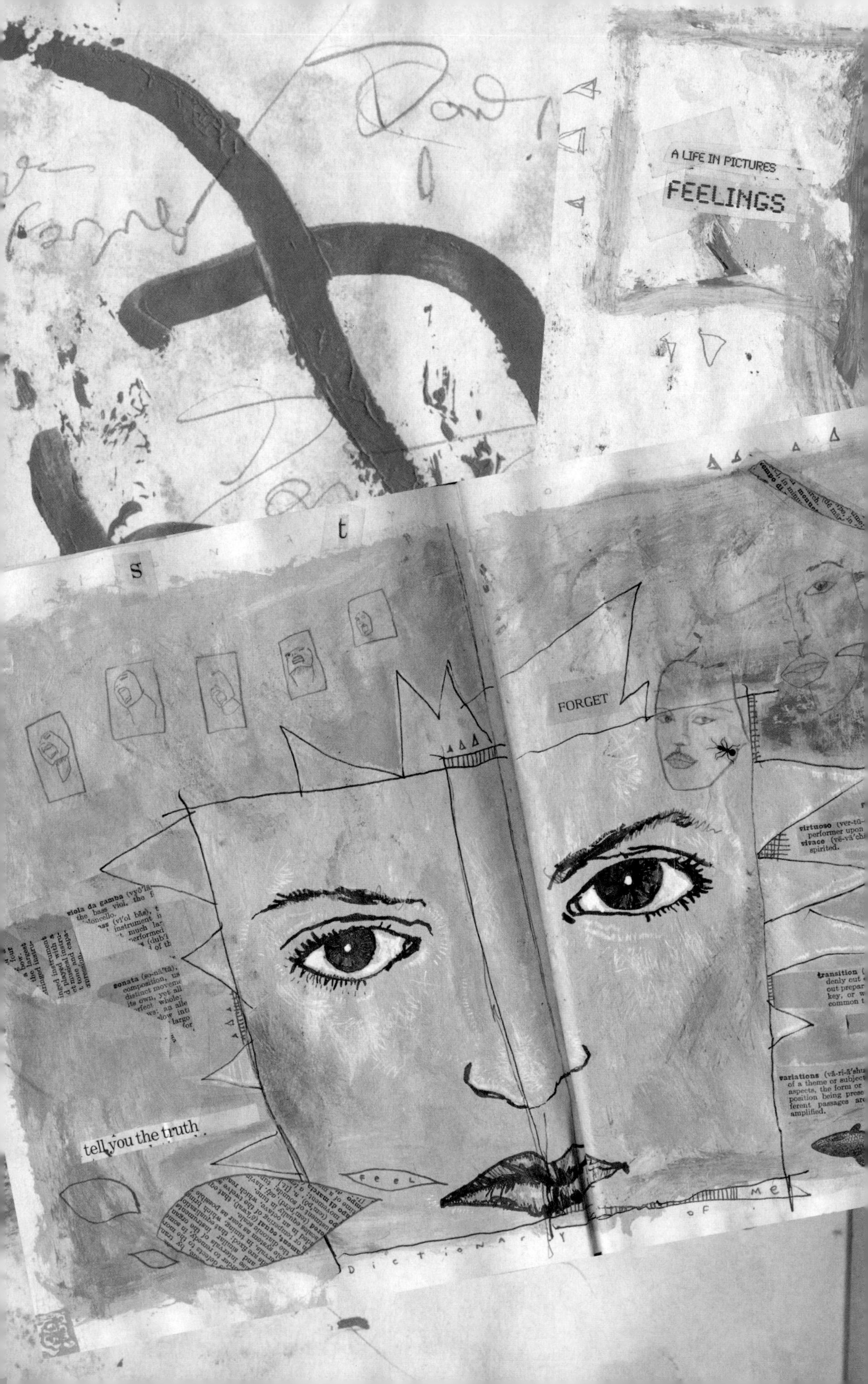
A LIFE IN PICTURES
FEELINGS
s
t
FORGET
tell you the truth
feel
of me
dictionary
virtuoso
performer upon
vivace
spirited.
transition
variations
of a theme or subject
aspects, the form or
position being prese
ferent passages are
amplified.

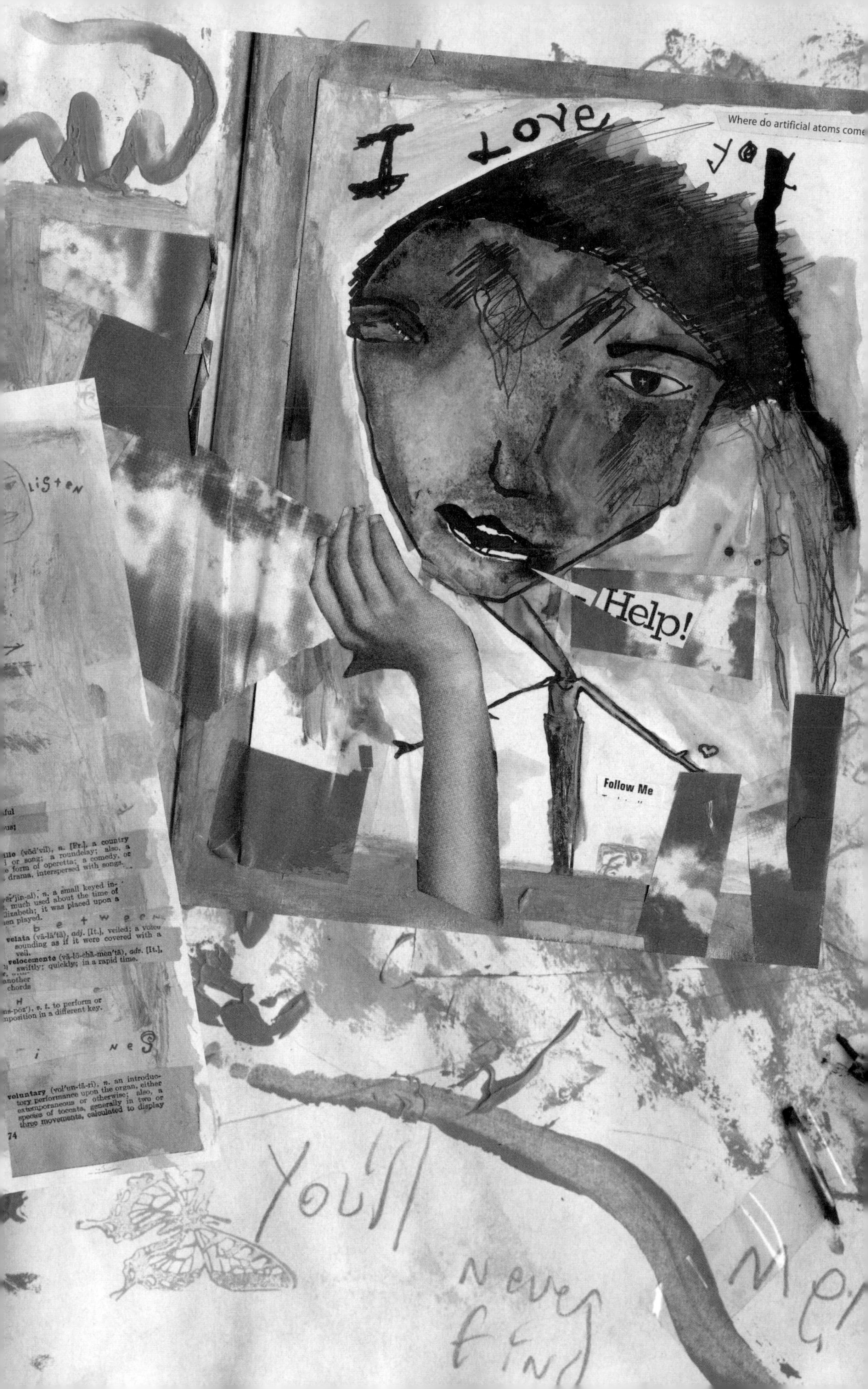
Where do artificial atoms come
I love yo
Listen
Help!
Follow Me
illo (vōd'vil), n. [Fr.], a country
i or song; a roundelay; also, a
e form of operetta; a comedy, or
drama, interspersed with songs.
ĕr'jin-al), n. a small keyed in-
much used about the time of
Elizabeth; it was placed upon a
hen played.
b e t w e e n
velata (vā-lä'tä), adj. [It.], veiled; a voice
sounding as if it were covered with a
veil.
velocemente (vā-lō-chā-men'tā), adv. [It.],
swiftly; quickly; in a rapid time.
another
chords
H
ns-pōz'), v. t. to perform or
nposition in a different key.
i N e S
voluntary (vol'un-tā-ri), n. an introduc-
tory performance upon the organ, either
extemporaneous or otherwise; also, a
species of toccata, generally in two or
three movements, calculated to display
74
You'll never find me

THE END